▲ *Chocolate-Vanilla Charlotte, Recipe 156*
◀ *Autumn Meringue Cake, Recipe 81*

Lenôtre's Desserts and Pastries

Gaston Lenôtre

Revised and Adapted by

Philip and Mary Hyman

Photos by Pierre Ginet

Barron's

Frontispiece Raisin Buns, Recipe 56

Photography by Mr. P. Ginet.

All inquiries should be addressed to:
Barron's Educational Series, Inc.
113 Crossways Park Drive
Woodbury, New York 11797

Library of Congress Catalog Card No. 77-13231

International Standard Book No. 0-8120-5137-8

Library of Congress Cataloging in Publication Data
Lenôtre, Gaston.
Lenôtre's desserts and pastries.
Translation of Faites votre pâtisserie comme
Lenôtre.
Includes indices.
1. Pastry. 2. Cookery, French. I. Title.
II. Title: Lenôtre's desserts and pastries.
TX773.L4413 1977 641.8'65 77-13231
ISBN 0-8120-5137-8

PRINTED IN HONG KONG

2345 041 12 11 10 9 8 7

CONTENTS

Foreword		7
Introduction		11
Dictionary of Terms and Procedures		15
1	Basic Recipes for Doughs and Batters	29
2	Basic Recipes for Creams and Syrups	57
3	Breakfast and Coffee Cakes	87
4	Large Cakes and Desserts	121
5	Pies and Tarts	165
6	Little Pastries	189
7	Hot Desserts—Omelettes and Soufflés	223
8	Cold Desserts—Charlottes and Stewed Fruit	241
9	Petits Fours and Cookies	281
Cross-Index: Ingredients and the Recipes that Use Them		306
Alphabetical Index to Recipes		307
Techniques		312

FOREWORD

Gaston Lenôtre was 12 years old when he made his first dessert, a rice pudding. He served it to his parents at their home in a little Norman village where they, and 150 other inhabitants, shared a quiet life in peaceful surroundings. This was in 1932. The next year Lenôtre's father became ill and the boy suddenly had to decide on a profession. Lenôtre loved to sculpt and mold things, even as a boy. He hesitated when making a choice between the two careers that then interested him most: cabinet making and pastry. These activities have more in common than might appear at first. They both demand skill and patience and involve detailed and decorative work. Almond paste and sugar finally won out over ebony and teak, and Lenôtre began a career that would lead to his being acclaimed the finest pastry chef in France.

From 1932 to 1936, Lenôtre worked as an apprentice with different bakers in his native Normandy. Then he left and went to Paris, hoping to find work with a famous Parisian baker. It was in the middle of the depression and few openings were available. Lenôtre eventually was employed by a pastry chef in a near suburb of Paris, and spent the next four years perfecting the skills he had begun to acquire at home in Normandy. In 1940 he returned home and worked as chief pastry chef in a small bakery in the town of Pont-Audemer (population 10,000). He married in 1944 and opened his own shop in the same town. Lenôtre was only 26 years old at that time, but he had already had 13 years of experience as a pastry cook. It was from then on that he really began to distinguish himself from others in his profession. His shop in Pont-Audemer was an immediate success. His reputation grew rapidly in the region, and people started coming from all around to taste his pastry. Lenôtre was constantly experimenting with new recipes and improving traditional pastries. In whatever he did, he made sure that only top quality ingredients were used; only the best butter and cream, the freshest eggs and fruits, were used in his shop. He knew all the farmers and dairymen in the region and searched out those who could supply him with the very best products. With these fine raw materials, he made desserts that were light and elegant, and his reputation grew greater each year.

For ten years, Lenôtre and his wife lived and worked in Pont-Audemer. She would greet the customers and serve them while he would prepare cakes and pastries in the kitchen behind the shop. Lenôtre could have continued happily working and living in these quiet surroundings if it hadn't been for an idea that kept bothering him. He had more and more orders for his pastries and not enough time to fill them all. He thought of building a large kitchen where all the basic ingredients could be assembled, and doughs and batters prepared. This was never to be a factory that turned out cakes and pastry—it was simply an extension of his own kitchen, but instead of baking for one shop, he could bake for several at the same time. His idea was impractical in Normandy, and his wife (a Parisian) encouraged him to return to the French capital. In 1957 Lenôtre, his wife, and family moved to Paris and he opened his first shop there. It was a traditional pastry shop similar to the one he had left in Pont-Audemer. His wife still greeted the customers, and he continued to do all the baking on the premises. In no time Parisians were flocking to his shop and his reputation soon spread throughout the city.

In 1960, Lenôtre enlarged his shop and began a catering service that was to bring him as much acclaim as his pastry. Finally, in 1968, he opened the independent kitchen, research headquarters, and distribution point he had dreamed of while working in Normandy. Thirty miles outside of Paris, in Plaisir-Grignon near Versailles, he built enormous kitchens and started training chefs in the different specialties that had made his reputation. He had butter and cream shipped to him from his native Normandy and continued to search out the best producers of each ingredient he used. His pastry was still the work of a skilled craftsman, an artisan, but now he had extra hands to help him. By 1970 Lenôtre had opened three more shops in Paris, each one serving pastry that was as perfect and distinctive as ever. All the basic doughs and creams were prepared under Lenôtre's supervision at Plaisir-Grignon and delivered to his shops in Paris for the finishing touches. The final baking and decoration of each cake was done in the Paris shops, and no article was ever sold that had been baked more than two hours in advance. Freshness and quality were always Lenôtre's first concern. That same year (1970) Lenôtre opened his own school for professional pastry chefs at Plaisir-Grignon. Unlike traditional French chefs, Lenôtre was willing to share his secrets with others. Not only were courses in pastry techniques made available to qualified professionals, but courses in catering and confectionary were begun as well. In recent years the school has welcomed up to 500 students a year. The central kitchens at Plaisir-Grignon today employ 308 people, and there are now six Lenôtre shops in Paris and the Paris region. The catering service offered by Lenôtre has continually grown in importance. In 1976, Lenôtre purchased one of the most beautifully located restaurants in Paris, Le Pré Catelan in the Bois de Boulogne, and turned it into a show place where individual customers or groups can experience the full range of Lenôtre's culinary expertise.

Despite this ever increasing number of activities, Gaston Lenôtre has never compromised the standards of excellence he began with. The freshness and lightness that characterize his work in pastry have been carried over to other realms and made his one of the most respected names in the history of French cooking.

Despite his unparalleled success in Paris, Lenôtre has never lost contact with his native Normandy. He still spends several months every year in a tiny village near the English Channel where he was born, and there is a definite Norman influence in the pastry that made him famous. Normandy is renowned for the fine butter, milk, and cream produced, and it's not surprising that large quantities of these ingredients, especially butter, are used in Lenôtre's desserts. Normandy is also the land of apples, and many of Lenôtre's recipes, made with either apples or cream, or both, are derived from traditional regional dishes he grew up with. But Lenôtre's imagination and interest have led him to experiment with many desserts that are far removed from the Norman tradition. For instance, both the Alsatian Kugelhopf and the Fruit Flan (a flan from the Limousin region in central France) figure among the recipes in this book. The Kugelhopf, in fact, appears twice, once as a Lenôtre specialty, and once in a more traditional form. These desserts, like every one Lenôtre makes, are not mere copies of standard preparations. Each dessert bears his mark. They include improvements and variants that make virtually every recipe in this book a Lenôtre specialty. Cooks familiar with traditional pâte brisée (short pastry dough), for instance, will be surprised when they read Lenôtre's version of it (it is much richer than the traditional version and *must* be chilled before rolling it out). Even the stewed fruits are enlivened and made more interesting by being poached in different wines with spices seldom seen in traditional French recipes. Three striking examples of Lenôtre's inventiveness are the Meringue d'Automne (Autumn Meringue Cake), the Rosace à l'Orange (Upside Down Orange Cake), and the Succès. It is interesting to note that two of them (the Meringue d'Automne and Succès) use baked meringue layered with a creamy filling in what could be called Lenôtre's version of a "layer cake." Using baked meringue in this way makes these desserts lighter, and what could have been a heavy cake is turned into an elegant, airy Lenôtre creation.

Most of Lenôtre's recipes are surprisingly easy to prepare. They simply require organization and the mastery of certain basic recipes given in the beginning of the book. Lenôtre, like all professional chefs, is used to working with much larger quantities than those given here. Creams and doughs are prepared for use in several desserts—rarely just for one. Most of these recipes involve "assembling" a cake with elements that have been prepared in advance. Certain doughs, the Génoise cake for instance, can be transformed into five or ten different desserts, and it is often advisable to bake several of the plain Génoise cakes at one time. Vanilla pastry cream (easy to make) is used often, and it is best to make a large amount so that some will always be on hand when called for. If meringues, ladyfingers, and at least one of the basic doughs are on hand, impromptu desserts are both easily and quickly made. Nevertheless, some of the recipes are admittedly difficult, and only time and experience will help the amateur cook if he fails in his first attempt to make them. Recipes which are simple enough for even an inexperienced cook are marked with one chef's hat

(♕). Those recipes that are a little more elaborate but should pose no problem for most cooks have two chef's hats (♕ ♕) after their name. Finally, recipes that are sometimes tricky, requiring more skill when making them (even experienced cooks might have to make them several times before mastering the techniques) are marked with three chef's hats (♕ ♕ ♕). It should be remembered that those recipes that are the easiest to prepare are just as good as the more complicated ones. The chef's hats are not indicative of quality, but are simply given as a guide to help beginners using this book. Beginners should start with the one chef's hat recipes and gradually work up to the three hat recipes. It is extremely important, when making any recipe, to read the instructions carefully, and make sure all the ingredients are assembled before beginning.

Few things will be wasted thanks to the cross indexing that is found at the end of the book. If, for instance, pastry cream or chocolate sauce remains after making one dessert, a look at this index will tell the reader what other desserts can be made with them.

Home bakers should not be afraid of making the large quantities of basic doughs and creams given early in the book. It takes no longer to make large amounts than small ones, and the leftover doughs or creams can be used to make a variety of desserts. Nevertheless, for those who only want to make small quantities, several lists of ingredients have been given with each basic recipe.

When using this book, it is extremely important to carefully read through the Dictionary of Terms and Procedures and to refer to it whenever a question arises in the course of a recipe. Many illustrations will help cooks understand techniques that are explained in the text, and the color photos often show how a dessert looks both before and after being baked. With these photos as a guide, following the advice given here, in the Dictionary, and in the course of the recipes, you will be able to serve desserts that are not the rival, but the equal of those produced by the finest pastry chef in France—Gaston Lenôtre.

Philip and Mary Hyman

INTRODUCTION

Respect for tradition and a familiarity with the past are certainly good things in cooking as in any other field. But the art of cooking is constantly changing, and this book was written as an effort to explain and illustrate La Nouvelle Pâtisserie Française. I have worked for many years to develop what is now called the new school of French pastry. Since the opening of my school for professionals in 1970, I have been able to share many of the techniques that have culminated in producing La Nouvelle Cuisine Française. In this book, for the first time, I would like to address myself to amateur cooks, anyone who loves to bake, and especially those disappointed in the past by desserts that didn't work because the recipes they followed were incomplete and vague. I am happy to share my recipes with others, and this book contains many of the secrets that other pastry cooks prefer to keep to themselves. My hope is that the home baker be able to produce desserts that are not only a pleasure to make, but of the highest possible quality as well. A beautifully made dessert gives a festive air to any dinner and will bring smiles to the faces of family or guests—what better reward can one ask for? But one thing must always be remembered—you can not prepare a truly fine dessert without top quality ingredients. There can be no skimping on ingredients; if a recipe calls for a pound of butter, then you *must* use a pound of the best butter, and no substitute, neither margarine nor other fats, will ever do. It is impossible to create fine desserts with mediocre products, and some products (artificial flavorings, for instance) might even prove harmful. Unfortunately, many bakers today no longer pay enough attention to the quality of the ingredients they use, and the result is a dessert that is only a parody of the real thing. Even with the best products, however, a fine dessert is often a delicate and fragile thing. Its preparation takes time and patience, and one day it might be perfect while the next it may not work as well—all pastry cooks experience this problem. Whatever happens, be patient and try again—you'll succeed in the end.

When making any of the recipes in this book, two things should always be remembered:

1) Pay great attention to the quality of the ingredients and utensils called for in any recipe.
2) Never begin a recipe until you have all the ingredients and utensils ready to use.

Now go ahead and try some of the recipes that follow. I've picked them because I believe they are those which would interest most cooks and be among the easiest to produce at home. I asked one of my best pastry chefs, Jean-Claude Dudoit, and my daughter Sylvie to go over all the recipes and simplify procedures whenever necessary. Sylvie made all the desserts at her own home and suggested many of the changes that, I hope, will make this book perfectly suited for both experienced and non-experienced cooks alike.

I have nothing more to add—any problems you previously had with pastry should disappear. I have revealed all my secrets to you in the pages that follow, and I wish you luck and hope you enjoy making and serving the desserts in this book.

Almond Paste Decorations, Recipe 36

Brioche Mousseline, Recipe 41; Brioche Nanterre, Recipe 42; Brioche Parisienne, Recipe 43

DICTIONARY OF TERMS AND PROCEDURES

Compiled for this translation by Philip and Mary Hyman

Read the Dictionary of Terms and Procedures before trying any recipes.

Bain-marie: This is a French term used when a substance in one container is placed in another which contains hot water for cooking. The effect is that produced by using a double boiler. Some desserts, however, are baked in the oven in a "bain-marie"—in this case the mold containing the dessert is placed in a platter large enough to hold both the mold itself and enough boiling water to come half way up the side of the mold. It is easiest to measure the amount of water needed ahead of time, bring it to a boil on top of the stove, place the dessert in the oven-proof platter, pour in the boiling water and bake.

Baking: All pastry should be baked in the center of the oven unless otherwise indicated. To speed glazing, pastry can be placed closer to the top of the oven toward the end of the baking time. Some recipes call for the oven door to be kept ajar during baking. To do this, a wooden spoon is simply left wedged between the door and the oven, leaving an opening of about one inch between the top of the oven door and the oven. (See PREHEATING and BAKING SHEET)

Baking Sheet: Several baking sheets are sometimes necessary (e.g., a large quantity of cookies is baked in consecutive batches). *The baking sheet should always be cold before it goes into the oven.* Remove the baking sheet before preheating the oven; always dress pastry, meringues, etc., on a cold baking sheet. When buttering or buttering and flouring a baking sheet, follow the instructions given under MOLDS AND PANS for buttering and flouring these utensils. A good baking sheet should be made of metal that is thick enough not to buckle when heated. Most baking sheets are thin and buckle, so it is often a good idea to buy a baking sheet from a professional supply house, or have one cut to the size of your oven, if necessary, to avoid this inconvenience. It is always better to bake only one baking sheet at a time, otherwise the baking may be uneven. Nevertheless, two cakes can often be baked on the same sheet, and this should be done whenever it is possible. (See BAKING)

Bowls: Pastry cooks in France often use the flat-bottomed metal mixing bowls pictured with the utensils (see photo page 27). These are not indispensable; china, porcelain, glass, or earthenware bowls will do. Whenever a large bowl is called for, this means that one full almost to the brim holds 3 quarts (3 liters); a medium-sized bowl holds 2 quarts (2 liters); and a small bowl holds 1 quart (1 liter) of water.

Bowls with covers that make them airtight are best for storage, but an ordinary bowl covered with aluminum foil is a good substitute.

Butter: Only the best unsalted butter should be used in these recipes. No substitutes for butter should ever be used. When butter is "softened" (or soft) this means that it is just soft enough to squeeze easily (usually an hour out of the refrigerator is sufficient).

Caramelized Almonds (Nut Brittle): Powdered caramelized almonds (called *praliné* in French) are often used to flavor and decorate desserts. Either hazelnuts or almonds can be used in the following recipe for preparing 5 cups (750 g) of powdered caramelized almonds (*praliné*):

INGREDIENTS	3⅓ cups (500 g) shelled almonds or hazelnuts
	2¼ cups (500 g) granulated sugar
	½ cup (12.5 cl) water

Preheat the oven to 350°F (180°C).

Warm the nuts for 7 minutes in the oven, then take them out and remove the skins by rubbing the nuts on the mesh of a drum sieve or other large sieve (if you are using almonds, this step can be omitted).

Place the sugar and water in a large saucepan and boil until the sugar reaches the hard ball stage—248°F (120°C) on a candy thermometer (this takes about 5 minutes). Add the nuts, then remove the pot from the heat. With a wooden spatula, slowly stir the mixture until the sugar has a grainy, sandy appearance. Put the pot back over medium heat for about 10 to 15 minutes to melt the sugar again, constantly stirring and scraping the bottom of the saucepan to keep the sugar from sticking. Cook until the sugar is a dark caramel color.

Pour the mixture out onto a greased baking sheet. Allow to cool for one hour, then break into small pieces.

To reduce the nut brittle to powder, either grind it in a heavy-duty blender for a few seconds, or pound it in a mortar until a coarse powder is formed.

Powdered caramelized almonds will keep for up to 3 months in a tightly closed container.

Chestnut Cream: Chestnut cream is made from fresh chestnuts, peeled and boiled with milk, sugar, and a little vanilla, then mashed to form a sweet thick cream. It is sold canned in some specialty shops. In French, it is called *créme de marrons*.

Cutting Dough: Often dough is rolled out and cut into different shapes with a sharp knife. When cutting some doughs, especially flaky pastry dough, the knife should simply be pressed straight down into the dough to cut it (like a cookie cutter). The knife should never be dragged through the dough since this presses the edges together and hinders its rising. Yeast doughs (e.g., brioche dough, etc.) on the other hand can be cut in the usual manner, but the dough should always be refrigerated before cutting for best results. In either case, a very large, extremely sharp straight-edged (not serrated) knife should be used.

Eggs: *All* the eggs used in this book should be medium. They should weigh approximately 1.75 oz. (49 g) or 21 oz. (596 g) a dozen. Since actual egg sizes may vary slightly, you should measure the volume of the eggs before using. If broken into a measuring cup, one beaten egg this size measures a scant ¼ cup (50 ml). If eggs of this size are not used, the measurements for eggs given in these recipes will have to be adjusted accordingly.

Egg Whites: Egg whites may be refrigerated (or frozen) for later use. When kept in a tightly closed jar they will keep in the refrigerator for 10 days or more. If they start to go bad they have an unpleasant odor that is easily recognizable. In these recipes 5 egg whites equal ¾ cup (155 g).

Egg whites are often beaten "until stiff." This means that the egg whites peak, and when held upright on the end of a beater or whisk, the peaks do not fall over. Egg whites should only be beaten just before they are to be used; they have to be folded into other ingredients rather than beaten in. (See FOLD)

Electric Mixer: Mixing times in this book are calculated for cooks using a mixer with only two or three speeds. Cooks using bigger and more sophisticated mixers (e.g., 8 to 10 speeds) should double the slow speed mixing times given here. Almost every recipe can be done with equal success by hand using a wire whisk. When a wire whisk is used, mixing times should be doubled.

Flan Rings: These are thin, smooth, metal circles of differing heights and diameters. They are used mainly by professional bakers in France. The ring is placed directly on the baking sheet and then lined with dough. After baking, the ring and tart are slid onto a rack to cool. The ring is removed by lifting it straight off of the tart or flan. Because there is nothing in between the bottom of the tart or flan dough and the baking sheet, the dough cooks quickly and evenly. Pie pans with removable bottoms are preferable when rings are unavailable.

Fold: This word is used primarily in connection with egg whites that have been beaten until very stiff. When beaten egg whites are to be mixed with other ingredients, they are "folded" in. This requires the use of a flat wooden spatula. Once the egg whites are in the same bowl as the ingredients they are to be mixed with, use the spatula to "cut" into the middle of the egg whites and scoop up, or fold over, half of the egg white mixture onto the other half. This cutting and folding should be done as carefully and quickly as possible. The airiness of the egg whites should not be lost, nor should particles of egg white remain in the final mixture, which should be absolutely homogenous.

Flour: Either all-purpose flour or pastry flour may be used in these recipes. *All measurements are for flour as it comes from the package.* If you wish to sift the flour, do so after measuring (see WEIGHTS AND MEASURES). Some flours absorb slightly more water than others. Sometimes it may be necessary to add extra liquid (a teaspoon at a time) when making certain doughs to achieve the desired consistency. All-purpose flour is preferable for doughs that contain yeast or baking powder. In the other recipes, either all-purpose or pastry flour, or a combination of both may be used.

Fondant: This is an opaque white icing preferred by French pastry chefs for glazing different cakes. It is shinier than ordinary icing, but when unavailable, an icing made by beating ⅔ cup (100 g) confectioners' sugar with 2 tablespoons of water can be used instead. Both this icing and fondant may be colored or flavored as desired.

The following recipe is for preparing 1½ cups (550 g) plain fondant.

INGREDIENTS
2¼ cups (500 g) granulated sugar
1 cup (¼ l) water
½ teaspoon lemon juice

Boil the sugar with the water and lemon juice until it reaches the soft ball stage—234°F (112°C) on the candy thermometer. This takes about 5 to 10 minutes. Pour it onto a clean, cool surface (preferably marble). Allow to cool for 1 minute, then begin working it with a wooden spatula in a back and forth, or figure eight, motion. Scrape the edges toward the center from time to time, working the entire surface of the melted sugar. It will slowly turn white and be more difficult to work. After about 15 minutes, when it is completely opaque and begins to look mat and slightly pasty in texture as the spatula is pulled through it, the fondant is ready. Scrape it up from the table with a metal spatula, place it in a glass jar, cover, and keep indefinitely in a cool place.

Fraiser: This is a way of kneading dough that consists of forming the dough into a ball and using the heel of your hand to break off a small piece of dough, pushing it against the table and away from you, and repeating this motion until the entire ball of dough has been parceled and pushed across the table. This operation should be done quickly and as many times as the recipe requires.

Glaze: This procedure makes the surface of a cake or tart shiny.

Tarts, tartlets, and flans are most frequently glazed with apricot jam. The jam should not contain any pieces of fruit. It is heated until it melts in a saucepan, then "painted" over the surface of the dessert and allowed to cool. Only a small quantity of apricot jam is necessary for a large tart. Water may be mixed with the warm jam if it is too thick.

Another method of glazing, often used with cakes, is to sprinkle the surface of the cake with confectioners' sugar and place the cake under the broiler or in a hot oven for a short time. The confectioners' sugar becomes transparent and makes the cake shine. Often the sugar is sprinkled over the cake 10 minutes before the end of baking. Only enough sugar to lightly cover the surface of the cake is used.

Finally, many pastries are brushed with beaten egg or egg yolk before baking. This actually makes the pastry a more beautiful, even brown when baked, but can be considered a kind of glazing.

Layer Cakes: Génoise cakes often are cut in half, or into three or four layers after baking. To do this properly, you need a very long serrated knife and several strips of cardboard, similar to those shown in photo 4, illustrating the flaky pastry (Recipe 3). It is essential that the blade of the knife be several inches longer than the diameter of the Génoise. Pile the cardboard strips on opposite sides of the Génoise so that they make two piles of equal height. The height of these piles is very important and depends on how many layers the cake has to be cut into. Use a ruler to measure the height of your Génoise. If you want to cut the cake into four equal layers, make the strips of cardboard into piles whose height is ¼ that of the Génoise (e.g., for a cake two inches tall, the piles of cardboard strips should be ½" high). Place the blade of the knife flat against the two piles of cardboard strips and saw into the cake, keeping the knife in contact with the strips, which will guide the blade. Lift off the top section of the cake and remove this first, bottom slice from between the strips. Replace the remaining cake in between the cardboard strips and cut through the cake again. Repeat this procedure once more, and the Génoise will be cut into four equal layers. The same procedure is used with cutting a Génoise into two, three, four, or five layers.

Molds and Pans: When a specific size cake or pie pan is called for, the measurement given for it is for the diameter of the utensil measured across the top. Most molds used are made of aluminum, tin, or stainless steel. *When a mold or pan is buttered (or buttered and floured) before baking, measurements for these ingredients are not included in the list preceding the recipe.* To butter a mold for baking, simply rub the inside of the mold all over with butter until the walls and bottom of the mold are covered by a *light* film of butter. If the mold is to be floured as well, sprinkle in a little flour then, turning the mold constantly in all directions, shake the flour around until a thin even coating of flour has stuck to the butter. Empty out whatever flour does not adhere to the mold (the same procedure is followed with sugar instead of flour in some recipes).

Orange-Flower Water: This is a fragrant liquid produced by distilling orange blossoms. It is always used in very small doses and can be found in specialty shops (it is often used in North African and Middle Eastern cooking as well as French). If orange-flower water is unavailable, vanilla extract, though completely different in taste, may be used instead, if the recipe does not already call for vanilla in one form or another. If vanilla is already used, it is best not to add the vanilla extract. Orange-flower water is not indispensable. It can be omitted in most recipes where it is called for without harming the result.

Parchment Paper: Specially treated non-stick parchment paper is often used in Lenôtre's recipes. It is used to line baking sheets and pans to avoid sticking. If you prefer, you can simply grease the pan or baking sheet with butter instead of using parchment paper. Instructions are included in each recipe.

Pastry Bag: Pastry bags are either plastified (for easy cleaning) or made of cloth. Several different-sized bags and a complete set of nozzles are indispensable. To fill the bag (it is easier if two people do this), place the nozzle in the bag, then bend the bag just above the nozzle by placing the nozzle on its side on a table and lifting the open end of the bag upward, perpendicular to the nozzle. Spoon the cream or batter into the bag held in this position.

When squeezing out the batter onto a baking sheet, it is best to hold the nozzle with one hand, very close to, but not touching, the baking sheet. Squeeze the pastry bag as evenly as possible with the other hand. Squeeze very hard only toward the very end, when the bag appears to be empty—there is usually batter or cream left just behind the nozzle. Never use a syringe type decorator instead of a pastry bag—the results would be disastrous.

Plastic Scraper: This is a very small and useful utensil that is often used when making different doughs (see photo, page 27). Chopping the butter and flour together with the scraper keeps the butter from softening too much and speeds the mixing of these two ingredients. The rounded side of the scraper is used to scrape batter or dough from bowls when emptying them.

Preheating: It is indispensable that the oven be sufficiently preheated before baking. Fifteen or twenty minutes before anything is baked, the oven should be turned on and set to the temperature called for in each recipe.

Pricking Dough: Pastry dough is pricked with a fork or needle to prevent it from puffing up too much when baked. When pricking the dough, make sure the prongs of the fork (or the needle) go completely through the dough, and that the whole surface of the dough is evenly pricked. This is especially important when pricking flaky pastry.

Quantities: It is often advisable to make the largest quantities of those doughs which have to rise before baking (especially brioche dough). Smaller quantities can be made, but the dough is generally easier to work in large batches and it saves well.

Refrigeration: It is extremely important that many doughs be refrigerated before being rolled out. Most doughs need to be prepared a day ahead of time because of the refrigeration. Cold dough is preferably rolled out on a cold (marble) table, but it can be worked on any flat surface. If the dough is not sufficiently refrigerated, the large amount of butter in it will make it impossible to roll out. Unless otherwise indicated, whenever dough is called for in a list of ingredients, it should be cold (see basic recipes for different doughs).

Ribbon: This term is used when a batter falls from a spoon or whisk in a smooth stream and piles up on itself like a ribbon before sinking into the rest of the batter.

Rum: Dark rum is traditionally used in French pastry. The best dark, 90 proof rum is to be preferred in making these recipes.

Spatula: Two kinds of spatulas are used in this book. One is a long, metal, flexible blade-spatula (see photo, page 27) and is used primarily in icing cakes. The other is made of wood, and has a large, rounded end that tapers down into a handle (see photo, page 25). The wooden spatula is primarily used when folding egg whites into other ingredients.

Table: It is essential that the table used for making pastry be perfectly flat. Any surface will do, although marble is traditionally considered the best. This is because marble is not only flat, but it cools quickly. Cold dough is best worked on a cold table, so ice trays are sometimes placed on the marble table top to cool it. The table should be absolutely clean before working on it (it is best to scrape the table with a rubber or plastic scraper while rolling out dough, and to flour the table often to avoid sticking).

Time: A clock, or wristwatch, is indispensable when making pastry. Precise times are given in these recipes as often as possible, but since neither stove nor utensils (or cooks!) are completely uniform, cooking times may have to be adjusted. Often, "signs" have been given to judge when something is ready (e.g., reached a certain consistency or color), and they are just as important as the times given for baking. Preparation times listed before each recipe are slightly arbitrary since an experienced cook works faster than a beginner; nevertheless, they give the reader some idea how long it takes to prepare a certain dessert.

Turn: This is a term used in connection with the rolling out of flaky pastry. To give the dough a turn means to roll it out into a long rectangle, then to fold it in thirds. Before rolling it out again, the folded pastry is given a quarter turn —hence the name. By turning the pastry in this way, the rolling pin will always roll in the direction of the fold in the pastry, never across it. Flaky pastry is usually given 6 turns (i.e., rolled out 6 times) before being rolled into its final shape.

Turn Out: This term is used throughout the book and always means to remove a finished dessert from the mold, pan, or ring it was prepared in. This is done either immediately after taking the dessert in question from the oven, once the dessert has been allowed to cool but is still warm, or after the dessert is completely cold. Individual recipes give precise instructions on this point.

Whenever a cake mold is used, the cake is turned out by placing a plate, larger in diameter than the cake itself, on top of the mold and in one quick motion, turning the cake "upside down." The result is that the cake is now on the plate and one can lift the mold up and off with no problem.

Sometimes, as in the recipe for Rolled Brioche with Candied Fruits, the operation described above results in the bottom of the dessert facing upwards. In this case another platter is placed on top of the dessert and the dessert is turned "upside down" once more before serving.

Whenever a tart is turned out, it is *never* turned upside down, since this would ruin the appearance of the fruit. Either a flan circle or pie pan with a removable bottom is used when cooking a tart (see FLAN CIRCLE). If this cannot be done, the tart should simply be served in the pan it cooked in (small tartlets can be lifted or slid out of their pans on to the serving platter).

Vanilla Sugar: This is vanilla-flavored sugar that is sold already prepared in France. It is better when prepared at home. To make it, you need one vanilla bean, 1⅓ cups (150 g) lump sugar, a pair of scissors, a mortar, and a pestle.

Hold the vanilla bean over the mortar and, using the scissors, cut it into tiny slices. Keep cutting until the entire vanilla bean has been sliced and has fallen into the mortar. Place half of the sugar in the mortar and begin pounding with the pestle. After about 10 minutes, pour the pounded vanilla and sugar into a very fine sieve and shake the sieve over a piece of waxed paper until all the finest pieces have gone through. Place what is left in the sieve back into the mortar, add the remaining sugar, and pound for another 10 minutes, then sift again. What remains in the sieve this time can be pounded once more, but no more sugar should be added. The vanilla sugar can be kept in an airtight container or tin for later use.

To make powdered vanilla, follow the instructions given here, but use only ½ cup (60 g) of sugar lumps instead of 1⅓ cups (150 g).

Vanilla sugar is seldom used in large quantities. If none is available, a few drops of vanilla extract can often be used instead.

Weights and Measures: The exact gram weights have been retained in parentheses in this book. Scales are inevitably more accurate than cups and tablespoons. When measuring in cups, the ingredient should never be packed in. The cup should be filled and shaken gently *only* to level the ingredient so that the measurement can be read easily. Ingredients such as butter should be placed in the cup so that no air bubbles or pockets remain, and the butter should be pressed until flat across the top. All spoon or cup measurements are level unless otherwise indicated. In referring to tablespoons or teaspoons, *generous* means that the contents of the spoon make a mound rather than being level with the edge of the spoon. *Scant* means that the spoon is not quite full, but approaches the measurement given. When applied to cup measurements, *generous* means that the contents of the cup are to come slightly above the line indicating the measurement given, but never more than 1 liquid ounce (⅛ cup) above it. *Scant* means that the contents are below the measurement given, but no more than 1 liquid ounce (⅛ cup) below it.

Whiten: When sugar is beaten with butter or egg yolks until very pale yellow, the mixture is said to whiten. This term is often used in conjunction with the term "form a ribbon" (see RIBBON).

Yeast: Compressed baker's yeast is to be preferred in the following recipes, however granulated dry yeast may be used instead. One cake of compressed baker's yeast equals one packet of granulated dry yeast.

Rolled Brioche with Candied Fruit, Recipe 44

1 Flan circle
2 Round metal nozzles, 1/16″ (0.2 cm) to 3/4″ (2 cm)
3 Flat-toothed nozzle
4 Star-shaped nozzle
5 Skimmer
6 Oven
7 Wire whisk
8 Pound cake mold
9 Kugelhopf mold
10 Individual oval flan rings
11 Individual flan circle
12 Tartlet circle
13 Dough hook
14 Pastry bag
15 Pastry brush
16 10-speed mixer
17 Wooden spatulas and spoon
18 Candy thermometer
19 Measuring cup

18
4
3
2
1
7
5
17
6
9
14
15
11
12
10
8
19
16
13

1 Scale and weights
2 Plastic pastry cups
3 Paper pastry cups
4 Plastic scraper
5 Serrated knife
6 Metal mixing bowls
7 Paper doilies
8 Cookie cutter
9 Cake rack
10 Individual ribbed brioche molds
11 Petit four molds
12 Ribbed brioche mold
13 Pie tin for tartlet
14 Cake pan
15 Cookie molds
16 Non-stick parchment paper
17 Rolling pin
18 Sugar dredger
19 Putty knife
20 Flexible blade-spatula
21 Small ladle
22 Paring knife
23 Vegetable peeler
24 Cutting board
25 Orange or lemon peeler

6
12
6
16
14
9
1
4
1
2
5
17
19
3
20
24
25
21
23
22
7
LENOTRE
18
LENOTRE
13
11
8
11
10
15

Chapter 1

BASIC RECIPES FOR DOUGHS AND BATTERS

RECIPES

1. Ladyfingers (Biscuits à la Cuillère)
2. Jelly Roll (Biscuit Roulé)
3. Classic Flaky Pastry (Feuilletage Classique)
4. Quick Flaky Pastry (Feuilletage Rapide)
5. Succès Batter (Fonds de Succès)
6. Génoise
7. French Meringue (Meringue Française)
8. Swiss Meringue (Meringue Suisse)
9. Brioche Dough (Pâte à Brioche Surfine)
10. Short Pastry (Pâte Brisée)
11. Cream Puff Pastry (Pâte à Chou)
12. Sweet Short Pastry (Pâte Sucrée)

1
Ladyfingers (Biscuits à la Cuillère)

Ladyfingers are used to garnish Bavarian cream molds and charlottes; they are also delicious served with whipped cream, fruit purées, stewed fruit, and vanilla or chocolate creams.

PREPARATION 25 minutes

BAKING TIME 18 minutes per baking sheet, with 24 ladyfingers per sheet

INGREDIENTS
For 24 ladyfingers
5 eggs
⅔ cup (150 g) granulated sugar
1 cup, scant (125 g), flour
Confectioners' sugar, to sprinkle on top

UTENSILS
2 mixing bowls
Electric mixer
1 spoon
Pastry bag with ¾" (2 cm) round metal nozzle
Parchment paper
Baking sheet
Sugar dredger

1

The Batter: Preheat oven to 350°F (180°C). Separate the whites from the yolks. Place the yolks in a mixing bowl. With the electric mixer set at medium speed, gradually beat in all but 1½ tablespoons of the granulated sugar. Beat for three minutes or until the mixture is thick, pale, and forms a ribbon. Carefully stir in the flour with a spoon, working the mixture as little as possible.

In another bowl, beat the egg whites for one and a half minutes with the mixer set at a high speed. Add the remaining 1½ tablespoons of granulated sugar and continue beating one and a half minutes more, or until stiff.

Carefully fold the egg whites into the batter as quickly as possible.

Baking: Line 2 baking sheets with parchment paper. To make the paper stick to the baking sheets, place a little batter under each corner of the paper. Fill the pastry bag with the batter. Squeeze out 24 ladyfingers 3½" long (9 cm) onto the baking sheet. Before baking, dust the ladyfingers with the confectioners' sugar. Bake for 18 minutes. After the first 12 minutes, check to see if the baking sheet needs to be turned in order to obtain even browning.

Note: If you do not have parchment paper, butter and flour the baking sheets before using them. You can add 4 teaspoons of vanilla sugar or 1 teaspoon of vanilla extract to the batter before folding in the egg whites. Two teaspoons of orange-flower water or the grated peel of ½ lemon could be added instead to the batter, especially if the ladyfingers are going to be eaten plain.

To Store: The ladyfingers will keep two to three weeks if placed in an airtight container.

To Freeze: You can also freeze the container with the ladyfingers. Before using them, however, let them thaw for 24 hours. Once thawed, the ladyfingers should be eaten within 3 or 4 days or else they will become moldy.

2

Jelly Roll Dough (Biscuit Roulé)

This dough can either be simply filled with jam to make a jelly roll or decorated to form one large, or several small Yule logs.

PREPARATION 15 minutes

BAKING TIME About 7 minutes

INGREDIENTS *For 1 roll, serving 8 persons*
4 egg yolks
⅓ cup (75 g) granulated sugar
½ cup (75 g) flour
3 egg whites
1½ tablespoons (25 g) butter, melted

UTENSILS Electric mixer
Narrow wooden spatula or spoon
2 mixing bowls
Parchment paper
1 jelly roll pan or baking sheet

The Batter: Preheat the oven to 450°F (240°C). In a bowl, place the yolks and the sugar. Beat for 3 minutes with the mixer set at medium speed, then stir in the flour. Beat the egg whites until stiff, adding 1 teaspoon of sugar halfway through. Pour the melted butter into the bowl with the egg yolks, then fold the egg whites into this mixture.

Baking: Spread the batter into a rectangle at least 10″x12″ (25x30 cm) and no more than ½″ (1 cm) thick over a thickly buttered paper placed on the baking sheet. The batter should be spread evenly in order to keep the dough from drying out in any one spot. Bake for 7 minutes.

When the cake is done, remove the paper from the baking sheet and turn it upside down onto a flat surface. Wet the paper with a brush dipped in water; 2 minutes later, remove the paper. Cover the cake with a cloth to prevent it from drying out and let it cool. The cake is now ready to be filled and rolled.

3

Classic Flaky Pastry (Feuilletage Classique)

Flaky pastry is made by wrapping cold butter inside cold dough, then rolling it out and folding it several times. This produces a very flaky dough, made up of many layers, which will rise to several times its original height when baked. It is difficult to make well, since it demands a great deal of care and patience, but the photographs will make the various steps easier to follow.

PREPARATION 30 minutes

RESTING TIME 5 hours

INGREDIENTS *For approximately 2 pounds 14 ounces (1,300 g) dough*
2 teaspoons (15 g) salt
1 cup (¼ l) water
3¾ cups (500 g) flour
5 tablespoons (75 g) softened butter
2¼ cups (500 g) cold butter

For approximately 1 pound 7 ounces (650 g) dough
1 teaspoon (8 g) salt
½ cup (12.5 cl) water

1¾ cups (250 g) flour
2½ tablespoons (38 g) softened butter
1 cup, generous (250 g), cold butter

For approximately 9 ounces (250 g) dough
½ teaspoon, scant (3 g), salt
3 tablespoons (5 cl) water
¾ cup (100 g) flour
1 tablespoon (15 g) softened butter
6½ tablespoons (100 g) cold butter
(for these small quantities, mix the dough by hand)

UTENSILS

Small bowl or glass
Large mixing bowl
Electric mixer with dough hook
Plastic scraper
Plastic wrap or waxed paper
Cardboard rulers

Making the Dough: In a small bowl or glass, dissolve the salt in the water. In the mixing bowl, place the flour and the softened butter. Beat for 30 seconds at low speed, then add the salt water. If necessary, finish mixing the dough by hand, cutting it with the plastic scraper. The butter should be completely incorporated. Form a ball with the dough and cut the top crosswise with a knife. Refrigerate covered for 2 hours.

Rolling out the Dough: Place the cold butter between 2 sheets of waxed paper or plastic wrap and tap it several times with a rolling pin in order to flatten it slightly and make it more pliable. Roll the dough into a square on a floured surface, place the butter in the center, and fold in the sides (see photo 2, page 34). The butter should be completely enclosed inside the dough.

Place the folded dough so that the line of the last fold is perpendicular to you. Lightly flour the surface of the dough and the rolling pin. If necessary, sprinkle a little more flour on the rolling surface as well.

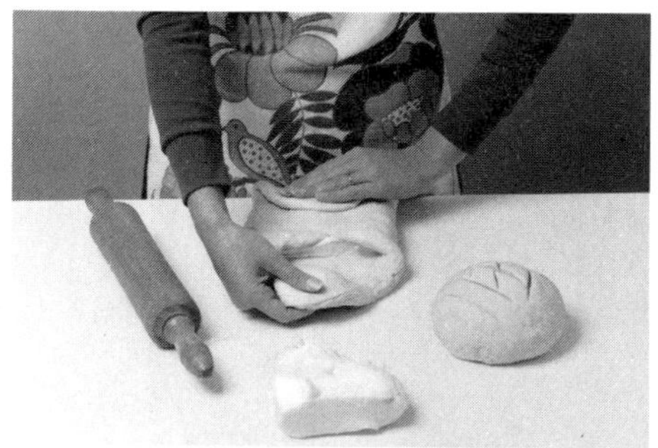
2

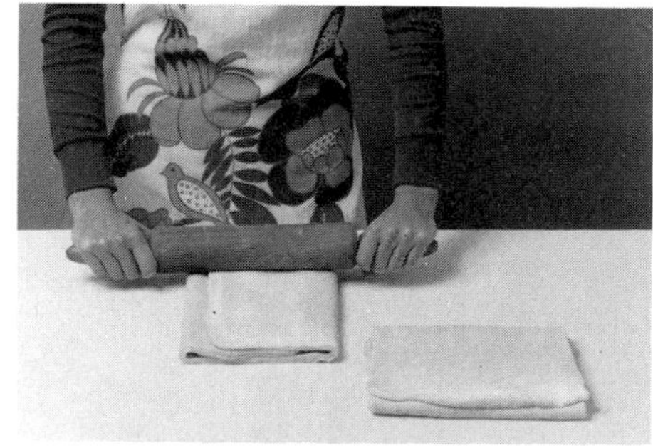
3

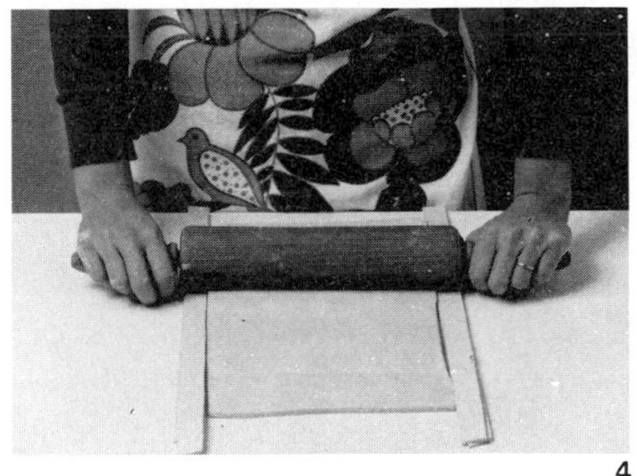
4

5

Roll the dough out into a long rectangle slightly more than ¼ inch thick, checking frequently to make sure the dough is not sticking to the table. Reflour the table and rolling pin when necessary, but do so as lightly as possible each time. When the desired thickness is reached, fold the dough into thirds.

Give the dough ¼ turn so the line of the fold is again perpendicular to you. You should never roll across this fold, but always roll along it (see photo 3, page 34). Roll the dough out a second time, and fold it in thirds once more. Refrigerate the dough, well covered, for 1 hour.

Give the dough 2 more turns (i.e., roll and fold it 2 more times). Refrigerate again for 1 hour. Just before using the dough, whether frozen or just refrigerated, give it 2 more turns and chill it for 1 hour in the refrigerator before rolling it into the shape asked for in any specific recipe.

Note: To roll the dough evenly, cut some cardboard rulers, 10″ long (25 cm). Place several of these rulers on top of each other until you reach the thickness you want the dough to be. The rulers will serve as a frame. You can then roll the dough 1/16″ (2 mm) or 1/8″ (3 mm), etc., to make small tarts (see photo 5, page 35), or other desserts, depending on the thickness the recipe calls for.

If the butter breaks through the dough, flour the broken places generously; also flour the rolling pin or table, depending upon whether the butter broke through the top or bottom. Continue rolling gently, until approximately the correct thickness, fold in thirds and refrigerate for 1 hour before continuing. Then proceed as directed, rolling the dough as gently and quickly as possible.

To Store: The dough will keep 3 to 4 days in the refrigerator if wrapped tightly in aluminum foil or plastic. After this time, however, it will begin to discolor and will eventually turn black.

To Freeze: Move the dough from the freezer to the refrigerator 24 hours before you intend to use it.

Croissants, Recipe 47; Chocolate Rolls, Recipe 55
Pithiviers, Recipe 58

4
Quick Flaky Pastry (Feuilletage Rapide)

This method of making flaky pastry differs slightly from the classic method, cutting the time needed to make it almost in half. However, it does not keep as well as classic flaky pastry, so it is best to use it the day it is made.

6

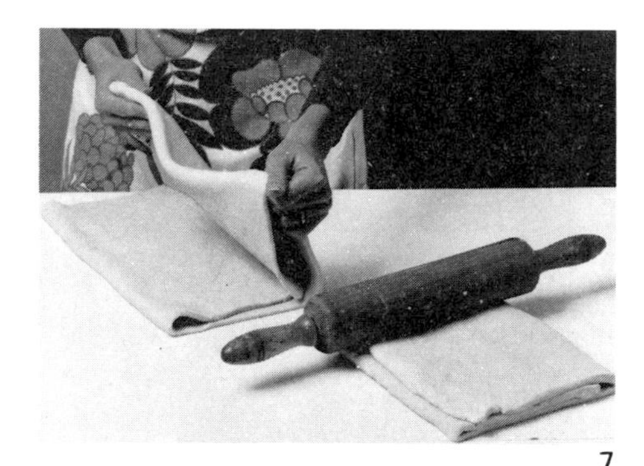

7

PREPARATION 20 minutes

RESTING TIME 3 hours

INGREDIENTS

For approximately 2 pounds 3 ounces (1 kg) dough
3¾ cups (500 g) flour
¾ cup, generous (200 g), softened butter
2 teaspoons (15 g) salt
¾ cup (2 dl) water
¾ cup, generous (200 g), cold butter

For approximately 1 pound 7 ounces (650 g) dough
2¼ cups (325 g) flour
⅔ cup, scant (130 g), softened butter
1½ teaspoons (10 g) salt
½ cup (1.25 dl) water
⅔ cup, scant (130 g), cold butter

For approximately 9 ounces (250 g) dough
1 cup, scant (125 g), flour

3 tablespoons (50 g) softened butter
½ teaspoon (4 g) salt
3 tablespoons (5 cl) water
3 tablespoons (50 g) cold butter
(for these small quantities, mix the dough by hand)

UTENSILS

1 large mixing bowl
1 medium-sized bowl
Electric mixer with dough hook
Plastic scraper
Rolling pin
Plastic wrap or waxed paper
Cardboard rulers

Making the Dough: In the mixing bowl, place the flour and softened butter, broken into pieces. Mix at low speed for 30 seconds, then add the salt and water. Finish kneading the dough by hand if necessary, using the scraper to completely incorporate the butter. Form a ball with the dough. Place the dough in the second bowl and cover it with a plate or a floured cloth. Let it stand for 1 hour in the refrigerator.

Rolling out the Dough: Place the butter between 2 sheets of waxed paper or plastic wrap and tap it several times with the rolling pin to make it more pliable.

Lightly flour the dough and the rolling surface. Roll the dough out into a rectangle about ¼ inch thick. Break the butter into pieces, and cover ⅔ of the dough with them. Fold the dough into thirds, beginning with the third which was not covered with butter (see photo 6, page 38).

Turn the dough so that the line of the fold is perpendicular to you. Roll it out into a rectangle again—this time slightly less than ½ inch thick. Check frequently to be sure the dough does not stick to the table. Reflour the table and the dough whenever necessary, but as lightly as possible. Fold the dough in fourths; i.e., fold the ends until they touch in the middle, then fold the dough in half (see photo 7, page 38).

Give the dough a ¼ turn so the folded edge is perpendicular to you. Roll it out again and fold it in fourths again. At this stage, the dough is said to have been given 2 double turns. Cover it well and chill it for 1 hour in the refrigerator.

If you don't intend to use all of the dough right away, it is best to freeze what is left over because it cannot be stored for more than a day in the refrigerator.

To Freeze: Wrap the dough tightly in aluminum foil or plastic wrap before freezing. Before using the dough, let it defrost for 24 hours in the refrigerator.

Using the Dough: Whether the dough has been frozen or simply chilled as described above, it should be given 2 more turns as described in Recipe 3 for Classic Flaky Pastry and set to chill for one hour more before being rolled out into the shape required for any specific recipe.

5

Succès Batter (Fond de Succès)

Succès batter can be used to prepare desserts such as Succès, Chocolatines, Hazelnut Cream Cakes, and Almond Butter Cream Pastries.

PREPARATION	15 minutes
BAKING TIME	1 hour, 20 minutes
INGREDIENTS	*For 2 8″ (20 cm) shells plus 2 6″ (15 cm) shells or 40 small shells* 5 egg whites 1 tablespoon, generous (20 g), granulated sugar ¾ cup (170 g) granulated sugar ⅔ cup, scant (90 g), confectioners' sugar ⅔ cup (90 g) powdered almonds 3 tablespoons (5 cl) milk Confectioners' sugar to sprinkle on top *For 2 8″ (20 cm) shells or 20 small shells* 3 egg whites 2½ teaspoons (12 g) granulated sugar ½ cup, scant (100 g), granulated sugar ⅓ cup (55 g) confectioners' sugar ⅓ cup, generous (55 g), powdered almonds 2 tablespoons (3 cl) milk Confectioners' sugar to sprinkle on top
UTENSILS	2 large mixing bowls Electric mixer Wooden spatula Parchment paper 2 pastry bags: one with a ¾″ (2 cm) nozzle and one with a ½″ (1 cm) nozzle 2 or 3 baking sheets, depending upon your purposes Sugar dredger

The Batter: Beat the egg whites until stiff; halfway through, add the smaller amount of granulated sugar. If you are using leftover egg whites and have forgotten how many you have, remember that 5 egg whites = ¾ cup (155 g) and 3 egg whites = ½ cup (95 g).

8

9

Preheat the oven to 275°F (135°C).

In a separate bowl, mix the larger amount of granulated sugar with the confectioners' sugar. Add the powdered almonds and the milk, then fold in a few spoonfuls of egg white. Pour this mixture on top of the remaining egg whites, and fold it in with a wooden spatula. Work carefully but quickly; there should be no particles of unblended egg white in the finished batter. Butter the baking sheets and dust them lightly with flour or line the sheets with parchment paper, sticking each corner down with a dab of batter.

Baking: *For large shells:* With a pencil, draw an 8″ (20 cm) circle and a 6″ (15 cm) circle on each baking sheet. Squeeze out the batter in a continuous spiral to fill the circles, using a pastry bag with a ¾″ (2 cm) nozzle (see photo 8, page 41). Dust the batter with confectioners' sugar and bake both baking sheets for 1 hour and 20 minutes. After 40 minutes, place the top baking sheet on the bottom and vice versa, so as to brown them both evenly.

For small shells: With a pencil, draw 20 1½″ (4 cm) circles on each pastry sheet to make small shells or Chocolatines. Fill each circle with the batter using a pastry bag with a ½ inch nozzle as described above. To prepare Colisées and Noisettines, draw oval shapes (see photo 9, page 41), and to prepare Succès, use the pastry bag set with a ¾″ (2 cm) nozzle and make mounds 1½″ (4 cm) in diameter. Dust them all with confectioners' sugar and bake both sheets at the same time for 45 to 50 minutes. Switch the sheets midway through the baking process.

Watch the browning of the Succès; you might have to lower the oven temperature because you find that they are browning too rapidly.

To Store: You can keep Succès for 15 days in a tightly sealed container.

6

Génoise

The Génoise is used to make many cream-filled cakes and desserts, but it can also be eaten plain.

PREPARATION 20 minutes

BAKING TIME 30 minutes

INGREDIENTS

For 2 8″ (20 cm) cakes
⅔ cup (155 g) granulated sugar
5 whole (1 cup) eggs
3 tablespoons (45 g) butter
1¼ cup, scant (155 g), flour
1½ teaspoons (8 g) vanilla sugar

For 1 8″ (20 cm) cake
⅓ cup (78 g) granulated sugar
3 whole (½ cup) eggs
1½ tablespoons (23 g) butter
½ cup, generous (78 g), flour
1 teaspoon, scant (4 g), vanilla sugar

UTENSILS

Mixing bowl
Electric mixer
Wire whisk
Large pot
Small saucepan
Wooden spatula
Flour sifter
2 8″ (20 cm) round cake pans

The Batter: Preheat the oven to 350°F (180°C). Place the eggs and sugar in a mixing bowl and set the bowl over a pot of boiling water; the water should not touch the bowl. Beat the eggs and sugar together for 1 minute, with the wire whisk. Then, with the bowl away from the heat, beat with the mixer at high speed for 2 minutes, then for 5 minutes more at low speed or until the mixture is very pale and falls from the wooden spoon in a smooth ribbon.

Clarify the butter in a small saucepan. Sift the flour and vanilla sugar, then fold into the egg-sugar mixture. Fold in the warm butter. Stop mixing as soon as all of the ingredients are well blended. This step should be done quickly and the Génoise should be baked right away.

Baking: Pour the batter into the buttered and floured pans and bake for 30 minutes or until golden brown. Let the cake cool for about 10 minutes, then turn out onto a rack, while still warm. Let cool completely before using.

Note: Do not overheat the egg mixture in the double boiler or the Génoise will dry out too fast when baking. For instructions on cutting the Génoise into layers, see the entry for Layer Cakes in the Dictionary of Terms and Procedures.

To Store: The Génoise will keep fresh for 8 days in the refrigerator if wrapped well in plastic or foil.

To Freeze: The Génoise will keep for 1 month if wrapped well, but be sure to allow it to thaw completely for 24 hours in the refrigerator before using it.

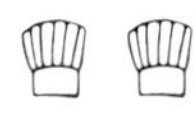

7

French Meringue (Meringue Française)

Meringue is used to make Têtes de Nègre, Autumn Meringue Cake, and Meringues Chantilly.

PREPARATION	15 minutes
BAKING TIME	1 hour, 15 minutes
INGREDIENTS	*For 3 7" (18 cm) circles or 20 individual shells or 1 pound (450 g) meringue* 5 egg whites 1 tablespoon, generous (20 g), granulated sugar ½ cup (125 g) granulated sugar, mixed with 1 cup, scant (125 g), confectioners' sugar *For 12 individual shells or 10½ ounce (300 g) meringue* 3 egg whites 2 teaspoons (12 g) granulated sugar ⅓ cup (75 g) granulated sugar mixed with ½ cup (75 g) confectioners' sugar
UTENSILS	Mixing bowl Electric mixer Pastry bag with ¾" (2 cm) nozzle Parchment paper 1 or 2 baking sheets

The Batter: Preheat the oven to 275°F (135°C). Beat the egg whites until very stiff; halfway through, add the smaller amount of granulated sugar. Sift the mixture of granulated sugar and confectioners' sugar together and fold into the egg whites.

Baking: Do not let the meringue sit; it tends to fall apart. Fill the pastry bag right away with it and squeeze it onto a buttered and floured baking sheet or onto a baking sheet lined with parchment paper (stick each corner of the paper to the pan with a dab of meringue). You can make 3 7″ (18 cm) circles for the Autumn Meringue Cake or 20 oval shells 1½″ by 2¾″ (3.5 cm by 7 cm) (see photo 10, page 44) or 20 2″ (5 cm) round shells to make Têtes de Nègre.

You can bake two sheets at once. Bake for 1 hour, 15 minutes. The meringues should be very light brown and completely dry on both the top and bottom, when done. If they brown too quickly, turn the oven down.

Note: When you use leftover egg whites, remember that 5 egg whites = ¾ cup (155 g) and 3 egg whites = ½ cup (90 g).

To Store: Meringues can be kept for 3 weeks in a metal box or a tightly closed container.

10

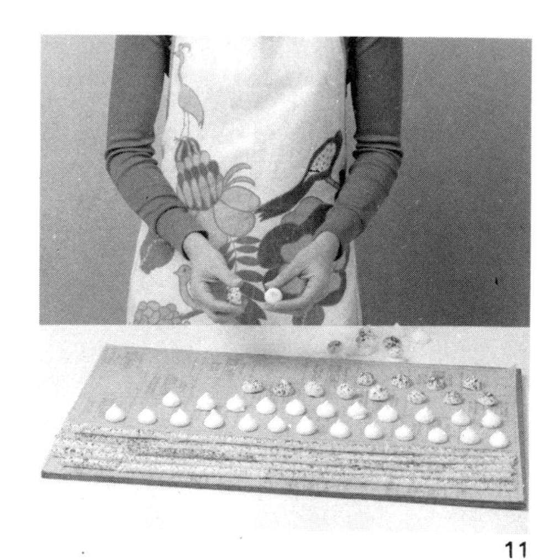

11

8

Swiss Meringue (Meringue Suisse)

Swiss meringue is used to make decorations, including snowmen, mushrooms, and Doigts de Fée (Chocolate Fingers).

PREPARATION	15 minutes
BAKING TIME	45 minutes
INGREDIENTS	4 egg whites = ⅔ cup (120 g) 1⅔ cups (250 g) confectioners' sugar *or* 1 cup, generous (250 g), granulated sugar Unsweetened powdered cocoa [optional] ¾ cup (120 g) powdered semi-sweet chocolate [optional]

UTENSILS	Large mixing bowl
Large pot
Electric mixer
Thermometer
Wire whisk
Pastry bag with ¼″ (0.6 cm) nozzle
Parchment paper
Baking sheets

The Batter: Preheat the oven to 275°F (135°C). Place the egg whites and sugar in a large mixing bowl and set the bowl over a large pot of boiling water; the water should not touch the bowl. Beat the egg whites and the sugar with the whisk until the mixture reaches 120°F (50°C). Remove from the heat and beat with the mixer at high speed for 5 minutes, then lower the speed and beat for 5 more minutes or until the meringue is very stiff. Fit the pastry bag with the nozzle; fill with the batter. Butter the baking sheet and dust it with flour or line it with parchment paper, sticking each corner to the sheet with a dab of meringue.

Squeeze the meringue onto the baking sheet in long strips or various shapes, such as mushroom caps and stems.

Note: If you wish, sprinkle the meringues with powdered unsweetened cocoa. Chocolate meringue can be made by adding the powdered semi-sweet chocolate while beating the egg whites at high speed.

Baking: Bake the meringues for 40 to 50 minutes in the oven, keeping the oven door ajar with a spoon. Taste a piece; it should be dry on the outside and soft inside. When baked, attach the stems to the mushroom caps by pressing them together gently. Cut the long strips into ½″ (1 cm) pieces to make Doigts de Fée (Chocolate Fingers), and into 1½″ (4 cm) pieces for Petits Fours (see photo 11, page 44).

To Store: Swiss meringue will keep for 3 weeks in a tightly closed box in a dry place.

9

Brioche Dough (Pâte à Brioche Surfine)

This dough should be made the night before intended use. If preferred, it can be frozen and used at a later time. Brioche dough may be mixed with an electric mixer equipped with a dough hook, but it is best to knead small quantities by hand.

PREPARATION 30 minutes

RISING TIME 3½ to 5½ hours

RESTING TIME 12 hours

INGREDIENTS

For approximately 2 pounds 10 ounces (1,200 g) dough
1 pound (450 g) butter
1 cake (15 g) compressed baker's yeast
2 teaspoons warm water
2 teaspoons (15 g) salt
2 tablespoons (30 g) granulated sugar
1½ tablespoons milk
3¾ cups (500 g) flour
6 eggs

For approximately 1 pound 5 ounces (600 g) dough
½ pound (225 g) butter
½ cake (8 g) compressed baker's yeast
1 teaspoon warm water
1 teaspoon (8 g) salt
1 tablespoon (15 g) granulated sugar
2¼ teaspoons milk
1¾ cups (250 g) flour
3 eggs

For approximately 12½ ounces (360 g) dough
½ cup, generous (135 g), butter
⅓ cake (5 g) compressed baker's yeast
¾ teaspoon warm water
¾ teaspoon (5 g) salt
2 teaspoons (10 g) granulated sugar
1½ teaspoons milk
1 cup, generous (150 g), flour
2 eggs

12

13

Strawberry Yule Log, Recipe 67

Traiteur
PARIS DEAUVILLE

UTENSILS

2 small bowls or glasses
1 large mixing bowl
Electric mixer with dough hook
Plastic scraper
Rolling pin
Plastic wrap or waxed paper

Note: This dough works best if made in large quantities. The following instructions are for making 2 pounds 10 ounces (1,200 g) of dough. The same method applies for making smaller amounts, but the amount of egg added at the various steps must be reduced according to the total number of eggs used.

Making the Dough: Take the butter out of the refrigerator 15 minutes before making the dough. Dissolve the yeast in the warm water. In another bowl, dissolve the salt and sugar in the milk. Never bring yeast into direct contact with salt or sugar.

Using an electric mixer: In the mixing bowl, place the salt-milk-sugar mixture. Add the flour, then add the yeast solution. Beat for 2 minutes at low speed, then all at once add 4 eggs and continue to beat until the dough is firm, homogenous, and smooth. Add the 2 remaining eggs one at a time, then beat at medium speed for 10 to 15 more minutes or until the dough is light and silky and no longer sticks to your fingers. Place the butter between 2 sheets of waxed paper or plastic wrap and tap it a few times with a rolling pin to flatten it. Break the butter into pieces the size of an egg. With the mixer on low speed, quickly add the butter to the dough—this should take no more than 2 minutes.

Kneading by hand: Have all the ingredients measured and ready for use. Place the flour on the table in a mound and make a well in the center. Put the yeast solution in the well and mix it with a little flour, then add 3 eggs. Incorporate about half the flour, then add the sugar-salt-milk mixture and 1 more egg, working with your fingers to mix all the ingredients together. When all the flour has been mixed in, knead the dough for 15 minutes, stretching it and slapping it back onto the table as you do so. When the time is up, add the remaining 2 eggs and keep working the dough until it becomes elastic and stretches easily without breaking. Now add the softened butter, prepared as described above for using an electric mixer, to ⅓ of the dough; then add the remaining dough, half of it at a time, using the plastic scraper to cut and mix the dough together (see photo 13, page 46). Try not to use your hands too much because the butter will melt too quickly.

14

Chocolate-Flavored Yule Log, Recipe 68

Rising: Place the dough in a large bowl, cover the bowl with a cloth, and let it stand for 1½ to 2½ hours at room temperature. When the dough has risen to twice its original bulk, punch it down and stretch it twice (see photo 14, page 49). Let the dough rise again in the refrigerator for 2 or 3 hours until double its bulk again — it should be rounded on top like a ball. Punch the dough down as before, cover tightly, and keep it refrigerated overnight.

The next day, place the dough on a floured board and flatten it quickly by hand, then place it in the molds that will be used for baking (see photos 15-17, page 50).

To Freeze: The dough will keep for 1 month if wrapped tightly in plastic or aluminum foil. If you are making a large quantity, divide it into 2 or 3 pieces before freezing. Let the dough thaw for 24 hours in the refrigerator before using.

15

16

17

10
Short Pastry (Pâte Brisée)

This pastry dough is used to make pie shells, Cherry Molds, or Clafoutis Tutti Frutti. The dough should be prepared a day in advance if possible.

18

19

PREPARATION — 5 to 10 minutes

RESTING TIME — 1 hour, minimum

BAKING TIME — 15-25 minutes

INGREDIENTS

For approximately 2 pounds (950 g) dough (3 9″ tarts)
3¾ cups (500 g) flour
1½ tablespoons (20 g) granulated sugar
2 teaspoons (15 g) salt
1⅔ cups (375 g) butter
2 eggs
2 tablespoons milk

For approximately 12 ounces (350 g) dough (1 10″ tart)
1⅓ cups, generous (185 g), flour
1½ teaspoons (7 g) granulated sugar
¾ teaspoon (5 g) salt
½ cup, generous (140 g), butter
¾ beaten egg
2¼ teaspoons milk

For approximately 9 ounces (250 g) dough (1 9″ tart)
1 cup (140 g) flour
1 teaspoon (5 g) granulated sugar
½ teaspoon (4 g) salt
6½ tablespoons (100 g) butter
½ beaten egg
2 teaspoons milk

UTENSILS

- Large mixing bowl
- Electric mixer [optional]
- Rolling pin
- Parchment paper
- Lentils for mold
- Pie plates, metal flan ring, or whatever else is needed for intended purpose

Making the Dough: *Using an electric mixer:* In a bowl, mix the salt and the sugar, add the butter in small pieces, then add the eggs and the milk. Beat the ingredients for a few seconds and then add all the flour at once.

Beat the ingredients just long enough to blend them. If the dough is worked too long, it will become elastic and tough when cooked. Don't worry if small pieces of butter are still visible.

Kneading by hand: Have all the ingredients measured and ready for use. Place the flour on the table in a mound, then make a well in the center of it. Sprinkle the sugar and the salt on the edges of the flour and in the well place the butter and the eggs. Mix all the ingredients together until crumbly, working very quickly with the tips of your fingers (see photo 18, page 51). Then, knead the dough gently (*fraiser*) by pushing it away from you against the table with the palm of your hand (see photo 19, page 51). Add the milk as you do so. Gather the dough into a ball and *fraiser* once more, working as quickly and gently as possible. Form the dough into a ball, wrap it in a floured cloth or place in a covered bowl and let it stand for at least 1 hour, or if possible overnight, in the refrigerator; the dough will be easier to work the next day.

Roll out the dough on a lightly floured table. Line the pie shells or flan circle with the dough (see photo 20, page 52); either cut the excess dough off flush with the mold by rolling the rolling pin over the mold, or leave a small border and crimp it by pressing the dough against the mold at regular intervals with the blunt edge of a knife (see photo 21, page 52). Leave in a cool place for 1 hour before baking.

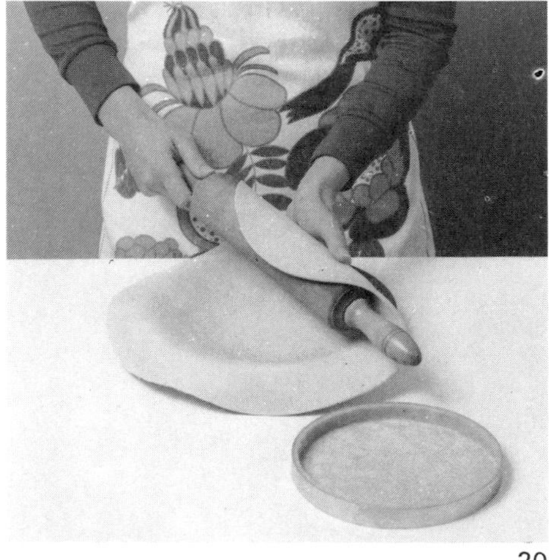

20

21

Baking: If you bake the shell empty, prick the bottom of it with a fork, then line the shell with parchment paper and fill it with lentils. This will prevent the dough from rising or forming bubbles as it bakes.

Once the shells are baked, remove the paper and the lentils; the lentils can be used in this way again.

If you decide to fill the unbaked shell with fruit and then bake it, do not prick the bottom of the shell because the juices will soak through the dough and make it soggy.

Note: To prevent the dough from becoming too elastic while working it by hand, first mix half the amount of butter into the flour until crumbly, work in the remaining butter, then continue the recipe as given above.

To Store: The dough will keep 8 days in the refrigerator. The pie shells can be prepared 24 hours before baking and filling.

11
Cream Puff Pastry (Pâte à Chou)

Do not work this dough too long or else the puffs will not rise correctly.

PREPARATION 15 minutes

BAKING TIME 20 to 30 minutes per baking sheet

INGREDIENTS *For approximately 1⅓ cups (600 g) dough*
4-5 eggs = 1 cup (¼ l), beaten
1 cup (¼ l) mixture of half milk, half water
¾ teaspoon (5 g) salt
1 teaspoon (5 g) granulated sugar
7½ tablespoons (110 g) butter
1 cup (140 g) flour
Confectioners' sugar

For approximately ⅔ cup (300 g) dough
2-3 eggs = ½ cup (12.5 cl), beaten
½ cup (12.5 cl) mixture of half milk, half water
¼ teaspoon, generous (2.5 g), salt
½ teaspoon (2.5 g) granulated sugar
3½ tablespoons (55 g) butter
½ cup (70 g) flour
Confectioners' sugar

For approximately ½ cup, scant (200 g), dough
1-2 eggs = ⅓ cup (8 cl), beaten
⅓ cup (8 cl) mixture of half milk, half water
¼ teaspoon (1.5 g) salt
¼ teaspoon, generous (1.5 g) granulated sugar
2 tablespoons (35 g) butter
⅓ cup (45 g) flour
Confectioners' sugar

UTENSILS

Large, thick-bottomed saucepan
Mixing bowl, warmed
Wooden spoon
Wire whisk
Pastry bag with ⅝" (1.5 cm) or ½" (1 cm) nozzle
Sugar dredger
Baking sheets, as needed

Making the Dough: Preheat oven to 425°F (220°C). Measure the eggs, since their volume can be more or less than the actual amount required by the recipe.

Place the water-milk mixture in the saucepan and add the salt, sugar, and butter. Bring slowly to a boil, then remove from the heat and add all the flour at one time. Beat the dough vigorously with a wooden spoon, replace the saucepan on the heat, and beat the dough for 1 minute or until it comes away from the sides of the pan and no longer sticks to the spoon. Transfer the dough to a warmed mixing bowl. Add a third of the beaten egg, beating the dough all the while with the spoon. When the egg is mixed in, add half the remaining egg, still beating the dough; finally, add the remaining egg and continue to beat until the dough is smooth.

Baking: Fill the pastry bag with the dough. Butter and flour the baking sheets or line them with waxed paper, sticking each corner of the paper to the sheet with some of the dough. Make 1½" (4 cm) rounds or, if you are experienced, make long eclairs or ovals 1¼" by 2¾" (3 by 7 cm), or 1 large round Paris-Brest (see photos 22 and 23, page 55). Dust the pieces of dough lightly with the confectioners' sugar so that their shapes will be more even after baking.

Bake as soon as the dough is ready. Bake each sheet at 425°F (220°C) for the first 15 minutes, then lower the heat to 400°F (200°C) for the next 15 minutes. This change in temperature will prevent the puffs from cracking open, but be

22

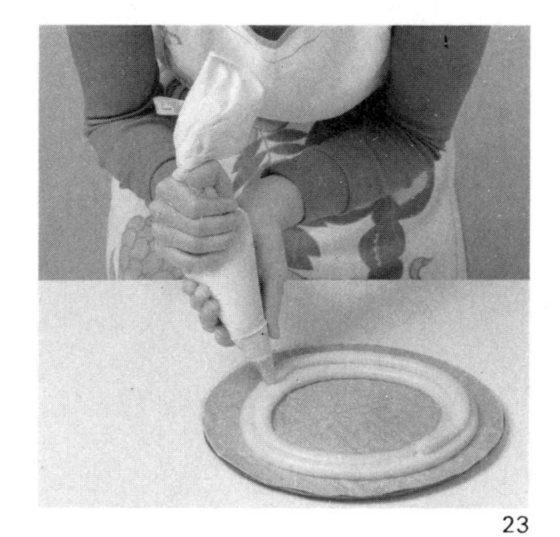

23

sure to keep the oven door ajar with a spoon. Watch the baking to see that the puffs are slightly moist. Small puffs bake faster than the larger ones, such as Paris-Brest or Saint-Honoré.

Note: Since the cooked puffs keep well, you should prepare and bake all the dough you make rather than trying to reserve leftover dough for later use.

To Store: The puffs can easily be kept a week in plastic bags in the refrigerator. They can be kept 1 month in the freezer but be sure to defrost frozen puffs for 24 hours in the refrigerator before using.

12

Sweet Short Pastry (Pâte Sucrée)

This dough is very delicate and breaks easily; it is used for pie crusts or small tarts, as well as for cookies. It is best to prepare it the night before.

PREPARATION	15 minutes
RESTING TIME	1 hour
BAKING TIME	15-25 minutes

INGREDIENTS

For approximately 2 pounds 10 ounces (1,200 g) dough
1½ cups (350 g) butter
½ cup (125 g) granulated sugar *or*
¾ cup (125 g) confectioners' sugar
1½ teaspoons (8 g) vanilla sugar
1 large pinch salt
3¾ cups (500 g) flour
1 cup (125 g) powdered almonds
2 eggs

For approximately 10½ ounces (300 g) dough
6 tablespoons (90 g) butter
2 tablespoons (30 g) granulated sugar *or*
3 tablespoons (30 g) confectioners' sugar
¼ teaspoon, generous (2 g), vanilla sugar
1 pinch salt
1 cup, scant (125 g), flour
3 tablespoons (30 g) powdered almonds
½ beaten egg

UTENSILS

Large mixing bowl
Electric mixer with dough hook
Plastic scraper
Rolling pin

Making the Dough: Place the butter between 2 sheets of plastic wrap or waxed paper, and tap it several times with a rolling pin to make it more workable.

Using an electric mixer: In a mixing bowl, blend together the butter (broken into pieces), sugar, vanilla sugar, salt, flour, and powdered almonds. Last of all, add the eggs.

Mix all the ingredients rapidly; this dough should not be worked for a long time. Wrap it well and let it stand for 24 hours in the refrigerator before rolling it out.

Kneading by hand: If kneading by hand, use the plastic scraper to cut and mix the dough. Follow the directions given for short pastry, Recipe 10.

Baking: Follow the directions given for short pastry, Recipe 10.

To Store: The dough will keep 15 days in the refrigerator if wrapped in foil.

To Freeze: You can freeze the dough for up to 2 months, if it is wrapped in foil. Before baking, defrost in the refrigerator for 24 hours.

Chapter 2

BASIC RECIPES FOR CREAMS AND SYRUPS

RECIPES

13. Chantilly Cream (Chantilly Nature Vanillée)
14. Chocolate Chantilly (Chantilly au Chocolat)
15. Fresh Fruit Sauce (Coulis de Fruits Frais)
16. Caramel Sauce (Caramel Liquide)
17. Almond Pastry Cream (Crème d'Amandes)
18. Homemade Almond Paste (Pâte d'Amandes à Faire Chez Soi)
19. Chiboust Pastry Cream (Crème Chibouste)
20. Butter Cream (Crème au Beurre Nature)
21. Coffee-Flavored Butter Cream (Crème au Beurre au Café)
22. Chocolate Butter Cream (Crème au Beurre au Chocolat)
23. Almond Butter Cream (Crème au Beurre Praliné)
24. Vanilla Pastry Cream (Crème Pâtissière Vanillée)
25. Coffee Pastry Cream (Crème Pâtissière au Café)
26. Chocolate Pastry Cream (Crème Pâtissière au Chocolat)
27. Chocolate Icing (Glaçage au Chocolat)

28. Fondant Icing (Glaçage au Fondant)
29. Dessert Syrup (Sirop à Entremets)
30. Chocolate Mousse (Mousse au Chocolat)
31. Chocolate Sauce (Sauce au Chocolat)
32. Vanilla Sauce (Sauce à la Vanille)
33. Bavarian Cream (Appareil à Bavaroise)
34. Charlotte Cream (Appareil à Charlotte)
35. Basic Soufflé (Appareil à Soufflé)
36. Almond Paste Decoration (Décors en Pâte d'Amande)

Concord Cake, Recipe 72

LENÔTRE
Traiteur
PARIS-DEAUVILLE-NEW YORK

13

Chantilly Cream (Chantilly Nature Vanillée)

Chantilly cream (vanilla-flavored whipped cream) can be mixed with other creams to make them lighter; it can also be flavored with chocolate. Avoid whipping the cream for too long; otherwise it will turn into butter.

PREPARATION 10 minutes

INGREDIENTS

For 4 cups (570 g) Chantilly
2 cups (450 g) crème fraîche, very cold
6 tablespoons (1 dl) cold milk
2 tablespoons (30 g) granulated sugar
1½ teaspoons (8 g) vanilla sugar
3 tablespoons (50 g) shaved ice or ice water

Or 2 cups, generous (500 ml), heavy cream
1½ teaspoons (8 g) vanilla sugar

For 2 cups (285 g) Chantilly
1 cup (225 g) crème fraîche, very cold
3 tablespoons (5 cl) cold milk
1 tablespoon (15 g) granulated sugar
¾ teaspoon (4 g) vanilla sugar
1½ tablespoons (25 g) shaved ice or ice water

Or 1 cup (250 ml) heavy cream
¾ teaspoon (4 g) vanilla sugar

UTENSILS

Electric mixer
Large mixing bowl, chilled

Whipping the Cream: Mix the crème fraîche with the milk in a chilled mixing bowl; add the sugar, vanilla sugar, and the shaved ice or ice water, whip at low speed for one minute, then whip at high speed for 1 to 3 minutes more or until it stands in soft peaks.

If using heavy cream, simply whip it with the vanilla sugar in a chilled bowl until it peaks. No other ingredients are necessary.

Refrigerate the Chantilly for later use or use immediately. It may either be used as it is or added to other pastry creams to make them lighter.

Note: Be sure to have all your ingredients very cold before you start, or else you will run the risk of turning the cream into butter.

To Store: Chantilly cream keeps for 24 hours if refrigerated in a tightly closed container.

14
Chocolate Chantilly (Chantilly au Chocolat)

PREPARATION 15 minutes

INGREDIENTS

For 4 cups, generous (700 g), Chantilly
7 ounces (200 g) semi-sweet chocolate
2 cups (450 g) crème fraîche
6 tablespoons (1 dl) cold milk
1½ teaspoons (8 g) vanilla sugar
3 tablespoons (50 g) shaved ice or ice water

Or 7 ounces (200 g) semi-sweet chocolate
2 cups, generous (500 ml), whipping cream
1½ teaspoons (8 g) vanilla sugar

For 2 cups, generous (350 g), Chantilly
3½ ounces (100 g) semi-sweet chocolate
1 cup (225 g) crème fraîche
3 tablespoons (5 cl) cold milk
¾ teaspoon (4 g) vanilla sugar
1½ tablespoons (25 g) shaved ice or ice water

Or 3½ ounces (100 g) semi-sweet chocolate
1 cup (250 ml) whipping cream
¾ teaspoon (4 g) vanilla sugar

UTENSILS

Double boiler
Electric mixer
Large mixing bowl, chilled
Wire whisk
Wooden spatula

Whipping the Cream: Melt the chocolate in the double boiler and let it cool to 70°F (25°C)—barely lukewarm.

Follow the instructions for preparing Chantilly cream (page 60). After the cream has been whipped, beat ⅓ of the cream into the cooled chocolate with the wire whisk; then gently fold the chocolate and cream mixture into the remaining whipped cream with the wooden spatula. Work as carefully but as quickly as possible, since the cream will fall apart if worked too long.

Note: All of your ingredients should be very cold, or the whipped cream is likely to turn to butter.

Confiture préparée selon
l'ancienne recette de ma
grand'mère Eléonore Lenôtre
Fraises

15
Fresh Fruit Sauce (Coulis de Fruits Frais)

This sauce can be served with a brioche, Génoise, charlotte, pudding, or Bavarian cream.

PREPARATION 10 minutes

INGREDIENTS *For approximately 4⅓ cups (1 l) sauce*
2¼ pounds (1 kg) fresh fruit
2⅔ cups (600 g) granulated sugar

For approximately 2 cups, generous (½ l), sauce
1 pound 2 ounces (500 g) fresh fruit
1⅓ cups (300 g) granulated sugar

UTENSILS Electric blender

Making the Sauce: Use any fruit of your choice, such as peaches, apricots, strawberries, raspberries, etc. Cut large fruits into quarters. Add the fruit to the sugar and blend at medium speed for 2 minutes, or until the ingredients are blended together well.

Note: When fruit is out of season, you can use canned fruit; just drain off the syrup and blend as described above, omitting the sugar.

To Store: Fruit sauce will keep for up to 8 days in a tightly closed container in the refrigerator.

To Freeze: This sauce can be frozen. When thawing, whip the sauce to make it smooth again.

Strawberry Almond Cake, Recipe 74

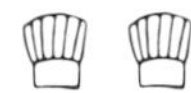

16

Caramel Sauce (Caramel Liquide)

This sauce may be served with a charlotte, vanilla custard, or ice cream.

PREPARATION 15 minutes

INGREDIENTS *To top a dessert serving 8 persons*
¾ cup, generous (200 g), granulated sugar
3 tablespoons water (to make caramel)
10 drops lemon juice
¼ cup water (to make sauce)

UTENSILS Thick-bottomed saucepan
Wooden spoon
Pastry brush

Making the Caramel: Place the sugar in the saucepan, add the water and heat slowly while stirring slowly with a wooden spoon. Be careful not to splash any sugar onto the sides of the pan. Add the lemon juice when the sugar begins to boil and form large bubbles. Stop stirring. If you are working on a gas stove, the flame should not extend past the bottom of the saucepan or the sugar will burn on the sides. If any sugar crystallizes on the sides of the pan and starts to brown, moisten the inside of the pan with a pastry brush dipped in water. When the melted sugar begins to brown, tip the pan and swirl it so that the sugar will color evenly. Do not stir.

Making the Sauce: Have ¼ cup of water measured and ready for use. When the caramel is a rich golden brown, remove the pan from the heat and pour half the water into it. The sugar will splatter so move your hands away from the pan as quickly as possible. When the splattering stops, add the remaining water. Stir the mixture with the spatula to mix the water and caramel completely. The caramel sauce should be very liquid, or else it will harden when it cools; add more water if necessary.

To Store: This sauce will keep for one month in the refrigerator in a tightly closed jar or bottle.

17

Almond Pastry Cream (Crème d'Amandes)

Almond pastry cream is used to garnish tarts, brioche, and other desserts. The almond mixture can be prepared as much as a week ahead of time.

PREPARATION — 15 minutes, plus 20 minutes to prepare the pastry cream

INGREDIENTS

For approximately 5½ cups (1 kg) cream
1½ cups (375 g) pastry cream (Recipe 24)
2 cups (250 g) powdered almonds
1⅔ cups (250 g) confectioners' sugar
3 eggs
2½ tablespoons (25 g) cornstarch
1½ tablespoons (25 ml) rum
1 cup, generous (250 g), soft butter

For approximately 2¾ cups (500 g) cream
¾ cup (185 g) pastry cream (Recipe 24)
1 cup (125 g) powdered almonds
¾ cup, generous (125 g), confectioners' sugar
1½ eggs, beaten
4 teaspoons (12 g) cornstarch
2½ teaspoons (12 ml) rum
¼ pound (125 g) soft butter

For approximately 2 cups (350 g) cream
½ cup (130 g) pastry cream (Recipe 24)
⅔ cup (90 g) powdered almonds
⅔ cup, scant (90 g), confectioners' sugar
1 egg
1 tablespoon (9 g) cornstarch
2 teaspoons (9 ml) rum
6 tablespoons (90 g) soft butter

UTENSILS

Electric mixer with paddle, or wooden spoon
Mixing bowl

Making the Cream: Prepare the pastry cream (Recipe 24) one hour ahead of time if you are planning to make the almond pastry cream the same day.

In the mixing bowl, cream the butter until soft, add the almond powder, beating until well mixed, then add the confectioners' sugar. Beat in the eggs one by one. Blend with the mixer set at medium speed until the batter is light and smooth, then add the cornstarch and the rum.

Add the chilled pastry cream to the almond base, mixing in one tablespoon at a time until blended.

To Store: Almond pastry cream will keep for up to 8 days in the refrigerator if stored in a tightly sealed container.

18

Homemade Almond Paste (Pâte d'Amandes à Faire Chez Soi)

Almond paste is used to prepare Genoa Cake, Pentecost Cake, Friands, Financiers, and Walnut Tartlets.

PREPARATION	5 minutes
INGREDIENTS	*For approximately 1 pound 2 ounces (500 g) paste* 1½ cups (200 g) powdered almonds 1⅔ cups (250 g) confectioners' sugar 2 egg whites from small eggs *For approximately 9 ounces (250 g) paste* ⅔ cup, generous (100 g), powdered almonds 1¾ cups, generous (125 g), confectioners' sugar 1 egg white from a small egg
UTENSILS	Wooden spoon Mixing bowl

Making the Paste: Mix the almond powder with the confectioners' sugar, then add the egg whites and blend until smooth.

Note: Leftover almond paste can be used to make simple candies by stuffing dates, plums, or candied cherries with it.

To Store: Almond paste will keep for up to one week in the refrigerator when stored in a tightly closed container or wrapped tightly in aluminum foil.

19
Chiboust Pastry Cream (Crème Chibouste)

Chiboust cream is a light pastry cream mixed with an Italian meringue. Everything must be done rapidly, so have all your ingredients ready before beginning.

PREPARATION 30 minutes

INGREDIENTS

For approximately 6 cups (450 g) cream

For pastry cream

1½ cups (3.75 dl) milk
¾ vanilla bean
4 egg yolks
3½ tablespoons (50 g) granulated sugar
3 tablespoons (30 g) cornstarch

For meringue

½ cup, scant (100 g), granulated sugar
3 tablespoons water
6 egg whites = 1 cup, scant (185 g)
2½ tablespoons (38 g) granulated sugar

For approximately 4 cups (300 g) cream

For pastry cream

1 cup (¼ l) milk
½ vanilla bean
3 egg yolks
2½ tablespoons (35 g) granulated sugar
2 tablespoons (20 g) cornstarch

For meringue

⅓ cup, scant (70 g), granulated sugar
2 tablespoons water
4 egg whites = ½ cup (120 g)
5 teaspoons (25 g) granulated sugar

UTENSILS

Pastry bag with ¾″ (2 cm) round metal nozzle
Small saucepan
Candy thermometer [optional]
Electric mixer
2 large bowls

Making the Pastry Cream: Prepare the pastry cream base using the above-listed ingredients but following the instructions for vanilla pastry cream (Recipe

24). This pastry cream is less sweet than the classic recipe. Keep the cream hot; cover it to prevent a skin from forming on top.

Making the Meringue: Place the larger amount of sugar with the water in a small saucepan. Bring to a boil, stirring until the sugar is dissolved. As the sugar cooks, beat the whites until very stiff, adding the smaller amount of sugar half-way through. This should take about 5 minutes. Check the sugar. When it reaches 248°F (120°C) or the hard ball stage, it is ready to use. (If you don't have a candy thermometer, let a drop of sugar fall from a spoon into a glass of cold water; the sugar should form a ball and hold its shape on the bottom of the glass.) With the mixer on high speed, pour the boiling sugar into the egg whites, being careful not to let it fall on the edge of the bowl or on the beaters.

Reduce the mixer to low speed and add the boiling pastry cream. Beat just long enough to blend the two mixtures together. Transfer the cream to a second bowl or directly into a pastry bag—this will cool it off and prevent it from becoming grainy.

Chiboust pastry cream should be used as soon as possible after being prepared. A Saint-Honoré, a Paris-Brest, or individual puffs may be decorated with it. It is important to fit the pastry bag with a large nozzle—star shaped or not —since using a smaller nozzle would place too much pressure on the cream and make it fall apart. Once decorated the dessert should be chilled for at least one hour before being served.

To Store: Chiboust pastry cream must be eaten within 24 hours of being made. Keep desserts decorated with it refrigerated until served.

20

Butter Cream (Crème au Beurre Nature)

This filling can be used as it is or flavored with chocolate, coffee, liqueur, etc. as shown in the following recipes.

PREPARATION 15 minutes

INGREDIENTS *For approximately 4 cups (750 g) cream*

1⅓ cups (300 g) granulated sugar
½ cup (12 cl) water
12 egg yolks
1½ cups, generous (375 g), soft butter, broken into pieces
Optional French Meringue (see Recipe 7 for procedure)
5 egg whites = ¾ cup (155 g)
⅓ cup (75 g) granulated sugar
½ cup (75 g) confectioners' sugar

For approximately 2⅔ cups (500 g) cream

¾ cup, generous (200 g), granulated sugar
⅓ cup (8 cl) water
8 egg yolks
1 cup (250 g) soft butter, broken into pieces

Optional French Meringue (see Recipe 7 for procedure)
3 egg whites = ½ cup (100 g)
3½ tablespoons (50 g) granulated sugar
⅓ cup (50 g) confectioners' sugar

For approximately 1⅓ cups (250 g) cream
½ cup, scant (100 g), granulated sugar
2½ tablespoons (4 cl) water
4 egg yolks
½ cup (125 g) soft butter, broken into pieces
Optional French Meringue (see Recipe 7 for procedure)
2 small egg whites = ¼ cup (55 g)
5 teaspoons (25 g) granulated sugar
2½ tablespoons (25 g) confectioners' sugar

UTENSILS
Small heavy-bottomed saucepan
Candy thermometer [optional]
Mixing bowl
Electric mixer or wire whisk

Preparing the Sugar: Boil the sugar with the water in a small saucepan until it reaches 250°F (120°C); this should take no more than 10 minutes. Use the thermometer or test the sugar by letting a drop fall from a spoon into a glass of cold water. If the temperature is correct, the sugar will form a ball and hold its shape on the bottom of the glass.

Making the Cream: Meanwhile, whip the egg yolks at medium speed in a mixing bowl, then add the boiling sugar little by little, being careful not to let it fall on the sides of the bowl or the beaters. Continue beating until the mixture is cool (2 to 3 minutes). When the cream is cool, add the butter and continue to whip the mixture at low speed for 5 more minutes. At this point, add the desired flavoring or, if you wish a lighter cream, fold in the French Meringue.

To Store: Unflavored butter cream filling will keep refrigerated for up to 8 days in a tightly closed container. Before using the cream, let it stand for 1 hour at room temperature and then work the cream with a wooden spatula until it is smooth before adding a desired flavoring.

21

Coffee-Flavored Butter Cream (Crème au Beurre au Café)

Preparing the Cream: Dissolve 1½ tablespoons of instant coffee in 2 teaspoons of hot water or, if you prefer, use 2 teaspoons of coffee extract and add it to 2⅔ cups (500 g) butter cream filling.

22

Chocolate Butter Cream (Crème au Beurre au Chocolat)

Preparing the Cream: Mix 5½ ounces (160 g) of melted sweet chocolate to 2⅔ cups (500 g) butter cream filling.

23

Almond Butter Cream (Crème au Beurre Praliné)

Preparing the Cream: Add 1 cup, scant (150 g), of powdered candied almonds to 4 cups (750 g) butter cream filling.

24

Vanilla Pastry Cream (Crème Pâtissière Vanillée)

This recipe can be used to prepare Millefeuilles, crêpes, almond pastry cream, and as a garnish for many other recipes.

PREPARATION
10 minutes

INGREDIENTS
For 2⅓ cups (580 g) cream
2 cups (½ l) milk
½ vanilla bean, split in half lengthwise
6 egg yolks
⅔ cup (150 g) granulated sugar
4 tablespoons (40 g) flour *or* cornstarch

For 1 cup, generous (290 g), cream
1 cup (¼ l) milk
¼ vanilla bean, split in half lengthwise
3 egg yolks
⅓ cup (75 g) granulated sugar
2 tablespoons (20 g) flour *or* cornstarch

UTENSILS
Saucepan
Wire whisk
Electric mixer [optional]
Mixing bowls

Easter Cake, Recipe 77

traiteur
PARIS-DEAUVILLE-NEW YORK

Traiteur
PARIS · DEAUVILLE · NEW YORK

Making the Pastry Cream: Place the milk and split vanilla bean in a saucepan and bring to a boil. Cover and keep hot. With the wire whisk (or mixer on medium speed), beat the sugar and egg yolks together, until the mixture whitens and forms a ribbon; then gently stir in the cornstarch or flour with the whisk.

Strain out the vanilla bean and pour the hot milk into the egg and sugar mixture, beating all the while with the wire whisk. Pour the mixture back into the saucepan and bring to a boil again, stirring constantly with the wire whisk so that the mixture does not stick to the bottom of the saucepan. Boil for 1 minute, stirring vigorously, then pour into a bowl and lightly rub the surface of the cream with a lump of butter to keep a skin from forming as it cools.

25

Coffee Pastry Cream (Crème Pâtissière au Café)

Preparing the Pastry Cream: With a wooden spoon, stir 1½ tablespoons of instant coffee or 3 teaspoons coffee extract into 2⅓ cups (580 g) hot pastry cream.

26

Chocolate Pastry Cream (Crème Pâtissière au Chocolat)

Preparing the Pastry Cream: Break 5½ ounces (160 g) of semi-sweet chocolate into small pieces and add to 2⅓ cups (580 g) of hot pastry cream. Let the chocolate melt, stirring occasionally with a wooden spoon to mix it into the cream.

To Store: These pastry creams will keep for a maximum of 2 days in the refrigerator in a tightly sealed container.

Autumn Meringue Cake, Recipe 81

Traiteur
PARIS-DEAUVILLE-NEW YORK

27
Chocolate Icing (Glaçage au Chocolat)

This icing can be made easily and is a good substitute for chocolate fondant icing. It is shiny, but soft; be careful not to touch the cake with your fingers once it is iced.

PREPARATION 10 minutes

INGREDIENTS *For 1½ cups (450 g) icing, sufficient for 2 cakes, each serving 6 persons*
7 ounces (200 g) semi-sweet chocolate
5 tablespoons (80 g) butter
4 tablespoons cold water
1 cup (160 g) confectioners' sugar

For ¾ cups (225 g) icing, sufficient for 1 cake serving 6 persons
3½ ounces (100 g) semi-sweet chocolate
2½ tablespoons (40 g) butter
2 tablespoons cold water
½ cup (80 g) confectioners' sugar

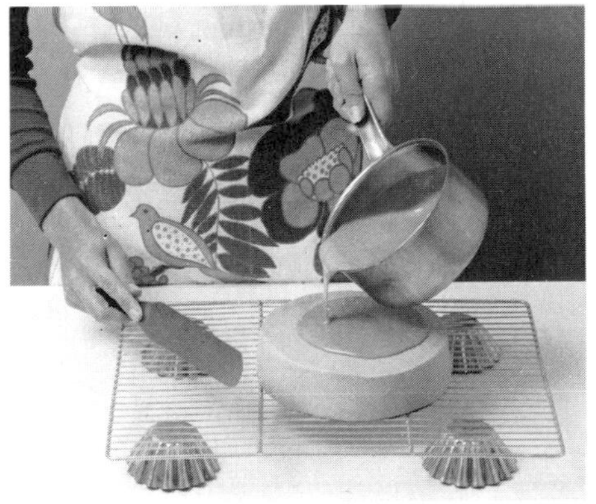
24

25

Paris-Brest, Recipe 87

UTENSILS	Wooden spatula Small mixing bowl Flexible blade-spatula Flat rack Sieve Saucepan

Making the Icing: Sift the sugar. Heat the chocolate in a double boiler until melted, then add the sifted sugar and the butter, cut into pieces. Stir until smooth, then remove the saucepan from the heat and add the water, one tablespoon at a time, to cool the mixture. This icing must be lukewarm to ice the cake. If it is too hot, it will run off; if it is too cold, it will not spread easily.

Icing the Cake: Place your cake on a plate that is smaller than the cake itself, then place on a rack. Spread the icing evenly on the cake, using the spatula (see photos 24 and 25, page 75).

28

Fondant Icing (Glaçage au Fondant)

PREPARATION	10 minutes
INGREDIENTS	*For 1 cup (350 g) icing, sufficient for 1 cake serving 6 persons* 1 cup (350 g) plain fondant 4 teaspoons cold dessert syrup (Recipe 29) 3 to 4 drops food coloring: coffee extract, carmine, red, yellow, *or* green
UTENSILS	Double boiler Flexible blade-spatula Wooden spatula Rack

Making the Icing: In a double boiler, melt the fondant until barely lukewarm. Stir in the dessert syrup, then add the food coloring, drop by drop so as to control the color. If you do not have coffee extract, dissolve 2 teaspoons of instant coffee in a little bit of water, then add the coffee to the syrup.

Icing the Cake: Ice the cake using the technique given for chocolate icing, Recipe 27.

29

Dessert Syrup (Sirop à Entremets)

PREPARATION 5 minutes

INGREDIENTS

For 1 cup (2½ dl) syrup
⅔ cup (1½ dl) water
½ cup, generous (135 g), granulated sugar
Flavorings
3 tablespoons (½ dl) alcohol of your choice: Kirsch, rum, Grand Marnier, etc. *or*
3 tablespoons (½ dl) water mixed with ¾ teaspoon vanilla extract or coffee extract

For ⅔ cup (1.5 dl) syrup
6 tablespoons (9 cl) water
⅓ cup (80 g) granulated sugar
Flavorings
2 tablespoons (3 cl) alcohol of your choice: Kirsch, rum, Grand Marnier, etc. *or*
2 tablespoons (3 cl) water mixed with ½ teaspoon vanilla extract or coffee extract

UTENSILS

Saucepan
Wooden spoon

Making the Syrup: Place the water and sugar in a saucepan and bring to a boil, stirring until the sugar is dissolved. Remove from the heat. When cool, add the flavoring of your choice.

This syrup is generally used lukewarm or cold.

To Store: Dessert syrup will keep for several weeks in the refrigerator in a tightly closed container.

30

Chocolate Mousse (Mousse au Chocolat)

Chocolate mousse may be eaten as it is, or decorated with chocolate shavings and confectioners' sugar. It may also be used as a filling for other desserts such as Charlotte Cécile, Meringue d'Automne, etc.

PREPARATION 15 minutes

INGREDIENTS *For approximately 5½ cups (750 g) mousse (serves 8 to 10)*
11 ounces (315 g) semi-sweet chocolate
¾ cup (190 g) butter, broken into pieces
5 egg yolks
8 egg whites = 1¼ cups (245 g)
3½ tablespoons (50 g) granulated sugar

For approximately 2 cups (300 g) mousse (serves 6)
4½ ounces (125 g) semi-sweet chocolate
⅓ cup (75 g) butter, broken into pieces
2 egg yolks
3 egg whites = ½ cup (90 g)
1½ tablespoons (20 g) granulated sugar

UTENSILS Double boiler
Mixing bowl
Electric mixer
Wooden spoon
Wooden spatula
Pastry bag with star-shaped nozzle [optional]

Making the Mousse: Melt the chocolate in a double boiler. Remove from the heat and add the butter, stirring it in with a wooden spoon. Allow the mixture to cool completely—it should be the consistency of a very thick cream—then stir in the egg yolks one by one.

Beat the egg whites until very stiff; halfway through, add the sugar. Fold the chocolate mixture into the egg whites with the wooden spatula, making sure the two elements are perfectly blended together.

Serving: If you are serving the mousse plain, pour into individual molds or into a deep bowl. It may be decorated by putting some of the mousse through a pastry bag set with a star-shaped nozzle. Chocolate shavings can be made with a vegetable peeler if desired. In any case, serve the mousse very cold, accompanied with a slice of brioche or petits fours.

31

Chocolate Sauce (Sauce au Chocolat)

Serve cold as a sauce with a Charlotte Cécile, a Chocolate Soufflé, a Chestnut Charlotte, or a Brioche Estelle. This sauce can also be served hot, on top of glazed profiteroles or vanilla ice cream.

PREPARATION 15 minutes

INGREDIENTS

For approximately 2 cups (½ l) sauce
9 ounces (250 g) semi-sweet chocolate
1 cup (2.5 dl) milk
5 teaspoons crème fraîche *or* heavy cream
¼ cup (60 g) granulated sugar
2½ tablespoons (35 g) butter

For approximately ¾ cup (2 dl) sauce
3½ ounces (100 g) semi-sweet chocolate
6½ tablespoons (1 dl) milk
2 teaspoons crème fraîche *or* heavy cream
5 teaspoons (25 g) granulated sugar
1 tablespoon (15 g) butter

UTENSILS

Double boiler
Wooden spatula
Saucepan

Making the Sauce: Melt the chocolate in the double boiler. Meanwhile, bring the milk to a boil, add the crème fraîche and bring back to a boil.

Remove the pot from the heat, then stir in the sugar, the melted chocolate, and the butter. Replace the pot on the fire and boil the sauce for a few seconds, then pour into a bowl and allow to cool.

32

Vanilla Sauce (Sauce à la Vanille)

This sauce is used with many desserts. Rich in egg yolks, it is also the base for Bavarian creams and charlottes.

PREPARATION	15 minutes
COOLING TIME	30 minutes
INGREDIENTS	*For 2⅔ cups (6 dl) sauce* 2 cups (½ l) milk 1 vanilla bean, split lengthwise 6 egg yolks ⅔ cup (150 g) granulated sugar *For 1⅓ cups (3 dl) sauce* 1 cup (¼ l) milk ½ vanilla bean, split lengthwise 3 egg yolks ⅓ cup (75 g) granulated sugar
UTENSILS	Saucepan Wooden spatula Electric mixer or wire whisk Mixing bowl Bowl filled with cold water

Making the Sauce: Place the milk and vanilla bean in a saucepan and bring to a boil. Lower the heat, cover the pot and let the vanilla bean infuse for 10 minutes.

Beat the egg yolks and the sugar on medium speed until the mixture whitens and forms a ribbon. Still beating, add the milk to the egg yolks. Pour the mixture back into the saucepan. Heat slowly, stirring constantly with a wooden spatula; do not allow the mixture to boil. When the liquid coats the spatula, remove the saucepan from the heat and immediately place the pan in a bowl of cold water to stop the cooking. Remove the vanilla bean.

Should the sauce accidentally come to a boil and separate, pour it into a blender and blend it at high speed, or pour a little of it at a time into a bottle, and shake vigorously.

Cool the mixture by leaving the pot in the bowl of cold water for about 30 minutes. Whip the sauce with a whisk from time to time while it is cooling.

33

Bavarian Cream (Appareil à Bavaroise)

This cream is used to prepare Bavarian cream or Brioche Estelle.

PREPARATION 5 minutes

INGREDIENTS

For approximately 2¾ cups (665 g) cream
1 tablespoon (4 sheets) unflavored gelatin
3 tablespoons cold water
2⅔ cups (6 dl) vanilla sauce (Recipe 32)
Optional
1½ tablespoons Kirsch + 1 teaspoon (1 sheet) gelatin

For approximately 1⅓ cups (330 g) cream
1½ teaspoons (2 sheets) unflavored gelatin
1½ tablespoons cold water
1⅓ cups (3 dl) vanilla sauce (Recipe 32)
Optional
¾ teaspoon Kirsch + ½ teaspoon (½ sheet) gelatin

UTENSILS	Small mixing bowl Wooden spatula Mold

Making the Cream: Dissolve the gelatin in the cold water, then add to the warm vanilla sauce, stirring with a spatula. If desired, add the Kirsch to the vanilla sauce, but in this case, be sure to add the extra gelatin in the beginning of the recipe. Allow to cool. The cream is then ready to be poured into a mold.

34
Charlotte Cream (Appareil à Charlotte)

Preparing the Cream: Charlotte cream is simply a Bavarian cream to which Chantilly is added. Since the proportions of the ingredients vary considerably from one charlotte to the next, the proportions are given in the list of ingredients that precedes each recipe (see charlotte recipes).

35
Basic Soufflé (Appareil à Soufflé)

This basic recipe is used to prepare many different types of soufflés. The soufflés differ from each other in the flavorings added to them; i.e., almonds, Grand Marnier, chestnuts, etc.

PREPARATION	30 minutes
BAKING TIME	20 minutes

Upside Down Orange Cake, Recipe 89

LENÔTRE
Traiteur
PARIS-DEAUVILLE-NEW YORK

INGREDIENTS

For 3 or 4 servings
1 cup milk (¼ 1)
⅓ cup, generous (60 g), granulated sugar
⅓ cup (45 g) flour
1½ tablespoons (20 g) butter
4 egg yolks
4 egg whites
1½ tablespoons (20 g) granulated sugar

UTENSILS

Soufflé mold 7″ (18 cm) wide and 2½″ (6 cm) deep
Saucepan with cover
Mixing bowl
Wooden spatula
Wire whisk
Sugar dredger
Knife

Making the Soufflé: Preheat the oven to 350°F (180°C). Generously grease the mold, then coat the inside with granulated sugar. Measure out the milk, then set 3 tablespoons aside. Place the remainder in the saucepan and bring it to a boil.

In the mixing bowl, place the sugar, flour, and 3 tablespoons of milk and beat with the wire whisk. Add a little of the boiling milk and mix well, then pour the mixture into the saucepan with the boiling milk. Boil for 2 minutes, then remove from the heat.

Add the butter, cover the saucepan, and allow to cool for 15 minutes. Then, stir in the egg yolks with the wire whisk. Add the flavoring desired, depending upon the recipe chosen.

Beat the egg whites until moderately firm, adding the granulated sugar half-way through. Gently fold the batter into the beaten egg whites with a wooden spatula.

Baking: Pour the mixture into the buttered and sugared mold; never fill the mold more than ¾ full. Dust lightly with confectioners' sugar, then bake for about 20 minutes or until done.

To test for doneness, plunge the blade of a knife into the center of the soufflé. If the knife comes out clean, the soufflé is done.

Note: The batter can stand for as long as 30 minutes before being baked, if covered and kept warm (90° to 100°F or 30° to 40°C). You can bake more than one soufflé at a time; you can also prepare 4 individual soufflés, using the same recipe.

36

Almond Paste Decorations (Décors en Pâte d'Amandes)

Desserts such as Strawberry Cake, Marly, or Ambassador Cake may be topped with almond paste. It may also be used to make holly leaves and other decorations for Yule logs.

PREPARATION — Variable

INGREDIENTS — *For 1 cake, serving 6 persons*
9 ounces (250 g) almond paste (Recipe 18)
⅔ cup (100 g) confectioners' sugar (approximately), to dust table
3 drops food coloring (approximately) for pastel colors

UTENSILS — Rolling pin
Knife

Preparing the Almond Paste: Mix the almond paste with the food coloring by working the paste as you would modeling clay. Add more food coloring if you wish the color to be more intense. Continue working the paste until it is of a uniform color.

Dust the surface of your work table with confectioners' sugar. Roll out the colored almond paste, turning the dough every time you roll it to keep it from sticking to the table, and dusting with more confectioners' sugar if necessary. If the dough should stick to the table and break, just pick it up, pack it into a ball and roll it out again.

Decorating the Cake: A cake must be covered with a thin layer of dessert cream—such as pastry cream—before being topped with almond paste. When this has been done, roll out the almond paste into a circle, then roll it around the rolling pin. Unroll it over the cake, as you would when lining a pie pan. To make the paste stick to the cake, press it gently with the palm of your hand against the surface of the cake, being careful not to wrinkle it.

Cut off the excess dough with a knife.

To make holly leaves, cut out the leaves with the point of a sharp knife, then twist the ends of the leaves slightly. To make green moss, press the paste through a sieve, held over a plate. With the blade of a knife, pick up the moss carefully, placing it on the surface of the cake, tapping it *very* lightly with the tips of your fingers to make it stick to the pastry cream.

Saint-Honoré Chiboust, Recipe 90

PARIS-DEAUVILLE-NEW YORK

Chapter 3

BREAKFAST AND COFFEE CAKES

Although these cakes may be eaten as desserts, they are especially good at breakfast or coffee breaks.

RECIPES

37. Cherry Almondines (Amandines aux Cerises)
38. Savoy Sponge Cake (Biscuit de Savoie)
39. Brioche Bordelaise
40. Individual Brioches
41. Brioche Mousseline
42. Brioche Nanterre
43. Brioche Parisienne
44. Rolled Brioche with Candied Fruit (Brioche Roulée aux Fruits Confits)
45. Fruit Cake (Cake aux Fruits Confits)
46. Pentecost Cake (Colombier de la Pentecôte)
47. Croissants
48. Friands
49. French Twelfth-Night Cake (Galette des Rois aux Amandes)
50. Basque Cake (Gâteau Basque)
51. Kugelhopf Lenôtre
52. Alsatian Kugelhopf
53. Linzer Torte

54. Mirlitons
55. Chocolate Rolls (Pains au Chocolat)
56. Raisin Buns (Pains aux Raisins)
57. Genoa Cake (Pain de Gênes)
58. Pithiviers
59. Dutch Pithiviers (Pithiviers Hollandais)
60. Brioche Almond Slices (Tranches de Brioche aux Amandes)

37

Cherry Almondines (Amandines aux Cerises)

PREPARATION 10 minutes

BAKING TIME 20 minutes

INGREDIENTS *For 16 individual pastries*
9 ounces (250 g) short pastry (Recipe 10) *or* sweet short pastry (Recipe 12)
2 cups (500 g) almond pastry cream (Recipe 17)
50 fresh cherries or stewed cherries

UTENSILS 16 small tartlet pans or 2 5″ (6.5 cm) circles
Spoon
Rolling pin

The Batter and Baking: Preheat the oven to 425°F (220°C). Roll out the dough, and cut it into circles large enough to line the pans. Butter the pans and line them with the dough. Place 3 pitted cherries in each pan and cover them with the almond cream, using a spoon to smooth the surface. Bake the cakes for 20 minutes. Turn out while still warm.

38

Savoy Sponge Cake (Biscuit de Savoie)

This cake, similar to a Génoise, can be served with a vanilla sauce, fruit sauce, compote, jam, or chocolate sauce.

PREPARATION 10 minutes

BAKING TIME 30 minutes

INGREDIENTS

For 2 cakes, 6 to 8 servings each
1 cup, generous (100 g), slivered blanched almonds [optional]
7 medium eggs, separated
1 cup, generous (250 g), granulated sugar
1 teaspoon orange-flower water
¾ cup (100 g) flour
¾ cup (100 g) cornstarch
4 teaspoons (20 g) granulated sugar
⅓ cup (80 g) butter, melted [optional]

UTENSILS

2 mixing bowls
Electric mixer
Wooden spatula
2 10″ (25 cm) Génoise molds

The Batter and Baking: Preheat oven to 350°F (180°C). Butter the molds, dust with flour, and line with slivered almonds [optional].

In a mixing bowl, place the egg yolks, the sugar, and the orange-flower water. Beat for 3 minutes at medium speed. Add the flour and the cornstarch. Mix well. Beat the egg whites until very stiff, adding the 4 teaspoons of granulated sugar halfway through. Using the wooden spatula, fold the egg whites and melted butter [optional] carefully into the batter. This batter should then be poured immediately into the molds and baked for 30 minutes. Turn out while still warm.

To Store: If well wrapped in aluminum foil, these cakes will stay fresh in the refrigerator for 3 or 4 days.

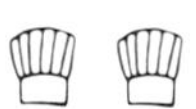

39

Brioche Bordelaise

The shape of this cake, and the candied fruits that decorate it, make it resemble a king's crown studded with jewels.

PREPARATION 1 hour

RESTING TIME 1 hour, 45 minutes

BAKING TIME 30 minutes

INGREDIENTS *For 8 servings*
1 pound 5 ounces (600 g) brioche dough (Recipe 9)
½ cup (100 g) candied fruit (plums, cherries, oranges, lemons, etc.), finely chopped
1 egg white, beaten

For decorating
3½ ounces (100 g) whole candied fruits sliced *or*
1¾ ounces (50 g) rock candy in small pieces *or*
crushed sugared almonds

UTENSILS Pastry brush
Baking sheet
Scissors

Forming the Dough: Prepare the broiche dough a day ahead.

On a lightly floured table, flatten the dough with your hands. Place all the chopped candied fruits on top of the dough and use your hands to press the candied fruits into it. Fold the corners of the dough toward the center, then roll it into a ball. Place the dough on a buttered baking sheet and let it stand for 5 to 10 minutes. Make a hole in the middle of the ball of dough by placing your thumbs in the center and turning and pulling until the hole in the center is 4″ (10 cm) in diameter. Be careful not to tear the dough while stretching it. Allow the dough to rest for a couple of minutes each time you stretch it if it looks like it's going to tear. Once the hole in the center is formed, let the dough rise at room temperature for 1 hour and a-half.

Baking: Preheat the oven to 400°F (200°C) at least fifteen minutes before baking. Brush the cake with beaten egg whites, then make slits in the surface of the dough at regular intervals using a pair of scissors that has been dipped in water. If you do not cut deep enough, the design will not remain once the cake is baked; if the cuts are too deep, the dough will fall. Bake for 30 minutes or until the brioche is golden brown. Remove from the oven and decorate the top of the brioche with slices of candied fruit, rock candy, or pieces of sugared almonds.

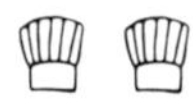

40
Individual Brioches

PREPARATION	15 minutes
RISING TIME	1 hour, 30 minutes
BAKING TIME	12 minutes
INGREDIENTS	*For 16 individual brioches* 1 pound (500 g) brioche dough (Recipe 9) 1 egg beaten with a pinch of salt
UTENSILS	16 individual brioche molds Pastry brush

Shaping the Dough: Prepare the brioche dough a day ahead.

On a lightly floured table, use your hands to roll the dough into a thick sausagelike shape. Divide it into 16 equal pieces. Dust the palms of your hands and the table with flour and roll each piece of dough into a ball. Don't press hard on the ball of dough while rolling it (see photo 15, page 50). Once a ball is formed, use the edge of your hand to dent the dough and form a smaller ball (or "head") for each brioche (see photo 16, page 50).

Butter each mold lightly with a pastry brush.

Place the dough in the molds with the small ball (or "head") on top. Use your fingers and gently press down the dough all around the bottom of the smaller ball or "head."

Let the dough rise for 1 hour, 30 minutes in a warm place.

Baking: Fifteen minutes before baking, preheat the oven to 450°F (230°C). Brush each brioche with a little beaten egg. Bake for about 12 minutes or until golden brown. Turn out while still warm.

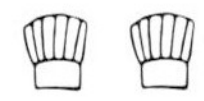

41
Brioche Mousseline
(Photo page 13)

PREPARATION	15 minutes
RESTING TIME	2 hours
BAKING TIME	30 to 35 minutes
INGREDIENTS	*For a brioche serving 6 persons* 12½ ounces (360 g) brioche dough (Recipe 9) 1 beaten egg
UTENSILS	Mousseline mold (or 1-quart can) 4″ (10 cm) wide and 4¾″ (12 cm) tall Parchment paper or aluminum foil Scissors

Shaping the Dough: Prepare the brioche dough a day ahead.

Fold a large sheet of parchment paper or aluminum foil in half. Lightly butter the outside of the paper and use it to completely line the sides of the mold. The paper should be twice as wide as the mold is tall; this way the paper will not only line the mold but will form a cylinder that is taller than the mold itself. Butter the bottom of the mold and butter generously the interior surface of the paper.

Place the ball of dough at the bottom of the mold; press it down with your fist. Let it rise for 2 hours at room temperature or until the dough has risen up to ½″ (1 cm) from the edge of the mold.

Baking: Preheat the oven to 400°F (200°C).

Brush the dough with the beaten egg and cut a cross on the top with a pair of scissors. Bake for 30 to 35 minutes or until golden brown and firm to the touch. Turn out while still warm.

To Freeze: See Brioche Nanterre (Recipe 42).

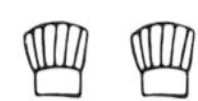

42

Brioche Nanterre

(Photo page 13)

You can bake two brioches at the same time. One of them can be served right away and the other frozen for later use.

PREPARATION	15 minutes
RISING TIME	2 hours
BAKING TIME	35 minutes
INGREDIENTS	12½ ounces (360 g) brioche dough (Recipe 9) 1 beaten egg
UTENSILS	1 bread or loaf pan Pastry brush Parchment paper Scissors

Shaping the Dough: Prepare the brioche dough a day ahead.

Line the mold with buttered paper; the paper should be 1¼″ (3 cm) higher than the mold.

Place the brioche dough on a lightly floured surface. Divide the dough into 6 equal parts. Shape each of the pieces into slightly oval balls.

Place the 6 balls of dough on the bottom of the mold. Let them rise for about 2 hours at room temperature or until they double in volume. They should then be all stuck together.

Baking: Preheat oven to 400°F (200°C).

Brush the dough with the beaten egg. With a pair of scissors that have been dipped into water, make a cross on the top of each mound of dough. Bake for 35 minutes or until golden brown and firm to the touch. Turn out while still warm.

To Freeze: The Brioche Nanterre should be frozen while still warm. To freeze, wrap in a plastic bag or aluminum foil. To thaw, let stand for 5 hours at room temperature or place in a 400°F (200°C) oven for 10 minutes, after letting it stand at room temperature for 1 hour.

Almond Succès, Recipe 92

43

Brioche Parisienne

(Photo page 13)

You can bake two of these large brioches at once and prepare a salpicon of fruit or a Brioche Polonaise with the extra.

PREPARATION	10 minutes
RISING TIME	1 hour, 30 minutes
BAKING TIME	35 minutes
INGREDIENTS	*For 1 large brioche* 12½ ounces (360 g) brioche dough (Recipe 9) 1 beaten egg
UTENSILS	Ribbed 7″ (18 cm) brioche mold Scissors Pastry brush

Shaping the Dough: Prepare the brioche dough a day ahead.

Place the dough on a lightly floured surface. Flour your hands and divide the dough into 2 balls, one large and one small (the small ball should be a little less than one third the size of the other). Roll the bigger ball of dough gently between your hands to make it smooth and round. Butter the mold and place the big ball of dough in it.

Roll the smaller ball of dough, shaping it like a pear. Make a depression in the top of the larger ball and place the narrow end of the smaller ball in the depression. Press lightly to make the two balls of dough stick together (see photo 17, page 50). Let the dough rise for an hour and a half at room temperature or until it has doubled in volume.

Baking: Preheat the oven to 400°F (200°C).

With scissors that have been dipped in water, cut slits on each side of the larger ball, then brush the dough with the beaten egg. Bake for 35 minutes or until golden brown. Turn out while still warm.

Note: Be careful not to let the beaten egg run down the sides of the mold; if it does, the brioche will stick to the mold.

To Store: This brioche will keep for up to 24 hours in the refrigerator if placed in a plastic bag or wrapped in aluminum foil.

To Freeze: Follow the instructions for Brioche Nanterre (Recipe 42).

Fruit Flan, Recipe 93; Apple Dartois, Recipe 94

44

Rolled Brioche with Candied Fruit (Brioche Roulée aux Fruits Confits)

(Photo page 23)

This cake is an unusual mixture of brioche dough, candied fruits, rum, and pastry cream. It is delicious either as a dessert or at breakfast time.

PREPARATION 45 minutes

RISING TIME 2 hours

BAKING TIME 35 minutes

INGREDIENTS *For 1 large brioche, serving 4 to 6 persons*
¼ cup (50 g) raisins
2 tablespoons rum
14 ounces (400 g) brioche dough (Recipe 9)
1⅓ cups (250 g) almond pastry cream (recipe 17) *or*
1 cup (250 g) vanilla pastry cream (Recipe 24)
¼ cup (50 g) chopped candied fruit
1 egg, beaten
⅔ cup (1½ dl) dessert syrup (Recipe 29)

For the glaze
⅔ cup (100 g) confectioners' sugar
2 tablespoons hot water
3 drops rum *or* apricot jam

UTENSILS Bowl
Rolling pin
Flexible blade-spatula
Knife
Cake pan 8″ (20 cm) round
Pastry brush

Assembling the Cake: Soak the raisins in the 2 tablespoons of rum for ½ hour. Take slightly more than a third of the chilled brioche dough (prepared a day in advance) and roll it out on a generously floured table until it is big enough to completely line the cake pan. Place it in the pan. Take one third of the pastry cream and spread it evenly over the bottom of the dough. Place the cake pan in the ice box while preparing the rest of the dough. On a generously floured table, roll out the remaining dough into a rectangle 10″ by 6″ (25 by 15 cm).

Spread the dough with the rest of the pastry cream, then sprinkle on the drained raisins and chopped candied fruit. Roll the dough into a 10″ (25 cm) long sausage and place in the refrigerator 15 minutes. Remove from the refrigerator and cut the roll of dough into 8 equal parts. Place these 8 pieces into the cake pan (see photo, page 19). There should be space between the rolls of dough and between the rolls and the sides of the cake pan. Put the cake pan in a warm place and leave to rise for about 2 hours, or until the dough has risen considerably and the rolls are touching.

Baking: Preheat the oven to 400°F (200°C).

Brush the top of the cake with the beaten egg, then bake for 35 minutes or until golden brown. If the top browns too quickly, cover it with aluminum foil.

When the cake is done, remove it from the oven and brush it with the dessert syrup (the cake will absorb all the syrup). Turn out while still warm, then let the cake cool. Decorate the surface of the cake with a white glaze made by mixing confectioners' sugar, rum, and water or make a shiny transparent glaze by painting the top of the cake with warm apricot jam.

To Store: This cake will stay fresh for 2 or 3 days in the refrigerator if it is kept covered.

45

Fruit Cake (Cake aux Fruits Confits)

This is a type of pound cake, generously flavored with candied fruits and basted with rum just before serving.

PREPARATION	15 minutes
RESTING TIME	30 minutes
BAKING TIME	45 minutes
INGREDIENTS	*For a cake serving 6 persons* 3 medium eggs = 1¾ ounces (50 g) each ¼ pound (120 g) butter

¾ cup (125 g) confectioners' sugar
1½ teaspoons (5 g) baking powder
1¼ cups (160 g) flour
1¼ cups (250 g) candied fruit, finely chopped
2 tablespoons rum
2½ tablespoons (50 g) apricot jam, warmed
⅓ cup (50 g) candied cherries

UTENSILS

Wooden spoon
Knife
Wire whisk
Mixing bowl
Pastry brush
Parchment paper
Waxed paper
Pound cake mold or loaf pan 10¼″ (26 cm) long

The Batter: Take the eggs and butter out of the refrigerator an hour before beginning the recipe. Place the softened butter in a bowl and whisk until creamy. Add the confectioners' sugar and the eggs, one by one. If the batter falls apart (separates), put the bowl into warm water and begin again.

On a piece of waxed paper, mix the baking powder with the flour and, using the wooden spoon, mix in the chopped candied fruit. This will prevent the fruit from falling to the bottom of the mold. Then add this mixture to the batter prepared earlier, stirring gently until all the ingredients are well mixed. Let stand for 30 minutes in the refrigerator.

Baking: Preheat oven to 475°F (240°C). Lightly butter cake mold. Line mold with parchment paper, allowing the paper to stick up over the rim of the mold. Pour the batter into the mold.

Start baking the cake at 475°F (240°C) for 5 minutes, then lower the heat to 350°F (180°C) for the next 40 minutes. To find out if the cake is done, insert a knife into the middle and if the blade comes out dry, the cake is done. Turn out while still warm.

Decorating: While the cake is still warm, spoon the rum over it and allow the cake to cool. When cool, brush on the warm apricot jam and decorate the cake with the glazed cherries cut in half.

To Store: This cake will stay fresh for 1 week in the refrigerator, wrapped in aluminum foil.

To Freeze: If you wish to freeze the cake, do not decorate the cake or brush on the apricot jelly. This last step should be done after the cake has been thawed for 24 hours in the refrigerator.

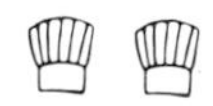

46

Pentecost Cake (Colombier de la Pentecôte)

Almond paste and candied fruit (especially oranges) dominate this holiday specialty.

PREPARATION	20 minutes
BAKING TIME	20 minutes
INGREDIENTS	*For a cake serving 6 persons* 7 ounces almond paste (200 g) 3 small eggs 3 tablespoons (30 g) flour 4 tablespoons (60 g) butter, melted and cooled ½ cup (100 g) candied fruit, chopped ½ cup (100 g) candied orange rind, chopped *For the icing* ⅔ cup (100 g) confectioners' sugar 3 drops rum 2 tablespoons water
UTENSILS	Mixing bowl Electric mixer with paddle or dough hook Small saucepan Parchment paper cut into 9″ (23 cm) circle Pastry brush Cake mold 9″ (23 cm) round Flexible blade-spatula

The Batter: Preheat the oven to 400°F (200°C). Generously butter the mold, especially the sides. Place the parchment paper on the bottom of the mold.

In the mixing bowl, mix the almond paste at low speed, then increase to medium for about one minute. Continue beating and add the eggs, one by one. When all the eggs have been added, beat until the mixture is light and smooth (5 to 10 minutes). Sift the flour. Continue beating the egg mixture and add the flour all at once, then add the cooled melted butter.

Fill the mold ¾ full with the batter. Decorate the surface of the batter with the candied fruit and candied orange rind.

Baking: Bake at 400°F (200°C) for 10 minutes, then lower the temperature to 350°F (180°C) for the next 10 minutes, or until golden brown. Turn out when cold, being careful, since this cake is very fragile.

Decorating: Mix the confectioners' sugar with the rum and water to make an icing. Brush this on the surface and the sides of the cake using the flexible blade-spatula. Refrigerate before serving.

Note: You can also line the buttered mold with a generous ½ cup (100 g) of chopped almonds instead of lining the bottom with paper.

To Store: The Pentecost Cake can stay in the refrigerator for up to 24 hours.

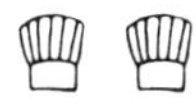

47

Croissants

(Photo page 36)

PREPARATION	20 minutes
RESTING TIME	7 hours minimum
BAKING TIME	15 minutes per baking sheet
INGREDIENTS	*For approximately 2 pounds 3 ounces (1 kg) dough; sufficient for 30 Croissants*

1 cake (18 g) compressed baker's yeast
1½ tablespoons warm water
3½ tablespoons (50 g) granulated sugar
2 teaspoons (15 g) salt
1½ tablespoons milk
3 tablespoons (40 g) butter
½ cup (125 ml) water
½ cup (125 ml) milk
3¾ cups (500 g) flour
1¼ cups, scant (260 g), butter
1 beaten egg (for glazing)

For approximately 1 pound 1½ ounces (500 g) dough; sufficient for 15 Croissants

½ cake (9 g) compressed baker's yeast
2¼ teaspoons warm water
5 teaspoons (25 g) granulated sugar
1 teaspoon (8 g) salt
2¼ teaspoons milk
1½ tablespoons (20 g) butter
¼ cup (65 ml) water
¼ cup (65 ml) milk
1¾ cups (250 g) flour
½ cup, generous (130 g), butter
½ beaten egg (for glazing)

UTENSILS

2 small mixing bowls
1 large mixing bowl
Small saucepan
Shallow baking dish
Electric mixer
2 baking sheets
Pastry brush

Making the Dough: Dissolve the yeast in the warm water. In another bowl, mix the sugar and the salt with 2 tablespoons of milk. When this is done, melt 3 tablespoons (40 g) butter in a small saucepan, then add ½ cup (125 ml) water and ½ cup (125 ml) milk and heat until the mixture is lukewarm. Then place the flour in the large mixing bowl, and with the mixer set at a low speed, add the sugar-milk mixture to the flour. Increase the speed of the mixer slightly and add the butter-milk mixture, beat for about a minute and add the dissolved yeast. The dough will be very light and lukewarm. Cover the bowl with a towel and let it rise in a warm place (80°F-25°C) for about 1 hour or until the dough has doubled in volume. Then place the dough in a lightly floured shallow baking dish, spreading it out evenly. Cover the dough and chill it in the refrigerator for 2 to 3 hours.

Half an hour before you intend to roll out the dough, remove the butter from the refrigerator and cut it in two. Leave one half at room temperature to soften. Put the remaining half back in the refrigerator.

Rolling out and Shaping the Dough: Place the dough on a lightly floured surface and roll it into a rectangle. Cover ⅔ of the dough with the softened half of the butter, which has been broken into small pieces. Fold the rectangle in thirds, starting with the side that was not buttered, then roll out the dough once and fold in thirds as for flaky pastry (see photo 3, page 34 and instructions for flaky pastry, Recipes 3 and 4). Return the dough to the refrigerator and let it stand, covered, for at least 2 hours, or for best results, overnight.

Roll out the dough again, softening and adding the remaining butter as described above. After folding in thirds, roll the dough in a rectangle 8″ by 10″ (20 by 25 cm). Return the dough to the refrigerator, covered, for 1 hour.

Roll the dough out until it is very thin (1/16" [3 mm] thick) and forms a rectangle 36" by 12" (90 by 30 cm), then cut the rectangle in two, lengthwise. Cut each band of dough into 15 triangles, and then roll each triangle into a sausage shape, rolling from the base toward the point of each triangle. Bend the edges of each little roll of dough inward to make them crescent-shaped.

Place the crescent-shaped rolls on buttered baking sheets, leaving spaces between them. Brush them with beaten egg, using a pastry brush. This will keep the rolls from drying out as they rise. Set the sheets in a warm place and allow the croissants to rise for 2 hours, or until they double in size.

Baking: Preheat the oven to 400°F (200°C).

Brush the croissants once more with beaten egg and bake for 15 minutes, or until golden brown. Watch the color because not all the croissants will bake at the same rate. If you wish to bake the entire recipe of 30 croissants, it would be better to bake them in 2 batches.

To Freeze: After baking, allow the croissants to cool for a few minutes. While still warm, put them on a plate, then place the plate in the freezer to quick-freeze the croissants. As soon as they are hard, put them in a plastic bag and return to the freezer.

When you want to eat them, preheat the oven to 475°F (250°C) for 15 minutes, then remove the croissants from the freezer and bake them for exactly 5 minutes to heat them through.

Once frozen, the croissants will stay good for 2 weeks.

48
Friands

PREPARATION	15 minutes
BAKING TIME	15-18 minutes
INGREDIENTS	*For 20 Friands* ¾ cup, scant (170 g), butter 1⅔ cups (250 g) confectioners' sugar 1 cup, generous (135 g), powdered almonds ⅓ cup (55 g) flour 5 egg whites = ¾ cup (150 g)
UTENSILS	Mixing bowl Small saucepan Baking sheet Wooden spoon

Pastry brush
Strainer
8 tartlet molds or 20 Friand molds

The Batter: Preheat oven to 475°F (240°C). Grease the molds generously with butter.

Clarify the butter by simmering it until it stops bubbling. It will taste like hazelnuts and will be of a very light brown color. In the mixing bowl, combine the sugar, the powdered almonds and the flour. Stir vigorously and add the egg whites, then add the warm butter by pouring it through a very fine strainer. Fill the molds with this batter using a spoon. The molds should be no more than ¾ full. Place them all on a baking sheet.

Baking: Bake the Friands at 475°F (240°C) for 5 minutes, then lower the temperature to 400°F (200°C), and bake for 10 minutes more. The baking time can be longer or shorter, depending upon the size of the molds. Turn off the oven and wait 5 minutes before taking the Friands out. Turn out onto a rack or waxed paper while still warm.

Note: The shape of the molds used is unimportant. Just be sure the molds are no more than ¾ full before they go in the oven.

To Store: These small tarts will stay fresh for up to 15 days in the refrigerator if kept in a tightly closed container.

49

French Twelfth-Night Cake (Galette des Rois aux Amandes)

This cake is traditionally served on Twelfth-Night (or Epiphany) in France. A tiny porcelain figurine is placed inside the cake before baking it and the person who is served a piece of cake containing the figurine is declared King or Queen for that day. A white bean, or broad bean, was once used instead of a figurine inside the cake and the name fève *(broad bean) is still given to the miniature statuette that is always included in this cake's filling.*

PREPARATION 25 minutes

RESTING TIME	1 hour
BAKING TIME	45 minutes
INGREDIENTS	*For 1 cake, 8 servings* 1 pound 5 ounces (600 g) flaky pastry dough, either the classic *or* the quick (Recipes 3 *or* 4) 1 whole egg, beaten 1¾ cups (300 g) almond pastry cream (Recipe 17) Confectioners' sugar
UTENSILS	Rolling pin Pastry brush Knife Spoon Pastry sheet Sugar dredger

Shaping the Dough: Divide the flaky pastry, while cold, into 2 equal pieces. Replace one piece in the refrigerator. Roll out the other piece until it is large enough to cut a circle 4″ wide out of its middle. Once you've cut the dough into a circular shape, place the trimmings in the middle of the circle and continue rolling out the dough until it forms a circle that is 11″ (28 cm) wide and approximately 1/16″ (2 mm) thick. Roll out the other piece of dough the same way.

If the dough is very elastic and shrinks, place it in the refrigerator for 15 minutes, then roll it out again. Place one of the circles on a pastry sheet and brush around the rim of the circle with the beaten egg. Spread the almond cream over the circle with a spoon being careful not to touch the moistened part of the dough, then cover the first circle of dough with the second one and press down the edges with your fingers or the back of a knife. Refrigerate for 1 hour.

Baking: Preheat the oven to 475°F (240°C).

Brush the surface of the cake with the remainder of the beaten egg. Draw diamond shapes on the top with a knife. Bake at 475°F (240°C) for 10 minutes, then lower the temperature to 400°F (200°C) for the next 35 minutes. About 10 minutes before the end of the baking time, dust the cake with confectioners' sugar and bake until the time is up or until golden brown. If the surface isn't completely glazed at the end of this time, place it under the broiler for 1 minute. Watch carefully to be sure the surface doesn't burn.

To Freeze: The cake can be frozen once the top and bottom have been pinched together. Quick freeze for 12 hours and, when it has become hard, place it in a plastic bag and seal tightly. To bake the cake, thaw it first, taking it out of the plastic bag. Baste with beaten egg and decorate as described above. When thawed, the baking will take 10 minutes longer than normal.

50
Basque Cake (Gâteau Basque)

This cake's batter contains both rum and orange juice, and surrounds a layer of pastry cream in this version of a specialty from the Basque region of France.

PREPARATION 15 minutes

RESTING TIME 15 minutes

BAKING TIME 40 minutes

INGREDIENTS *For 1 cake, 6 servings*
¾ cup, generous (200 g), butter, melted and cooled
2 cups (270 g) flour
1½ teaspoons (5 g) baking powder
3 whole eggs
1 cup (240 g) granulated sugar
Juice of ½ medium orange
2-3 drops vanilla extract
2 teaspoons rum
⅔ cup, generous (190 g), vanilla pastry cream (Recipe 24)
1 whole egg, beaten

UTENSILS Mixing bowl
Wire whisk
Wooden spoon
Knife
Pastry brush
Baking sheet
Waxed paper
Pastry bag with ½″ (1.2 cm) nozzle
Cake pan 9″ (23 cm) round

The Batter: Preheat the oven to 400°F (200°C). Butter the cake pan. On a piece of waxed paper, mix the flour and the baking powder together. In the mixing bowl, beat the eggs and sugar lightly then, one at a time, slowly add the cool melted butter, the flour-baking powder mixture (a third at a time), the orange juice, and finally the vanilla extract and the rum. Let the batter stand for 15 minutes.

Shaping the Dough: Fill the pastry bag with the batter and press the dough in a spiral shape into the mold. Start with the outer edge and finish at the center of the mold. Spread the vanilla pastry cream on the batter, leaving ½ inch of the batter uncovered all around the rim of the mold. Do not let the pastry cream touch the edges of the mold, or else the cake will be difficult to turn out after it is baked. Cover the pastry cream with a spiral of dough, using the pastry bag as you did to form the bottom layer. Brush the top layer of dough with beaten egg.

Baking: Bake the cake for 40 minutes then allow to cool for 10 minutes. Turn out while still warm. Serve cold.

To Store: If covered, this cake will stay fresh in the refrigerator for 3 days.

51

Kugelhopf Lenôtre

(*Photo page 109*)

This cake is prepared with a brioche dough, and it is richer than the Alsatian Kugelhopf, which follows (Recipe 52). It is a good idea to bake two at the same time and freeze one for later use.

PREPARATION	15 minutes
RISING TIME	2 hours
BAKING TIME	30 minutes
INGREDIENTS	*For 1 cake, serving 8 persons* 3 tablespoons rum ½ cup, scant (100 g), granulated sugar 6½ tablespoons (1 dl) water ½ cup (100 g) raisins 1 cup, generous (100 g), slivered almonds 12½ ounces (360 g) brioche dough (Recipe 9) 1 whole egg, beaten Confectioners' sugar (to decorate) Melted butter to brush the top of the cake
UTENSILS	Small saucepan Pastry brush Kugelhopf mold 9½″ (24 cm) Sugar dredger

Kugelhopf Lenôtre, Recipe 51

Shaping the Dough: Prepare a syrup by mixing the rum, sugar, and water in a saucepan. Bring this mixture to a boil, then remove from the heat. Soak the raisins for about 1 hour in this syrup (the syrup can be kept for several weeks in the refrigerator if placed in a tightly sealed container).

Butter the mold and sprinkle all over with slivered almonds. On a lightly floured board, roll the chilled brioche dough into a long rectangle. Drain the raisins, place them on top of the dough and roll the dough tightly in a long roll; bring the ends together to form a circle and stick them together with some beaten egg. Place the dough in the mold; let the dough rise at a temperature of about 80°F (25°C) for 2 hours or until the dough fills ¾ of the mold.

Baking: Preheat the oven to 400°F (200°C). Bake the cake for 30 minutes; check the color after 20 minutes. If the Kugelhopf is already brown on top, finish the baking after covering it with aluminum foil. To find out if the Kugelhopf is done, insert a knife; if the blade comes out dry, it is cooked. Turn out the Kugelhopf while it is still warm. Brush the surface of the cake with melted butter and dust with confectioners' sugar just before serving.

To Freeze: You can freeze the Kugelhopf while it is still lukewarm, but do not brush on the butter or dust with confectioners' sugar. When you take the cake out of the freezer, let it thaw for 2 hours at room temperature and then bake at 325°F (150°C) for 10 minutes to warm the cake. Brush the surface of the cake as indicated above and serve.

52
Alsatian Kugelhopf

PREPARATION	15 minutes
RESTING TIME	2 hours
BAKING TIME	30 minutes
INGREDIENTS	*For 1 cake, serving 8 persons* 1 cake (15 g) compressed baker's yeast 2 teaspoons warm water 1 teaspoon (7 g) salt ¼ cup (60 g) granulated sugar 6½ tablespoons (1 dl) milk 3¾ cups (500 g) flour 4 whole eggs ¾ cup, generous (200 g), butter

Preparing the Dough: Using the ingredients listed here, make a dough following the instructions given for the brioche dough (Recipe 9). This dough will not be as rich as the brioche dough given in Recipe 9. Use it instead of brioche dough to make a Kugelhopf, following the instructions given in the previous recipe.

53
Linzer Torte

This is an Austrian dessert made with raspberry jam, flavored with cinnamon and hard-boiled eggs!

PREPARATION	25 minutes
RESTING TIME	1 hour

BAKING TIME 20 minutes

INGREDIENTS *For 2 tarts, each serving 8 persons*
2 cups, generous (300 g), flour
1⅔ cups (280 g) butter
6 hard-boiled egg yolks, worked through a sieve
⅓ cup (50 g) powdered almonds
⅓ cup (50 g) confectioners' sugar
½ teaspoon (2 g) cinnamon
2 teaspoons rum
¾ cup (200 g) apple sauce (Recipe 179), cooled
1½ cups (500 g) raspberry jam, unstrained

UTENSILS Large mixing bowl
Wooden spoon
Jagged-edged pastry wheel or knife
2 metal flan rings 9″ (23 cm) or 2 pie pans with moveable bottoms, such as springform molds

Making the Dough: In the mixing bowl, blend together the flour, butter, egg yolks, powdered almonds, confectioners' sugar, cinnamon, and rum. Mix all the ingredients together with a spoon, without working it too much. Cool for 1 hour in the refrigerator.

Assembling and Baking the Tarts: Preheat the oven to 425°F (220°C). Take ⅔ of the dough and divide it into two equal parts. On a lightly floured table, roll out each piece of dough, making two circles—one for each mold. Line each mold with dough. Mix the apple sauce with the raspberry jam, then divide this mixture into 2 equal parts, filling each mold with the mixture.

Work the remaining dough between the palms of your hands. The dough will become elastic and easy to use. Roll the dough into a long rectangle, then cut it into strips ⅝″ (1½ cm) wide. Lay strips of dough across the top of each tart, forming a diamond-shaped pattern. Press the ends of the strips to the edges of the mold.

Bake for about 20 minutes or until done. Remove from the rings or pans while still warm.

Note: The dough can be prepared in advance because it will keep for several days in the refrigerator.

To Store: This cake will keep 3 or 4 days.

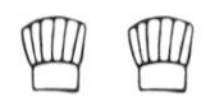

54
Mirlitons

This recipe is an excellent way of using leftover pieces of flaky pastry dough and almond pastry cream; it can also be made from scratch on the day you intend to serve it.

PREPARATION	15 minutes
RESTING TIME	30 minutes
BAKING TIME	30 minutes
INGREDIENTS	*For 15 small tarts* 9 ounces (250 g) leftover flaky pastry dough (Recipe 3) 2 whole eggs ⅓ cup (80 g) heavy cream ½ cup (80 g) almond pastry cream (Recipe 17) *or* 4 tablespoons (40 g) powdered almonds 3½ tablespoons (50 g) granulated sugar 1½ tablespoons (20 g) vanilla sugar 3 drops orange-flower water Confectioners' sugar
UTENSILS	Large mixing bowl Wooden spatula Rolling pin Round cookie cutter, 3½″ (9 cm), or 1 cup with a thin rim 15 tartlet molds Sugar dredger

Shaping the Dough: On a lightly floured board, roll out the dough to a thickness of 1/16″ (2 mm). Cut this dough into circles, using a pastry cutter or glass. Line each mold with enough dough so that ¼″ (½ cm) of dough sticks up over the rim of each mold. Prick the dough with a fork and then let it stand at room temperature for ½ hour.

Baking: Preheat the oven to 350°F (180°C).

In the mixing bowl, prepare the filling by lightly beating together the eggs, heavy cream, almond pastry cream (or the powdered almonds), granulated sugar, vanilla sugar, and orange-flower water.

Spoon some filling into each of the molds and sprinkle each generously with confectioners' sugar.

Bake for 30 minutes. Turn out while still warm and serve hot or cold the same day.

55

Chocolate Rolls (Pains au Chocolat)

(Photo page 36)

These rolls are made with the same dough as Croissants (Recipe 47). They are a favorite with schoolchildren in France who usually buy them around five in the afternoon to eat as a snack on their way home from school.

PREPARATION	10 minutes
RESTING TIME	1 hour
BAKING TIME	18 minutes per sheet
INGREDIENTS	*For 15 rolls* 1 pound 1½ ounces (500 g) Croissant dough (Recipe 47) 15 small, semi-sweet chocolate bars, ⅓ ounces (10 g) each *or* 5 ounces (150 g) semi-sweet chocolate chips 1 egg, beaten
UTENSILS	Rolling pin Knife Waxed paper Pastry brush Baking sheet

Assembling the Rolls: Follow the recipe given for preparing Croissants, but when you roll this dough for the second time before cutting it, roll it into a rectangle 6″ by 35″ (15 cm by 90 cm). Then cut the dough into 15 smaller rectangles, 6″ by 2⅜″ (15 cm by 6 cm). Place a chocolate bar across each rectangle, about 1½″ (4 cm) from one end and roll the dough around the chocolate (see photo, page 36). Place these small rolls on a well-buttered baking sheet and cover with waxed paper. Let the rolls rise at room temperature for 1 hour.

Baking: Preheat the oven to 475°F (250°C).

Remove the waxed paper and brush the rolls with beaten egg; bake for 3 minutes at 475°F (250°C), then lower the temperature to 400°F (200°C) and continue baking for 15 minutes longer. Watch the color because the Chocolate Rolls will not all bake at the same rate. Bake until golden brown.

Note: If using chocolate chips, sprinkle them in a thin line across each rectangle of dough, then roll the dough around the line of chips as if they were a chocolate bar.

To Freeze: Chocolate Rolls can be frozen. Freeze them as soon as they are shaped, but before they are set to rise. Place them first separately on a plate, leaving space between them and let them harden in the freezer. Then place them in plastic bags and place back in the freezer. When you want to use them, thaw them first in the refrigerator for 24 hours, then let them rise at room temperature for 1 hour and bake them according to instructions given above.

56

Raisin Buns (Pains aux Raisins)

(Photo page 2)

These buns are found in every Parisian bakery. The brioche dough used in making them is best prepared a day ahead of time.

PREPARATION 45 minutes

RESTING TIME 1 hour

BAKING TIME 10 minutes

INGREDIENTS *For 10 individual buns*
¼ cup (50 g) raisins
1 cup (¼ l) boiling water
3 tablespoons (½ dl) rum
9 ounces (250 g) brioche dough (Recipe 9)
½ cup (100 g) almond pastry cream (Recipe 17) *or* vanilla pastry cream (Recipe 24)
1 egg, beaten

For the icing
⅔ cup (100 g) confectioners' sugar
3 drops rum
2 tablespoons water *or*
3 tablespoons apricot jam

UTENSILS Small mixing bowl
Rolling pin
Pastry brush
Parchment paper
Baking sheet

Shaping the Buns: Soak the raisins in the boiling water for 15 minutes. Drain, then soak them in the rum while you roll out the dough. On a lightly floured board, roll the brioche dough into a rectangle 10″ by 6″ (25 cm by 15 cm). Cover the dough with the pastry cream of your choice, then drain the raisins and place them on top of the cream. Roll the dough tightly into a 10″ (25 cm) long roll. Place in the refrigerator for 30 minutes, then cut into 10 equal pieces (see photo, page 2). Place each piece of dough on a lightly buttered baking sheet (or a baking sheet lined with parchment paper), and let them rise for about 1 hour.

Baking: Preheat the oven to 425°F (220°C).

Brush the top of the buns with beaten egg. Bake the buns for 10 minutes. Remove the baking sheet from the oven and let the buns cool. While they are still warm, brush them either with an icing made by mixing confectioners' sugar, rum, and water or with a glaze made by melting a little apricot jam.

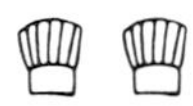

57

Genoa Cake (Pain de Gênes)

This soft cake can be served either with vanilla sauce, chocolate sauce, or a fruit sauce; or you can serve just as it is with tea or coffee.

PREPARATION 30 minutes

BAKING TIME 20 minutes

INGREDIENTS *For 2 cakes, each serving 6 persons*
½ cup, generous (50 g), slivered almonds
13 ounces (375 g) homemade almond paste (Recipe 18)
6 medium eggs
¾ teaspoon rum
¾ teaspoon Grand Marnier
2 cups, generous (300 g), flour
6½ tablespoons (100 g) butter, melted and cooled

UTENSILS Mixing bowl
Electric mixer with paddle or dough hook
Wooden spatula
2 round pieces of parchment paper 7″ (18 cm)
2 round cake pans 7″ (18 cm)

The Batter: Preheat the oven to 400°F (200°C).

Butter the cake pans and line the sides with slivered almonds. On the bottom of the pans, place the round pieces of parchment paper. The paper will stick to the butter and will keep the cake, which is very fragile, from sticking to the pan.

Place the almond paste in the bowl and mix at low speed for 2 or 3 minutes, then increase the speed to medium, adding the eggs one by one, beating continuously. The dough should be very light; then add the rum and Grand Marnier and continue beating 5 to 10 minutes more.

Then, using a wooden spatula, gently fold the flour and the melted butter into the batter. The batter must be baked immediately.

Baking: Fill each pan ¾ full and bake at 400°F (200°C) for 10 minutes, then lower the heat to 350°F (180°C) and bake for 10 minutes more. Turn out the cakes when completely cold and place them each on a plate, paper side down.

To Store: This cake will keep for 4 days in the refrigerator if wrapped in aluminum foil.

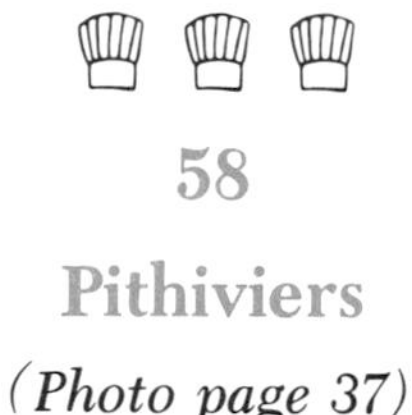

58

Pithiviers

(Photo page 37)

This is a dessert made from flaky pastry and almond cream. It was once a specialty of the town of Pithiviers but is now prepared all over France and is very similar to the Twelfth-Night Cake (Recipe 49).

PREPARATION	20 minutes
RESTING TIME	30 minutes
BAKING TIME	45 minutes to an hour
INGREDIENTS	*For 1 cake, serving 8 persons* 2 cups, generous (400 g), almond pastry cream (Recipe 17) 1 pound 5 ounces (600 g) classic *or* quick flaky pastry dough (Recipe 3 or 4) 1 egg, beaten 1½ tablespoons (15 g) confectioners' sugar

UTENSILS

Rolling pin
Saucer
Pastry brush
Knife
Baking sheet
Sugar dredger

Assembling the Cake: Preheat the oven to 475°F (245°C).

Divide the dough into two equal parts. On a lightly floured board, roll each piece of dough into a circle. To roll the dough into a perfect circle, roll it first into a small square barely larger than a saucer, place the saucer upside down on the dough and cut around it with a knife. Place this excess dough in the center of the circle and continue rolling the dough until it forms a large circle 10½" (26 cm) wide and ⅛" (3 mm) thick. Roll out the other piece of dough, so you will have two circles of dough the same size and thickness.

Place one circle on the baking sheet and brush a ½" (1 cm) band of beaten egg around the rim of the circle; don't get any egg on the edge of the dough. Place the almond pastry cream in the center of this circle of dough and spread it to within about 1" (3 cm) of the edge. Cover this circle of dough with the remaining circle and press down the edges so that they will stick together. Refrigerate the cake for 30 minutes.

Baking: Brush the top of the cake with the remaining beaten egg. Using the point of the knife, make a decorative design, drawing semi-circles in a spiral shape, starting from the center of the cake out to the edges (see photo page 37). Bake the cake at 475°F (245°C). When the Pithiviers has risen (after about 15 minutes), lower the heat to 400°F (200°C). Continue baking for 30 to 40 minutes more. Ten minutes before the cake is done, sprinkle the top with confectioners' sugar. Serve the cake warm.

To Freeze: This cake must be frozen before it is baked and before brushing on the beaten egg and decorating the surface. Follow the directions as given for the Twelfth-Night Cake (Recipe 49). Do not thaw the cake before baking but rather increase the baking time by 15 minutes.

59

Dutch Pithiviers (Pithiviers Hollandais)

This cake is just a slight variation on the preceding one. Only the decoration differs, since this version has a dome shape and the decoration is made with a mixture of sugar, almond powder, and egg white. Follow the general instructions for the Pithiviers in the preceding recipe with the following additional ingredients and instructions.

PREPARATION	20 minutes
RESTING TIME	90 minutes
BAKING TIME	45 minutes
INGREDIENTS	*For decoration* 2 tablespoons (30 g) granulated sugar 3 tablespoons (30 g) almond powder ½ egg white

Assembling the Cake: Make the two circles of dough slightly smaller and thicker than in the previous recipe. Place the almond pastry cream in the center of the first circle of dough in the shape of a dome. Cover the cream with the second circle of dough and press the edges together. Refrigerate for 1 hour.

Take the cake out of the refrigerator, press the edges together again to flatten them so that they will not come apart during baking and return the cake to the refrigerator for another half hour.

Baking: Preheat the oven to 400°F (200°C).

Mix the sugar, almonds, and egg white together and spread this mixture over the top of the cake. Sprinkle the cake generously with confectioners' sugar and then draw a star on the sugar, using the point of the knife. Bake the cake for 45 minutes.

60

Brioche Almond Slices (Tranches de Brioche aux Amandes)

Serve these cakes warm with coffee, tea, or fruit juice.

PREPARATION	15 minutes
BAKING TIME	5 minutes

INGREDIENTS

For 8 servings
1 Brioche Mousseline (Recipe 41)
2 cups, generous (400 g), almond pastry cream (Recipe 17)
6½ tablespoons (1 dl) water
½ cup, generous (135 g), granulated sugar
6½ tablespoons (1 dl) rum
3 drops orange-flower water
¾ cup (60 g) slivered almonds
Confectioners' sugar (for glazing)

UTENSILS

Saucepan
Knife
Flexible blade-spatula
Pastry brush
Baking sheet
Sugar dredger

Making the Syrup: Prepare a dessert syrup by mixing the water, granulated sugar, rum, and orange-flower water in a pot. Bring to a boil, then remove from the heat.

Assembling and Baking: Preheat the oven to 475°F (245°C).

Cut the Brioche Mousseline into ⅜" (1 cm) slices. With the pastry brush, brush the sides of each slice with the dessert syrup. On one side of each slice, spread a ⅛" (3 mm) layer of almond pastry cream, then sprinkle with some slivered almonds and dust with confectioners' sugar.

Place the slices on a buttered baking sheet and bake for a few minutes, or until the slices are golden brown, then serve.

Banana Tart, Recipe 100

Chapter 4

LARGE CAKES AND DESSERTS

RECIPES

61. Ambassador Cake (Ambassadeur)
62. Basic Baba Dough (Pâte à Babas)
63. Rum Baba (Babas au Rhum)
64. Strawberry Cake (Bagatelle aux Fraises)
65. Uncle Tom's Cake (Biscuit de l'Oncle Tom)
66. Rolled Cakes (Biscuits Roulés)
67. Strawberry Yule Log (Bûche Fraisier)
68. Coffee-Flavored Yule Log (Bûche au Café)
69. Chocolate Yule Log (Bûche au Chocolat)
70. Chestnut Yule Log (Bûche aux Marrons)
71. Chataigneraie
72. Concord Cake (Concorde)
73. Ivory Coast Cake (Côte d'Ivoire)
74. Strawberry Almond Cake (Fraisier)
75. Gâteau de Madame
76. Mexican Cake (Gâteau Mexicain)
77. Easter Cake (Gâteau de Pâques)
78. Raspberry Marly (Marly aux Framboises)
79. Chocolate Marquise (Marquise au Chocolat)
80. Chestnut Cake (Marronier)

81. Autumn Meringue Cake (Meringue d'Automne)
82. Millefeuille (Preparation and Baking)
83. Millefeuille with Vanilla Pastry Cream (Millefeuille à la Crème Pâtissière)
84. Loire Valley Millefeuille (Millefeuille Val-de-Loire)
85. Strawberry or Raspberry Millefeuille (Millefeuille aux Fraises ou aux Framboises)
86. Mocha Cake (Moka au Café)
87. Paris-Brest
88. Apricot Cake (Régent â l'Abricot)
89. Upside Down Orange Cake (Rosace à l'Orange)
90. Saint-Honoré Chiboust
91. Apricot-Pineapple Cake (Singapour aux Abricots)
92. Almond Succès (Succès Praliné)

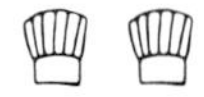

61
Ambassador Cake (Ambassadeur)

This is a Génoise cake filled with pastry cream and chopped candied fruit, flavored with Grand Marnier, and decorated with almond paste.

PREPARATION	25 minutes
RESTING TIME	1 hour
INGREDIENTS	*For 1 cake, serving 6 persons* 1 8″ (20 cm) Génoise cake (Recipe 6) 3½ tablespoons (40 g) candied fruit, finely chopped 3 tablespoons Grand Marnier 1¼ cups (300 g) vanilla pastry cream (Recipe 24) 1 cup (2½ dl) dessert syrup (Recipe 29) 14 ounces (400 g) pink or green almond paste decoration (Recipe 36) Candied cherries for decoration
UTENSILS	Small mixing bowl Flexible blade-spatula Serrated knife Rolling pin Pastry brush Cardboard disk 8″ (20 cm)

Assembling the Cake: A day ahead, prepare the Génoise cake and soak the diced candied fruit in Grand Marnier. The following day, prepare the pastry cream and let it cool. Set aside and refrigerate half of the cream. To the other half, add the diced and drained fruit. Prepare the dessert syrup.

With the knife, cut the Génoise cake horizontally in 3 equal layers. Place one layer on the cardboard disk and soak it with syrup by dipping the pastry brush into the syrup and "painting" it onto the cake. Cover it with half the pastry cream mixed with the diced fruit. Then cover this layer with a second layer of cake, which should be brushed with syrup as described above. Spread the remainder of the pastry cream-candied fruit mixture over this layer, then cover it with the third layer and brush it with syrup as well. Cover the whole cake with the refrigerated pastry cream and then chill the cake for 1 hour.

To decorate, roll out the prepared almond paste to cover the whole cake and decorate the top with candied cherries cut in two.

62

Basic Baba Dough (Pâte à Babas)

Although this recipe is for 1 large baba, you might want to double the recipe and prepare enough dough to bake 2 desserts at the same time, freezing one for later use.

PREPARATION 15 minutes

RESTING TIME 15 minutes

INGREDIENTS *For 1 baba, 4 to 5 servings, plus 10 individual Savarin cakes (approximately 1 pound)*
1½ ounces [500 g] dough)
½ cake (7 g) compressed baker's yeast
1½ tablespoons warm water
6½ tablespoons (1 dl) milk
1¾ cups (250 g) flour
1 teaspoon (6 g) salt
3 whole eggs
1 teaspoon, generous (6 g), granulated sugar
5 tablespoons (75 g) butter, cut into pieces

UTENSILS Mixing bowl
Electric mixer with dough hook

Making the Dough: Take the butter out of the refrigerator 30 minutes before preparing the dough.

Dissolve the yeast in the warm water. In a mixing bowl, place the yeast, 1 tablespoon of the milk, the flour, and the salt. Mix the ingredients at low speed, adding the eggs one by one, then increase the speed to medium and mix for 3 to 4 minutes or until the dough, which is firm in the beginning, becomes smooth and elastic. Soften the dough by gradually adding the remaining milk, sugar, and butter.

The dough should stretch easily between your fingers without breaking. Place the dough in a clean, large bowl and let it rise in a warm place for about 15 minutes. The dough should not rise for too long, or else the baba will become too crumbly. Punch the dough down once during this time.

63

Rum Baba (Babas au Rhum)

This cake, flavored to your taste with rum, Kirsch, or Grand Marnier, can be filled with whipped cream, pastry cream, stewed fruit, or a fruit salad.

PREPARATION 15 minutes

RESTING TIME 30-40 minutes

BAKING TIME 12-15 minutes

INGREDIENTS

For 1 baba, 4 to 5 servings
9 ounces (250 g) Basic Baba Dough (Recipe 62)
1½ cups (350 g) granulated sugar
2 cups, generous (½ l), water
1½ tablespoons rum, Kirsch, *or* Grand Marnier
⅓ cup (100 g) apricot jam, hot

For the decoration
Either candied cherries or stewed fruit of your choice, *or* a dessert cream (Chantilly, vanilla pastry cream, etc.)

UTENSILS

1 ring mold 8″ (20 cm)
Knife
Spoon
Cake rack
Plate
Small saucepan
Pastry brush
Pastry bag with star-shaped nozzle [optional]

Baking: Preheat the oven to 400°F (200°C).

Lightly butter the mold, place the dough in it, and let it rise in a warm place for 30-40 minutes or until the dough almost fills the mold.

Bake the baba for 12 to 15 minutes, or until done. To see if the cake is done, insert the blade of a knife into the cake; the knife should come out clean.

Turn out while still warm. If the baba sticks to the mold, wrap the warm cake and mold entirely in aluminum foil. The vapor will make the baba turn out more easily.

Flavoring and Decorating: As the baba cools, prepare a syrup by placing the sugar and water in a pot, bring just to a boil, then remove from the heat. Let this syrup cool, then add the alcohol of your choice. Place the baba on a rack over a plate and spoon the syrup over the cake, until almost all the liquid has been absorbed. As the syrup drips onto the plate, reuse it to baste the baba again before serving it. Another way to "soak" the baba is to place the syrup in a large bowl and dunk the baba in the liquid until thoroughly soaked. Then place the baba on a rack over a plate to drain.

Just before serving the baba, spoon a little remaining syrup over the cake, then glaze the baba with the hot apricot jam. Use a pastry brush to spread the jam onto the cake. Decorate with large candied cherries or slices of stewed fruit or fill the center with a cream of your choice (Chantilly cream [Recipe 13] or vanilla pastry cream [Recipe 24]). To fill the center of the baba, use a pastry bag fitted with a star-shaped nozzle.

To Store: The baba will keep for 10 to 15 days if well wrapped and placed in refrigerator, before being soaked with syrup or decorated.

To Freeze: Wrap the cake while it is still warm and before it is soaked with syrup, and place in the freezer. Before using, let the baba thaw in the refrigerator for 24 hours, then proceed to soak and decorate the cake as described above.

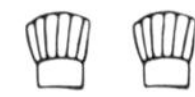

64

Strawberry Cake (Bagatelle aux Fraises)

(Photo page 129)

This cake is filled with a butter cream filling and fresh strawberries, then topped with a layer of almond paste.

PREPARATION	25 minutes
INGREDIENTS	*For 1 cake, serving 6 persons* 1½ cups (300 g) butter cream filling (Recipe 20) 1 Génoise cake, (Recipe 6) either 6″ (15 cm) square *or* 8″ (20 cm) round ⅔ cup (1 ½ dl) dessert syrup, flavored with Kirsch (Recipe 29)

10½ ounces (300 g) fresh, small strawberries (some cut in half) for the filling
6 large strawberries

For the decoration
⅓ cup (100 g) red currant jelly and
12 large strawberries *or*
5¼ ounces (150 g) almond paste decoration (Recipe 36)

UTENSILS

Pastry brush
Flexible blade-spatula
Bowl
1 piece of cardboard 8″ (20 cm) round or 6″ (15 cm) square
Serrated knife
Pastry bag with star-shaped nozzle [optional]
Rolling pin

Assembling the Cake: If you prepared the butter cream filling a day ahead, take it out of the refrigerator one hour before using it. Cut the Génoise in half with a serrated knife. Place the bottom half on the cardboard and, using the pastry brush, soak the cake with the dessert syrup. Spread a layer of butter cream filling on the cake to a thickness of between ⅛″ and ¼″ (3 mm to 5 mm).

Place whole strawberries all over the cream and those cut in half along the edges of the cake. All the strawberries should be "standing" on their base in the cream (see photo, page 129). Cover the strawberries completely with a second layer of butter cream filling.

Place the second layer of Génoise on top of the butter cream filling and soak this layer of cake with the dessert syrup, using a pastry brush. Cover this layer completely with another thin layer of butter cream filling.

Decorating: Either dip the 12 large strawberries into red currant jelly and place them on top of the cake, then cover the entire cake with the red currant jelly, or decorate the cake with almond paste in one of the following ways.

Use green-colored almond paste, and roll it out until you have a sheet large enough to cover the top of the cake *or* (if the strawberries around the side of the cake aren't perfectly even and erect) roll out enough almond paste to wrap around the sides of the cake as well.

Once the almond paste has been applied, cover the top of the cake with roses made from the butter cream filling or any other decorations made with the pastry bag. You could also place a multi-colored almond braid (see photo, page 12) on top, then place some large strawberries alongside and coat them with red currant jelly. Refrigerate the cake before serving. This cake should be eaten the same day it is prepared, or the following day at latest.

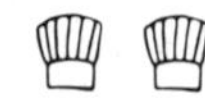

65

Uncle Tom's Cake (Biscuit de l'Oncle Tom)

This cake can be served with tea or as a dessert with a vanilla sauce.

PREPARATION 15 minutes

BAKING TIME 50 minutes

INGREDIENTS

For 2 cakes, each serving 6 persons

3½ ounces (100 g) semi-sweet chocolate
5 eggs, separated
¾ cup (180 g) granulated sugar
3½ tablespoons (50 g) butter, melted
2 tablespoons (20 g) flour
2 tablespoons (20 g) cornstarch
1½ tablespoons (20 g) granulated sugar

For the decoration

Confectioners' sugar

UTENSILS

Large mixing bowl
Electric mixer
Double boiler
Wooden spatula
2 waxed paper or parchment paper disks to line the bottom of the cake pans
2 cake pans 8″ (20 cm) round and 1½″ (4 cm) high
Sugar dredger
Paper doilies

The Batter: Preheat the oven to 400°F (200°C).

Butter the pans and place a paper disk at the bottom of each one. Dust the sides of the pans with flour so the cakes will turn out easily.

Melt the chocolate in a double boiler.

Beat the egg yolks with the sugar until the mixture forms a pale ribbon; then, still beating, add the melted butter. Beat the egg whites until very stiff, adding 1½ tablespoons granulated sugar halfway through.

Pour the yolk-sugar mixture over the warm chocolate, stirring vigorously.

Strawberry Cake, Recipe 64

Then gently fold the flour and cornstarch into the chocolate. Using the spatula, fold the chocolate mixture into the egg whites, working quickly but carefully. This batter must be baked immediately.

Baking and Decorating: Pour the batter into the pans; they should be no more than ¾ full. Bake in a 400°F (200°C) oven for 1 minute, then lower the heat to 350°F (180°C) and bake for 50 minutes more, keeping the oven door ajar with a spoon.

Remove the cakes from the oven and allow to cool. While still warm, turn out and place the paper doilies on top of them. Sprinkle the cakes with confectioners' sugar, then remove the doilies and serve. (You may use paper cuttings of your choice: e.g., stars, circles, or letters, instead of doilies.)

To Store: This cake will keep for 2 to 3 days if well wrapped and placed in the refrigerator.

66
Rolled Cakes (Biscuits Roulés)

This recipe uses a variety of fillings and decorations to achieve a range of tastes. Try each combination out, one at a time, and decide which one you like the best.

PREPARATION 30 to 40 minutes

INGREDIENTS *For 1 roll serving 10 persons*
1 jelly roll (Recipe 2)
⅔ cup (1½ dl) dessert syrup with flavoring of your choice (Recipe 29)

For the filling
1 cup (250 g) vanilla pastry cream (Recipe 24), plus ⅔ cup (125 g) stewed fruit (peaches, pears, cherries, pineapple, apricots) *or*

2⅔ cups (500 g) butter cream with flavoring of your choice (Recipes 20 to 23)—half for filling, half for decoration *or*

3½ cups, generous (500 g), chocolate mousse (Recipe 30) —half for filling, half for decoration *or*

1⅓ cups (330 g) Bavarian cream (Recipe 33) *or*

1½ cups (500 g) jam of your choice

For the decoration
2 tablespoons (40 g) apricot glaze *or* jam
⅓ cup (25 g) slivered almonds
Confectioners' sugar

UTENSILS Flexible blade-spatula
Long platter
Pastry bag with a star-shaped nozzle
Pastry brush
Sugar dredger

Assembling the Cake: Remove the paper from the cake (see Recipe 2). With a pastry brush, "paint" the papered side of the cake with dessert syrup. Then with a spatula, spread an even layer of the desired filling.

If you are using a pastry cream, mix in the thinly sliced fruit before spreading it on the cake. Roll the cake tightly; serve as is or decorate.

Decorating: Using a pastry bag with a star-shaped nozzle, completely cover the cake with a layer of butter cream or chocolate mousse, respectively, if either of these two fillings was used. Otherwise, completely cover the cake with apricot glaze.

If it is filled with Bavarian cream, serve it simply covered with the apricot glaze. But if the cake is filled with jam or pastry cream, cover the apricot glaze with slivered almonds and sprinkle with confectioners' sugar, then place the cake under the broiler for 1 to 2 minutes until golden brown. Refrigerate until ready to serve.

To Store: If the cakes are filled with pastry cream or Bavarian cream, they will keep in the refrigerator 48 hours. If they are filled with jam or butter cream, they will keep 4 days in the refrigerator.

67

Strawberry Yule Log (Bûche Fraisier)

(Photo page 47)

This is a rolled cake decorated with Italian meringue.

PREPARATION 15 minutes

BAKING TIME 10 minutes

INGREDIENTS *For 1 roll serving 10 persons*
1 jelly roll (Recipe 2)
⅔ cup (1½ dl) dessert syrup, flavored with Kirsch (Recipe 29)
1½ cups (500 g) strawberry jam
Confectioners' sugar
Almond paste decorations (Recipe 36)
Swiss meringue mushrooms (Recipe 8)

For the meringue
4 egg whites
1 cup, generous (250 g), granulated sugar

UTENSILS

- Large mixing bowl
- Electric mixer
- Small saucepan
- Candy thermometer [optional]
- Glass
- Flexible blade-spatula
- Pastry brush
- Fork
- Sugar dredger
- Baking sheet

Preparing the Meringue: Prepare the Italian meringue by beating the egg whites until very stiff; halfway through, add 2 teaspoons of the granulated sugar.

Boil the remaining sugar with 4 tablespoons of water until the syrup reaches 248°F (120°C)—hard ball stage. Use the thermometer to determine temperature or test by dropping one drop of sugar into a glass of cold water; if ready, it will form a ball and hold its shape at the bottom of the glass. Very quickly, pour the sugar onto the egg whites, being careful not to let the sugar fall on the edges of the bowl or the beaters. Keep beating at low speed for about 5 minutes or until the mixture has cooled.

Baking: Preheat the oven to 475°F (240°C).

Brush the cake with the dessert syrup and then spread the strawberry jam over it. Roll the cake up, then with a spatula, completely coat the cake with an even layer of Italian meringue. Sprinkle with confectioners' sugar. To decorate, draw lines on the meringue with a wet fork. The log is now ready.

Bake for about 10 minutes to harden the meringue and give it a golden color. Turn off the oven after 5 minutes if you see that the meringue is golden brown, but leave the cake in the oven for another 5 minutes to complete cooking.

Let the cake cool, then decorate with almond paste decorations and Swiss meringue mushrooms.

To Store: The Yule Log will keep for 4 days if refrigerated.

68

Coffee-Flavored Yule Log (Bûche au Café)

(Photo page 48)

This is a rolled cake with a coffee mousse filling and almond paste decorations. Its elaborate decoration always delights children, especially at Christmas time when Yule Logs are traditionally made in France.

PREPARATION 15 minutes

RESTING TIME 1 hour

INGREDIENTS *For 1 roll serving 10 persons*
2 cups, generous (500 g), butter
1½ teaspoons coffee extract
French meringue made with 3 egg whites, unbaked (Recipe 7)
1 jelly roll (Recipe 2)
⅔ cup (1½ dl) coffee syrup
3½ ounces (100 g) almond paste decoration, green (Recipe 36)
10 Swiss meringue mushrooms (Recipe 8)

UTENSILS Mixing bowl
Electric mixer
Flexible blade-spatula
Pastry bag with star-shaped nozzle
Sieve

Preparing the Mousse: Take the butter out of the refrigerator 1 hour before using it. Place the butter in a mixing bowl and whip it for a minute or two at low speed until it is very soft and light. Then add the coffee extract and carefully fold in the French meringue.

Assembling and Decorating the Cake: Brush the coffee syrup onto the cold jelly roll, then spread ¾ of the mousse over the surface of the cake. Roll the cake very tightly and refrigerate for 1 hour.

To decorate, cut two slices from the cake each about ¾″ (2 cm) thick. Place these slices on top of the log to simulate two cut off branches of a tree. With a pastry bag fitted with the star-shaped nozzle, cover the cake with the remaining mousse. Decorate by placing Swiss meringue mushrooms on top. Cut holly leaves out of green-colored almond paste to decorate as well. Press some of the almond paste through a large sieve onto the log to simulate moss. You can also place small almond paste figurines on the log. Cover the two ends and the branches with sheets of almond paste. Refrigerate until ready to serve.

To Store: The Yule Log will keep 3 or 4 days in the refrigerator.

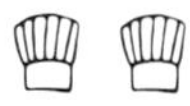

69

Chocolate Yule Log (Bûche au Chocolat)

This is a chocolate Génoise batter, baked like a jelly roll, then flavored with vanilla or rum and filled with chocolate mousse.

PREPARATION 30 minutes

BAKING TIME 7 to 8 minutes

RESTING TIME 1 hour

INGREDIENTS *For 10 servings for the Génoise batter*
¾ cup (100 g) flour
1½ tablespoons (15 g) bitter cocoa powder
¾ teaspoon (3 g) baking powder
3½ tablespoons (35 g) cornstarch
4 eggs
⅔ cup, scant (140 g), granulated sugar
2 tablespoons (35 g) butter, melted and cooled

For the decoration
⅔ cup (1½ dl) dessert syrup, flavored with rum *or* vanilla (Recipe 29)
5½ cups (750 g) chocolate mousse (Recipe 30)
5 mushrooms made of Swiss meringue (Recipe 8)
3½ ounces (100 g) light green almond paste (Recipe 36)

UTENSILS
- Bowl and electric mixer
- Small saucepan
- Baking sheet or jelly roll pan
- Parchment paper
- Flexible blade-spatula
- Pastry bag with star-shaped nozzle
- Sieve

Batter and Baking: Preheat the oven to 450°F (235°C).

Follow directions of Recipe 6 to prepare the Génoise batter, using the quantities given above. After measuring, sift the flour, cocoa, baking powder, and cornstarch, then add these ingredients to the egg-sugar mixture; add the butter, still following the directions of Recipe 6. With the spatula, spread this batter on the parchment paper lined baking sheet or jelly roll pan in an even ½″ (1 cm) thick layer.

Bake at 450°F (235°C) for 7 to 8 minutes, then remove from the oven and take the cake off the baking sheet when it comes from the oven.

Decorating: Prepare the dessert syrup with vanilla or rum flavor depending upon your taste.

Prepare the chocolate mousse; set aside 1⅓ cups (200 g) for decoration. Remove the paper from the cake while it's still warm by turning the cake upside down on a table and moistening the paper with a brush dipped in water. Cover the cake with a cloth and let it cool.

With a pastry brush, brush the dessert syrup on the side the paper was attached to. Spread the mousse over the surface of the cake, then roll the cake very tightly and refrigerate for 1 hour.

To decorate, cut two ¾″ (2 cm) thick slices off one end of the cake, place them on the log to simulate two sawed-off branches. With the pastry bag fitted with a star-shaped nozzle, cover the top of the log with the reserved chocolate mousse to simulate the bark of a tree. Add small Swiss meringue mushrooms and holly leaves made from the light green colored almond paste. Press the remaining almond paste through a sieve to simulate moss on the log. You can also decorate the log with small figurines made of almond paste; then cover both ends and the two branches with small sheets of almond paste. Refrigerate until ready to serve.

To Store: This cake will keep 48 hours in the refrigerator.

70
Chestnut Yule Log (Bûche aux Marrons)

This is a rolled cake filled with chestnut cream and candied chestnuts.

PREPARATION 30 minutes

RESTING TIME 1 hour

INGREDIENTS *For 1 roll, serving 10 persons*
1 jelly roll (Recipe 2)
⅔ cup (1½ dl) dessert syrup, flavored with rum *or* vanilla (Recipe 29)
1¾ cups (600 g) chestnut cream
1⅓ cups (300 g) butter, softened
6½ tablespoons (1 dl) rum [optional]
3½ ounces (100 g) candied chestnuts, broken
3½ ounces (100 g) almond paste decoration (Recipe 36)
10 Swiss meringue mushrooms (Recipe 8)

UTENSILS Mixing bowl
Electric mixer
Double boiler
Flexible blade-spatula
Pastry brush
Pastry bag with star-shaped nozzle

Assembling the Cake: In the double boiler, combine the chestnut cream, the softened butter, and the rum. When the batter is homogenous, pour it into a bowl and beat for another 5 minutes at low speed or until the batter becomes light and airy. Brush the cake with the dessert syrup and then spread ¾ of the chestnut filling over the surface of the cake. Sprinkle the candied chestnuts on top of the filling and then roll the cake very tightly. Refrigerate for 1 hour.

Decorating: Cut off two slices ¾″ (2 cm) thick from the "log." Place these slices on top of the log to simulate 2 sawed-off branches. With the pastry bag fitted with the star-shaped nozzle, cover the cake with the remaining chestnut cream to simulate the bark. Decorate with Swiss meringue mushrooms and holly leaves made out of almond paste. Press the remaining almond paste through a sieve to simulate moss on the log. You could also add some almond paste figurines. Cover both ends of the log and the two branches with the sheets of almond paste. Refrigerate until ready to serve.

To Store: This Yule Log will keep for 3 or 4 days in the refrigerator.

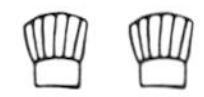

71
Chataigneraie

Peeling chestnuts requires a great deal of patience but the resulting cream you make with them is well worth the effort. This dessert is a favorite with children.

PREPARATION	45 minutes
COOLING TIME	About 30 minutes
RESTING TIME	1 hour, 30 minutes
INGREDIENTS	*For 1 dessert, serving 8 persons* ¾ cup, generous (200 g), butter 1 pound (450 g) fresh chestnuts 2 cups, generous (½ l), milk 1 vanilla bean, split lengthwise 1½-4 tablespoons rum (according to taste) ⅔ cup (150 g) granulated sugar 1½ cups (450 g) chocolate icing (Recipe 27) Confectioners' sugar
UTENSILS	Large mixing bowl Hand whisk Food mill, set with finest grill Wooden spatula Aluminum foil Flexible blade-spatula Pound-cake pan, 10¼″ (26 cm) long Sugar dredger Fork Knife

Making the Filling: Take the butter out of the refrigerator an hour before working with it. With a sharp knife, slit open the skin of each chestnut and peel off the outer skin. Cook the chestnuts in milk, along with the split vanilla bean, for 30 minutes. While hot, remove the inner skin of each chestnut (it peels off easily). Grind the chestnuts through a food mill and then pour in some of the strained milk the chestnuts cooked in until a thick purée is obtained. Cool at room temperature and then add the rum, according to taste.

In the mixing bowl, cream together the butter and sugar with the whisk.

Then, using the wooden spatula, add the chestnut purée. Line the cake pan with aluminum foil and fill the pan with the chestnut batter. Refrigerate for 1 hour.

Decorating: Prepare a thick chocolate icing (Recipe 27). Turn out the cake carefully and coat the whole cake, using a flexible blade-spatula, with half of the icing. Refrigerate the cake for 30 minutes, then give it a second coat with the remaining chocolate icing.

Finish decorating the cake by making lines with a fork to simulate the bark of a tree. Sprinkle some confectioners' sugar on top to simulate snow just before serving.

To Store: This cake will keep up to 8 days in the refrigerator.

72

Concord Cake (Concorde)

(Photo page 59)

This cake is made of chocolate mousse between three layers of chocolate meringue and covered with a chocolate meringue decoration.

PREPARATION	40 minutes
RESTING TIME	1 hour
BAKING TIME	1 hour, 5 minutes
INGREDIENTS	*For 1 cake, serving 10 persons for the meringues (including the decoration)* 3½ tablespoons (35 g) bitter cocoa powder 1 cup (150 g) confectioners' sugar 5 egg whites = ¾ cup (155 g) ⅔ cup (150 g) granulated sugar *For the mousse* (Recipe 30) 5½ ounces (160 g) semi-sweet chocolate

6½ tablespoons (100 g) butter
3 egg yolks
4 egg whites = ⅔ cup (120 g)
5 teaspoons (25 g) granulated sugar

UTENSILS

Pastry bag with ½″ (1 cm) nozzle
Pastry bag with ⅛″ (0.3 cm) nozzle
Mixing bowl and electric mixer
Wooden spatula
Baking sheet
Sugar dispenser
Parchment paper
Flexible blade-spatula
Oval cardboard 10″ by 5½″ (26 x 14 cm)

Preparing the Meringues: Preheat the oven to 300°F (150°C). Butter and lightly flour the baking sheet or cover the baking sheet with parchment paper. Mix the cocoa powder with the confectioners' sugar and sift together. Beat the egg whites until firm (about 5 minutes) adding 1½ tablespoons sugar halfway through. As soon as the egg whites are stiff, add the remaining sugar at low speed, then with the wooden spatula, quickly fold in the cocoa-sugar mixture.

Draw three ovals 10″ by 5½″ (26 x 14 cm) on the baking sheet to guide you when making the meringues. Take the pastry bag with the ½″ (1 cm) nozzle, fill it with chocolate meringue, and make three ovals by squeezing out the meringue in a spiral as shown in photo number 10,(page 44). Once this is done, using another pastry bag with a ⅛″ (0.3 cm) nozzle, squeeze out all the remaining meringue into long strips as in photo 11.

Baking: Bake in a 300°F (150°C) oven for 1 hour and 5 minutes. Check the color of the meringue after 15 minutes of baking. The meringues should not brown. If they do, lower the heat of the oven. The meringue strips will be done first and should be removed while the large ovals might need 10 minutes extra baking. When they are cooked, the meringues are hard and can easily be detached from the baking sheet.

Both the ovals and the meringue strips can be prepared a day ahead.

While the meringue is baking, prepare the chocolate mousse following the instructions given with Recipe 30 but using the measurements listed above.

Assembling the Cake: Once the meringue has cooled completely, place one of the ovals on a decorative piece of cardboard, or simply place it on a serving platter.

With the flexible blade-spatula, spread a layer of chocolate mousse over the meringue. Then place on top of the chocolate mousse a second layer of meringue, then a second layer of chocolate mousse and finally the last layer of meringue. Cover the cake completely with the remaining mousse.

Cut the chocolate strips into ½″ (1 cm) sticks. Cover the sides and the top of the cake with these strips. Refrigerate for 1 hour. Lay a broad ribbon (or piece of cardboard) across the cake, then sprinkle the cake all over with powdered sugar. Remove the ribbon (this part of the cake will be darker since it was not covered with sugar) and serve.

To Store: The cake can keep 48 hours in the refrigerator.

73

Ivory Coast Cake (Côte d'Ivoire)

This is a chocolate Génoise cake flavored with rum and filled with Chantilly cream.

PREPARATION 30 minutes

RESTING TIME 1 hour, minimum

BAKING TIME 30 minutes

INGREDIENTS *For 1 cake, serving 8 persons, for the Génoise (Recipe 6)*
3 whole eggs
⅓ cup (80 g) granulated sugar
6 tablespoons (60 g) flour
1 tablespoon (10 g) bitter cocoa powder
¾ teaspoon baking powder
2 tablespoons (20 g) cornstarch
1½ tablespoons (20 g) butter, melted and cooled

For the decoration
¾ cup (2 dl) dessert syrup, flavored with rum (Recipe 29)
2 cups, generous (350 g), chocolate Chantilly (Recipe 14)
1 tablespoon (10 g) bitter cocoa powder

UTENSILS Sifter or fine strainer
Pastry brush

Serrated knife
Metal flan circle 8″ (20 cm) wide by 2″ (5 cm) high (or circle this size made of strips of cardboard)
Flexible blade-spatula

The Batter: Break the eggs into a measuring cup; you need a generous ½ cup (⅛ l) of eggs. (Three eggs can be more or less than the quantity required, so be sure to check the volume before beginning). Preheat the oven to 350°F (180°C).

Follow the instructions given for Recipe 6 to prepare the Génoise but use the quantities given above. Sift the flour, cocoa, baking powder, and cornstarch, then add this mixture just as you would the flour alone when making the Génoise.

Pour the batter into the cake pan and place it immediately in the oven. Bake for 30 minutes. Turn out while still warm.

Decorating: While the cake is baking, prepare the dessert syrup flavored with rum. Let it cool while you prepare the chocolate Chantilly.

To assemble the cake, cut the Génoise into 3 equal layers with the serrated knife. Place the bottom layer in the metal flan circle or inside a circle made from strips of cardboard. With a pastry brush, coat the cake with dessert syrup, then using the flexible blade-spatula, cover the dessert syrup with a layer of Chantilly. Place a second layer of Génoise on top of the cream and brush with dessert syrup and cover with a layer of Chantilly. Place the third layer on top, brush it with syrup, and then cover the top of the cake with a thick layer of Chantilly, spreading the cream with the spatula dipped into hot water. (The last layer of cream should come just to the top of the circle.) Sprinkle the cake generously with bitter cocoa and refrigerate for at least 1 hour.

To remove the cake from the metal circle, pass a sponge that has been dipped in hot water around the exterior of the ring. If cardboard was used, simply loosen and remove it with the aid of a knife. Smooth the Chantilly around the edge of the cake with the spatula.

Use the edge of the spatula to decorate the top of the cake by drawing 8 lines from the center of the cake toward the edges.

To Store: The cake will keep for up to 24 hours in the refrigerator.

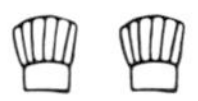

74

Strawberry Almond Cake (Fraisier)

(Photo page 62)

This is a strawberry jam-filled cake, flavored with Kirsch and surrounded with meringue and almonds.

LE NÔTRE
CUVÉE RÉSERVÉE
CIDRE FERMIER
Vallée d'Auge
GARANTI PUR JUS
Traiteur
PARIS DEAUVILLE NEW YORK

PREPARATION 20 minutes

BAKING TIME A couple of seconds under the broiler

INGREDIENTS *For 1 cake, serving 8 persons*
1 Génoise cake 8″ (20 cm) round (Recipe 6)
⅔ cup (1½ dl) dessert syrup, flavored with Kirsch (Recipe 29)
10½ ounces (300 g) French meringue (Recipe 7)
1 cup (350 g) strawberry jam
⅓ cup (50 g) slivered almonds

UTENSILS Cardboard disk 8¼″ (22 cm)
Flexible blade-spatula
Serrated knife
Pastry bag with ½″ (1 cm) nozzle

Assembling the Cake: With the serrated knife, cut the cake into 2 equal layers. Brush the cake with the cold dessert syrup.

Place a layer of Génoise on the cardboard disk, which should be slightly larger than the cake. With a pastry bag filled with French meringue, draw a circle around the rim of the cake. Fill the center with all the strawberry jam, spreading it with the spatula. The jam will be inside the meringue circle and will not run out. Cover the jam with a second layer of Génoise. Cover the entire cake with a ½″ (1 cm) layer of meringue. Sprinkle the surface of the cake with slivered almonds. Place the cake under the broiler for a few seconds to lightly color the meringue and brown the almonds. Serve the cake warm.

To Store: This cake will keep up to 24 hours in the refrigerator.

75

Gâteau de Madame

This is a chocolate Génoise cake, filled with Chantilly cream and covered with shaved chocolate.

PREPARATION 60 minutes

Eleanor's Apple Tart, Recipe 102

RESTING TIME 1 hour

BAKING TIME 30 minutes

INGREDIENTS *For 1 cake, serving 8 persons for the Génoise (Recipe 6)*
5¼ tablespoons (80 g) granulated sugar
3 whole eggs = ½ cup, generous (⅛ l)
⅓ cup, generous (60 g), flour
2 tablespoons (10 g) bitter cocoa powder
¾ teaspoon baking powder
2 tablespoons (20 g) cornstarch
1½ tablespoons (20 g) butter, melted and cooled

For the decoration
¾ cup (2 dl) dessert syrup, flavored with Kirsch *or* vanilla (Recipe 29)
1¾ cups (250 g) Chantilly cream (Recipe 13)
3½ ounces (100 g) semi-sweet chocolate for decoration, in a bar *or* large squares

UTENSILS
Sifter
Serrated knife
Pastry brush
Flexible blade-spatula
Génoise pan 8″ (20 cm)
Cardboard disk 8″ (20 cm)
Vegetable peeler

The Batter: Preheat the oven to 375°F (180°C).

Prepare a Génoise as described in Recipe 6 but use the ingredients listed above. Sift together the flour, cocoa, baking powder, and cornstarch, and add these ingredients as you would add the flour in Recipe 6. Pour the batter into the buttered cake pan and bake immediately. Bake for 30 minutes; turn out while still warm.

With the serrated knife, cut the Génoise into 4 equal layers. Place one layer on the cardboard disk and brush it with the dessert syrup. Cover the syrup with the Chantilly cream, spreading it with the flexible blade-spatula. Repeat this procedure until the last layer is covered with cream. Cover the cake completely with the remaining Chantilly cream and refrigerate for 1 hour.

Decorating: Cover the cake with shaved chocolate. To obtain the chocolate shavings, scrape the chocolate with a vegetable peeler.

Note: Three tablespoons of pastry cream can be added to the Chantilly cream. Do this by folding the pastry cream into a third of the Chantilly cream, then folding this mixture into the rest of the Chantilly cream.

To Store: Refrigerate this cake until you are ready to serve. It will keep for 1 day in the refrigerator.

76

Mexican Cake (Gâteau Mexicain)

This is a coffee-flavored Génoise, filled with coffee or hazelnut-flavored pastry cream.

PREPARATION 30 minutes

RESTING TIME 1 hour

INGREDIENTS *For 1 cake, serving 8 persons*
1 Génoise (Recipe 6), flavored with 1½ teaspoons coffee extract
2 cups, generous (300 g), Chantilly cream (Recipe 13)
⅔ cup (100 g) hazelnuts, whole
1 cup (2½ dl) dessert syrup, coffee-flavored (Recipe 29)
1 cup, generous (290 g), coffee-flavored pastry cream (Recipe 25)

UTENSILS 1 8″ (20 cm) cardboard disk
Flexible blade-spatula
Pastry brush
Serrated knife
Mortar and pestle or nut chopper
Pastry bag with star-shaped nozzle

Assembling the Cake: Prepare the Génoise a day ahead, adding the coffee extract just before adding the flour. Whip the Chantilly cream and set aside 1 cup for decorating the cake; place this reserved cream in the refrigerator.

In the oven, roast the hazelnuts and when browned, set aside 20 for decorating the cake. Chop or pound the remaining nuts. Cut the Génoise into 3 equal layers, using the serrated knife.

Place one layer of cake on the cardboard disk and brush it with dessert syrup. Add ½ cup of Chantilly cream to the coffee pastry cream, then add the chopped nuts. Cover the first layer of cake completely with this cream, spreading it with a spatula. Place a second layer of cake on top, brush with dessert syrup, then cover with the remaining Chantilly. Place the third layer of cake on top and brush with dessert syrup. Cover the whole cake with the refrigerated Chantilly cream. Refrigerate for 1 hour.

Decorating: Fill the pastry bag, fitted with a star-shaped nozzle, with the remaining Chantilly cream and make 20 small stars on top of the cake. Decorate with the 20 whole hazelnuts.

77

Easter Cake (Gâteau de Pâques)

(Photo page 71)

This is a Génoise filled with a very light cream cheese and decorated with cherries, strawberries or raspberries.

PREPARATION	20 minutes
RESTING TIME	1 hour
INGREDIENTS	*For 1 cake, serving 8 persons* 1 Génoise (Recipe 6) *For the dessert syrup* ¾ cup, generous (200 g), granulated sugar ⅔ cup (1½ dl) water 2-3 drops vanilla extract *or* 3 tablespoons (½ dl) Kirsch *For the filling* 1¾ cups (250 g) Chantilly cream (Recipe 13) 3½ tablespoons (50 g) granulated sugar ⅓ cup (75 g) farmer's cheese ⅔ cup (200 g) raspberry jam *For the decoration* 40 candied cherries or cherries in syrup *or* 1¾ cups (200 g) fresh strawberries *or* raspberries (whichever is in season) 3 tablespoons (50 g) raspberry jelly *or* jam Confectioners' sugar [optional]
UTENSILS	Flexible blade-spatula Serrated knife Pastry brush Pastry bag with ½″ (1 cm) nozzle 1 8″ (20 cm) cardboard disk

Assembling the Cake: Using the serrated knife, cut the Génoise into 2 equal layers. Prepare the dessert syrup and allow it to cool. Mix the sugar and the farmer's cheese; then fold all but 3 generous tablespoons of the Chantilly cream into the sugar-cheese mixture. Brush the 2 layers of cake with the dessert syrup. Place one layer on the cardboard disk or simply on a serving platter and cover with a layer of raspberry jam and a 1″ thick layer of cream-cheese mixture. Place the second cake layer on top of the filling and cover the whole cake with more of the cream-cheese mixture, smoothing the top and sides with the spatula. Fill a pastry bag with the remaining cream-cheese mixture and make a decorative border all around the top of the cake (see photo, page 71). Refrigerate for 3 hours.

With the remaining Chantilly cream, again smooth the sides of the cake and place the cake back in the refrigerator. The cake needs to be kept very cold.

Decorating: Place the cherries or the fresh fruit inside the border on top of the cake. Brush the fruit with jam or jelly or simply decorate the cake with fresh fruit and confectioners' sugar. Refrigerate before serving; serve the same day as prepared.

78

Raspberry Marly (Marly aux Framboises)

This is a Kirsch-flavored cake filled with butter cream and fresh raspberries.

PREPARATION	25 minutes
RESTING TIME	1 hour
INGREDIENTS	*For 1 cake, 8 servings* 1 Génoise (Recipe 6) 1 cup (2½ dl) dessert syrup, flavored with Kirsch (Recipe 29) 1⅓ cups (250 g) butter cream (Recipe 20) ½ pound (250 g) fresh raspberries ¼ cup (75 g) raspberry jam, mixed with ½ teaspoon Kirsch 10½ ounces (300 g) pink-colored almond paste (Recipe 36)
UTENSILS	Flexible blade-spatula Serrated knife

Pastry bag with ½″ (1 cm) nozzle
Cardboard disk 8″ (20 cm)
Pastry brush

Assembling the Cake: With a serrated knife, cut the Génoise into 2 equal layers. Place a layer on the cardboard disk or serving platter and brush on the dessert syrup. Set aside two tablespoons of the butter cream for decorating the top of the cake, then with the spatula, spread a thin layer of butter cream over the bottom layer of the Génoise. Using a pastry bag containing more butter cream filling, draw a circle around the rim of the cake. Fill the center with all but 10 of the raspberries. Cover the fruit with the raspberry jam mixed with Kirsch. Place the second layer of cake on top; cover the whole cake with the butter cream filling. Refrigerate for 1 hour.

Decorating: Roll out the almond paste decoration and cover the cake completely. On top of the almond layer, set the 10 reserved raspberries, using the reserved butter cream filling to stick the raspberries to the almond paste.

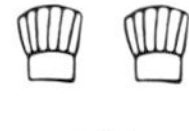

79

Chocolate Marquise (Marquise au Chocolat)

This is a rich chocolate layer cake that is refrigerated before serving.

PREPARATION 25 minutes

RESTING TIME 1 hour

INGREDIENTS *For 1 cake, serving 8 persons*
1 Génoise (Recipe 6)
1 cup (2½ dl) dessert syrup, flavored with vanilla (Recipe 29)
1 cup, generous (290 g), chocolate pastry cream (Recipe 26)
5 teaspoons (25 g) butter, creamed
¾ cup (225 g) chocolate icing (Recipe 27)

For the decoration
5 tablespoons Chantilly cream (Recipe 13) *or*
Confectioners' sugar

UTENSILS

Mixing bowl
Wire whisk
Flexible blade-spatula
Pastry brush
Serrated knife
Pastry bag with ¼″ (0.6 cm) nozzle or sugar dredger
Cardboard disk 8″ (20 cm)

Assembling the Cake: With the serrated knife, cut the Génoise into 3 equal layers. Place the first layer on the cardboard disk or serving platter and brush with dessert syrup. Cover the cake with a layer of chocolate pastry cream, using the spatula to smooth the cream. Place a second layer of the cake on top of the first, brushing it with dessert syrup and covering it with chocolate pastry cream. Place the third layer on top, again brushing with dessert syrup.

Whip the remaining chocolate pastry cream with the creamed butter and, using the spatula, cover the cake completely with this cream. Refrigerate for 1 hour.

Decorating: Spread the chocolate icing on the whole cake. With the pastry bag, decorate the surface of the cake with Chantilly cream. Or decorate by dusting the chocolate icing with confectioners' sugar, using cut-outs such as stars or circles to form patterns on the top. Refrigerate until ready to serve.

Note: You can vary this cake by using a coffee-flavored dessert syrup and coffee-flavored icing.

To Store: This cake will keep for 48 hours in the refrigerator.

80

Chestnut Cake (Marronier)

This is a rum-flavored Génoise filled with chestnuts.

PREPARATION 20 minutes

RESTING TIME 1 hour

INGREDIENTS

For 1 cake, serving 8 persons
5 tablespoons (75 g) butter, softened
¾ cup (250 g) chestnut cream
¾ teaspoon rum
1 Génoise (Recipe 6)
⅔ cup (1½ dl) cooled dessert syrup, flavored with rum (Recipe 29)
⅔ cup (100 g) chopped candied chestnuts

For the decoration
1 cup (300 g) chocolate icing (Recipe 27) *or* green-colored almond paste decoration (Recipe 36), plus| 8 candied chestnuts

UTENSILS

Mixing bowl
Electric mixer
Flexible blade-spatula
Serrated knife
Pastry brush
Cardboard disk 8″ (20 cm)

Assembling the Cake: Whip together the softened butter, chestnut cream, and rum with the mixer set at low speed for 2 minutes; the mixture should be creamy.

With a serrated knife, cut the Génoise into 3 equal layers. Place one layer on the cardboard disk and brush it with the dessert syrup. With the spatula, spread the cake with a layer of the chestnut-butter mixture, then sprinkle on half of the chopped chestnuts. Repeat with the second layer. Place the third layer on the cake and brush with the syrup. Cover the entire cake with the remaining chestnut mixture. Refrigerate for 1 hour.

Decorating: Cover the entire cake with the chocolate icing.

Note: For variety, you could omit the icing and roll out some green-colored almond paste (Recipe 36) and place it on top of the cake. Top the almond paste with glazed chestnuts. The almond paste decoration will keep longer than the chocolate icing.

To Store: This cake will keep up to 3 days in the refrigerator.

81

Autumn Meringue Cake (Meringue d'Automne)

(Photo page 72)

PREPARATION	30 minutes
COOKING TIME	15 minutes
RESTING TIME	1 hour minimum
INGREDIENTS	*For 1 cake, 6 servings* 3 circles of baked French meringue (Recipe 7) 2 cups, generous (300 g), chocolate mousse (Recipe 30) 5¼ ounces (150 g) semi-sweet chocolate
UTENSILS	Double boiler Flexible blade-spatula Flexible putty knife (see photo, page 72), 3½″ (9 cm) wide at base Baking sheet Cardboard disk 7″ (18 cm)

Assembling the Cake: Take half of the chocolate mousse and save for coating the outside of the cake. Place 1 layer of meringue on top of the cardboard disk and, using the spatula, spread a layer of mousse onto the meringue. Place the next meringue layer on top of the mousse and cover this second layer with another layer of mousse. Place the third meringue on top of the mousse. Cover the top and sides of the cake with the reserved Chocolate mousse. Refrigerate for 1 hour.

Decorating: Melt the chocolate in the double boiler, then with the putty knife, spread a *very* thin layer of chocolate onto the baking sheet. Place in the refrigerator.

After about 10 minutes, with the putty knife nearly horizontal to the baking sheet, scrape off a band of chocolate. The chocolate should form pleated ribbons 1½ to 2″ (4 to 5 cm) wide; if the chocolate is too cold, it will break; in this case, let the chocolate stand at room temperature for 5 minutes and try again. If the chocolate is not cold enough, it will be too soft and you will not be able to pick it up; in this case, place the chocolate back in the refrigerator and let it harden some more before trying to form the ribbons. Once you have several bands of chocolate, place them around the sides of the cake, then begin to scrape chocolate to decorate the top.

Try to get fan-shaped chocolate ribbons by placing your thumb against one edge of the chocolate ribbons as you scrape.

Form a circle with the least pleated strips of chocolate placed around the rim of the cake, and in the center, place the most fan-shaped strips to form a rose (see photo page 72).

82

Millefeuille (Preparation and Baking)

Bake the dough in advance and fill as desired at the last possible minute (they are best if eaten no longer than an hour after they are assembled).

PREPARATION	20 minutes
BAKING TIME	20 minutes per sheet
RESTING TIME	1 hour, minimum
INGREDIENTS	*For 1 cake, serving 6 persons, or 6 individual pastries* 1 pound 7 ounces (650 g) quick flaky pastry dough (Recipe 4) *or* classic flaky pastry dough (Recipe 3)
UTENSILS	Baking sheet Rolling pin Fork Serrated knife

Preparing the Dough: On a lightly floured board, roll out the dough into 3 rectangles, 8″ by 12″ (20 by 30 cm) and about 1/16″ (2 mm) thick. So that the dough does not shrink during baking, lift each rectangle of dough and let it fall back onto the board several times while rolling it out. Fold each rectangle of dough in 2 and leave for 1 hour (or overnight) in the refrigerator.

Baking: Preheat the oven to 425°F (220°C).

Unfold 1 rectangle of dough and place it on a slightly damp baking sheet. Prick all over with a fork. Bake for 20 minutes. Prepare and bake the remaining 2 rectangles of dough as you did the first one.

Note: To make individual portions: once the Millefeuille is assembled, cut it carefully into 6 rectangles using a serrated knife.

83

Millefeuille with Vanilla Pastry Cream (Millefeuille à la Crème Pâtissière)

This recipe uses the dough prepared in the previous recipe and combines it with pastry cream to form one large Millefeuille pastry.

PREPARATION — 30 minutes

INGREDIENTS — *For 6 servings*
1 pound 7 ounces (650 g) flaky pastry dough (Recipe 3 *or* 4)
2 cups (500 g) vanilla pastry cream (Recipe 24)
¾ cup (100 g) Chantilly cream (Recipe 13)
Confectioners' sugar
Jam of your choice

UTENSILS — 2 round cookie cutters ¾″ and 1¼″ (2 cm and 3 cm)
Flexible blade-spatula
Sugar dredger

Assembling the Cake: Roll out the dough into 3 rectangles and bake as described in the previous recipe. With the scraps left from cutting out the rectangles, make a ball, roll it out and cut it into 1¼″ (3 cm) circles. With the ¾″ (2 cm) cutter, cut out the center of each circle. (Make as many circles as possible, but no more than 20). These pastry rings can be baked with one of the sheets of pastry (the rings should be done after 8 to 10 minutes of baking, so watch their color carefully). When the three sheets and all the rings have been baked, select the best rectangle to serve as the cover or top layer of the cake. Turn this rectangle over and dust generously with confectioners' sugar. Broil for 1 minute, watching carefully to see that the sugar does not burn. Allow to cool.

Fold the vanilla pastry cream into the Chantilly cream. On the first rectangle of pastry, spread a layer of this cream. Place the second rectangle on top, spread it with the cream as well, then cover with the glazed rectangle of pastry. Sprinkle half the flaky pastry rings with confectioners' sugar, then place all the rings on top of the cake. Use a little jam to attach each ring to the top of the cake, alternating "brown" and "white" rings to form a decorative pattern.

84

Loire Valley Millefeuille (Millefeuille Val-de-Loire)

PREPARATION 15 minutes

INGREDIENTS *For 6 servings*
1 pound 7 ounces (650 g) flaky pastry dough (Recipe 3 *or* 4)
⅔ cup (200 g) raspberry jam
2¾ cups (400 g) Chantilly cream (Recipe 13)
Confectioners' sugar

UTENSILS Pastry bag with star-shaped nozzle
Sugar dredger
Flat metal rod or kitchen knife

Assembling the Cake: Use the flaky pastry dough to prepare 3 rectangles and bake as described in Recipe 82. Allow to cool. Set aside the nicest pastry rectangle for the top of the cake. On one rectangle, spread all the raspberry jam; place the second rectangle on top and with a pastry bag fitted with a star-shaped nozzle, cover it with the Chantilly cream. Place the last rectangle on top of this and sprinkle generously with confectioners' sugar; then heat the metal rod or knife until red hot and use it to draw a checkerboard pattern on the confectioners' sugar.

85

Strawberry or Raspberry Millefeuille (Millefeuille aux Fraises ou aux Framboises)

This recipe is for a Millefeuille cake filled with fresh strawberries or raspberries.

PREPARATION 30 minutes

INGREDIENTS — *For 1 pastry, serving 6 persons*
1 pound 7 ounces (650 g) flaky pastry dough (Recipe 3 *or* 4)
1 cup (250 g) vanilla pastry cream (Recipe 24)
1⅓ cups, generous (200 g), Chantilly cream (Recipe 13)
1 pound (450 g) fresh strawberries or raspberries

UTENSILS — Flexible blade-spatula
Pastry brush
Pastry bag with star-shaped nozzle

Assembling the Cake: Prepare three rectangles with the flaky pastry dough and bake them as described in Recipe 82. Allow to cool. With a spatula, spread the vanilla pastry cream onto the first rectangle and then cover the cream with a second layer of pastry. Cover this layer with half the Chantilly cream and spread the fresh fruit on top. (The fruit should be cleaned with a soft brush and not washed). Place the last layer of pastry on top of the fruit and decorate with small Chantilly roses made with a pastry bag fitted with a star-shaped nozzle. Garnish the top of the cake with a few pieces of fruit before serving.

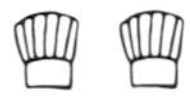

86

Mocha Cake (Moka au Café)

This is a Génoise filled with coffee mousse and glazed with coffee-flavored icing.

PREPARATION — 30 minutes

RESTING TIME — 1 hour

INGREDIENTS — *For 1 cake, 6 servings*
1 Génoise (Recipe 6)
⅔ cup, generous (160 g), butter
¾ teaspoon coffee extract
10½ ounces (300 g) French meringue (Recipe 7)
¾ cup (2 dl) dessert syrup, flavored with coffee *or* vanilla
¾ cup, generous (300 g), fondant icing, flavored with coffee (Recipe 28)
16 candy coffee beans, filled with liquor *or* chocolate

UTENSILS	Mixing bowl Electric mixer Flexible blade-spatula Pastry brush Serrated knife 8″ (20 cm) cardboard disk Cake rack

Assembling the Cake: Using the serrated knife, cut the Génoise into 3 equal layers. In the mixing bowl, cream the butter until smooth, then add the coffee extract. Whip until the mixture is light and very creamy; gently fold this mixture into the meringue. If you find the mixture hardening, place in a bain-marie and mix lightly.

Place one layer of cake on the cardboard disk, brush with dessert syrup, and cover with the meringue mixture. Then place a second layer of cake on top, following with dessert syrup and a layer of meringue. Finally place the last layer on top. Cover the entire cake with the remaining meringue mixture. Refrigerate for 1 hour or until the mocha hardens.

Decorating: Place the cake on a rack and cover with the fondant icing. Decorate the top of the cake with the liquor-filled or chocolate-filled candy coffee beans.

To Store: This cake must be served within 24 hours.

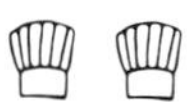

87

Paris-Brest

(*Photo page 74*)

This cake can be filled with any of 3 different creams. Prepare several rings of dough; they can be frozen easily or they will keep fresh for at least 1 week, if kept refrigerated.

PREPARATION	40 minutes
BAKING TIME	30 minutes

INGREDIENTS

For 1 cake, 6 servings
⅔ cup (300 g) cream puff pastry (Recipe 11)
⅓ cup (50 g) chopped almonds *or*
½ cup, generous (50 g), slivered almonds

For the Paris-Brest cream filling
1 cup (250 g) vanilla pastry cream (Recipe 24)
3½ tablespoons (50 g) butter, softened
½ cup (75 g) caramelized almonds (powdered)
Confectioners' sugar

For the Chiboust pastry cream filling
3⅓ cups (250 g) Chiboust pastry cream (Recipe 19)
Confectioners' sugar

For the light pastry cream filling
¾ cup (200 g) vanilla pastry cream (Recipe 24)
¾ cup (100 g) Chantilly cream (Recipe 13)
Confectioners' sugar

UTENSILS

Serrated knife
Wooden spoon
Baking sheet
Waxed paper [optional]
Pastry bag with ½″ (1 cm) nozzle and pastry bag with ¾″ (2 cm) star-shaped nozzle
Sugar dredger

Shaping and Baking the Dough: Preheat the oven to 450°F (230°C).

On a buttered baking sheet, or a sheet lined with waxed paper, draw an 8″ (20 cm) circle or 12 small circles 2½″ (6 cm). With a pastry bag fitted with the ½″ (1 cm) nozzle, draw a circle of cream puff pastry dough on the baking sheet (see photo 23, page 55). Draw a second circle inside and touching the first one, then place a third circle on top of the 2 other circles. Dust the rings with the chopped or slivered almonds.

Bake for about 30 minutes, keeping the oven door ajar with a wooden spoon. Begin by baking at 450°F (230°C) until the cake has risen (about 15 minutes), then lower the temperature to 400°F (200°C). When the cake has cooled, cut the cake in half so that you can fill it.

Assembling the Cake: Fill the cake with the cream of your choice. Sprinkle generously with confectioners' sugar and refrigerate. Serve the same day. The following are instructions for three possible fillings.

Paris-Brest cream: Prepare the vanilla pastry cream; add the softened butter and the powdered candied almonds while the cream is cooling. Whip the cream for one minute at slow speed so that it becomes fluffy. Place in the pastry bag fitted with a ¾″ (2 cm) nozzle and use it to fill the cake.

Chiboust pastry cream: Prepare the cream and fill a pastry bag fitted with a ¾″ (2 cm) nozzle. The nozzle does not have to be star-shaped but it has to have a large enough opening so as not to flatten the light Chiboust cream.

Light pastry cream: Prepare the vanilla pastry cream and let it cool. Whip the Chantilly cream and fold it very delicately into the cooled pastry cream. Use the ¾″ (2 cm) nozzle with the pastry bag.

88
Apricot Cake (Régent à l'Abricot)

This is a Génoise filled with apricot jam and flavored with Kirsch or vanilla.

PREPARATION 30 minutes

INGREDIENTS

For 1 cake, 6 servings
1 Génoise (Recipe 6)
⅔ cup (1½ dl) dessert syrup, flavored with Kirsch *or* vanilla (Recipe 29)
¾ cup, generous (250 g), apricot jam

For the decoration
⅔ cup (100 g) confectioners' sugar, mixed with 2 tablespoons of water and 2 drops of Kirsch
8 stewed apricots, cut in half
8 large candied cherries

UTENSILS

Small mixing bowl
Small saucepan
Flexible blade-spatula
Serrated knife
Pastry brush
8″ (20 cm) cardboard disk

Assembling the Cake: Cut the Génoise into 3 equal layers with the serrated knife. Place the first layer on the cardboard disk, brush it with dessert syrup, then, using the spatula, spread it with the jam. Place the second layer on top and follow the same procedures. Place the third layer on the cake and again brush with syrup.

Decorating: Heat the remaining jam and cover the whole surface of the cake with the hot jam. Prepare the icing by mixing the confectioners' sugar with the water and Kirsch. With a spatula, spread the icing over the top and sides of the cake. Place the apricot halves on top, along with the candied cherries. Refrigerate until ready to serve.

To Store: The cake will keep for 48 hours in the refrigerator.

89

Upside Down Orange Cake (Rosace à l'Orange)

(*Photo page* 83)

PREPARATION	45 minutes
COOKING TIME	2 hours a day ahead, 20 minutes next day
RESTING TIME	2 hours
INGREDIENTS	*For 1 cake, 6 servings* 4 oranges 4 cups water 2¾ cups (600 g) granulated sugar ⅔ cup (1½ dl) dessert syrup, flavored with Grand Marnier (Recipe 29) Juice of ½ orange 1 cup, generous (150 g), Chantilly cream (Recipe 13) 1¼ cups (300 g) vanilla pastry cream (Recipe 24) 1 Génoise (Recipe 6)
UTENSILS	Mixing bowl Electric mixer Saucepan Serrated knife Pastry brush 8½" (22 cm) cake pan

Preparing the Oranges: Cut the 4 oranges into very thin slices. Boil the water with the granulated sugar, then add the orange slices to the syrup and simmer slowly for 2 hours. Pour the oranges and the syrup into a bowl and leave until the next day.

Assembling the Cake: Prepare the dessert syrup (Recipe 29), flavored with the Grand Marnier and the juice of half an orange.

Whip the Chantilly cream. Set aside half of the orange slices for decorating the cake and cut the remaining ones into small pieces. Mix the pieces with the vanilla pastry cream, then fold the cream and oranges very delicately into the whipped Chantilly cream.

Butter the cake pan and dust with sugar. Line the mold with the orange slices, as shown in the picture on page 83. Half fill the mold with the orange-flavored pastry cream. Cut the Génoise into 2 layers with the serrated knife and brush both with the syrup. Place one layer on top of the pastry cream (trim it if necessary to fit the pan). Cover the layer with the remaining orange-flavored pastry cream and place another layer of Génoise on top. Press the cake with a dinner plate (with a small weight on top) and refrigerate for 2 hours.

To turn out, remove the plate and weight, dip the cake pan into hot water and turn it over onto a plate. Serve within 48 hours and keep refrigerated until ready to eat.

90

Saint-Honoré Chiboust

(Photo page 86)

This is a ring of cream puff pastry, placed on top of flaky pastry and filled with the Chiboust pastry cream.

PREPARATION 1 hour

BAKING TIME 25 minutes

INGREDIENTS *For 1 cake*
6¾ ounces (190 g) flaky pastry dough
(either Recipe 3 *or* 4)
⅔ cup (300 g) cream puff pastry (Recipe 11)

For the Chiboust cream (Recipe 19)
Pastry cream
1⅓ cups, generous (350 dl), milk
1 vanilla bean
5 egg yolks
3 tablespoons (45 g) granulated sugar
3 tablespoons (30 g) cornstarch
Meringue
⅓ cup, scant (70 g) granulated sugar
2 tablespoons water
4 egg whites = ½ cup (120 g)
5 teaspoons (25 g) granulated sugar

For the caramel
¾ cup, generous (200 g), granulated sugar
3 tablespoons water

UTENSILS

Small saucepan
Baking sheet
Parchment paper [optional]
Mixing bowl
Wire whisk
Rolling pin
Wooden spoon
Fork
3 pastry bags with ⅝″ (1.5 cm), ½″ (1 cm) and ⅛″ (0.3 cm) nozzles
1 pastry bag with ¾″ (2 cm) star-shaped nozzle

Baking: On a buttered baking sheet (or one lined with parchment paper), roll a circle of flaky pastry dough that is 9½″ (24 cm) round. Lift the dough up and let it fall to the table several times as you roll it out, to allow for shrinkage. When the right size, prick the dough all over with a fork.

Preheat the oven to 450°F (240°C).

Prepare the cream puff pastry and place it in a pastry bag fitted with the ⅝″ (1.5 cm) nozzle. Make a circle of cream puff pastry on top of the flaky pastry dough. Alongside, on the baking sheet, make 16 small puffs using the ½″ (1 cm) nozzle. If there is any dough left, make a spiral in the middle of the circle (see photo, page 86).

Bake for 10 minutes, then lower the temperature to 400°F (200°C) and bake for 15 more minutes, keeping the oven door ajar with a wooden spoon. Watch the color but try to avoid opening the oven door completely because the dough will fall. The small puffs will cook first—remove them after about 15 minutes of baking. When the large cake is done, remove from the oven and allow to cool.

Making the Chiboust Cream: While the dough is baking, prepare the Chiboust cream, following the instructions given for Recipe 19 but using the ingredients listed above. But, before adding the meringue, set aside ¾ cup (200 g) of the pastry cream to fill the cream puffs. Add the meringue to the remaining pastry cream.

Assembling the Cake: To fill the small puffs with the pastry cream, make a small hole in the bottom of the puffs with a knife and fill them with a pastry bag fitted with the ⅛″ (0.3 cm) nozzle.

Prepare a very light caramel by mixing the sugar and the water in a small saucepan and heating until it begins to darken.

With the pan away from the heat, dip the tops of the puffs in the caramel (to avoid burning yourself, hold the small puffs on the tip of a knife) and place the puffs, caramel side down, on a buttered baking sheet (or on waxed paper) to cool. As soon as the puffs are cool (it will only take a couple of minutes), place them at regular intervals on top of the larger circle of cream puff pastry, attaching them with some more caramel.

Fill the center of the cake with the Chiboust pastry cream, using the pastry bag fitted with the ¾″ (2 cm) nozzle. The nozzle need not be star-shaped but it should be large enough so as not to crush the cream.

Refrigerate the cake until you are ready to serve it. This cake should be served the same day it is prepared.

91

Apricot-Pineapple Cake (Singapour aux Abricots)

This is a Génoise filled with apricots and pineapple and decorated with pineapple and candied cherries.

PREPARATION	30 minutes
COOKING TIME	8 minutes
INGREDIENTS	*For 1 cake, serving 8 persons* 3 fresh apricots ½ cup, scant (100 g), granulated sugar 6 slices pineapple in syrup 3 tablespoons Kirsch [optional] 1 Génoise (Recipe 6)

8 large, red, candied cherries
⅓ cup (50 g) slivered almonds
⅔ cup (200 g) apricot jam, hot

UTENSILS

2 small saucepans
Serrated knife
Flexible blade-spatula
Pastry brush
Baking sheet
8″ (20 cm) round cardboard disk

Assembling the Cake: Remove the pits and cut the apricots into small pieces. Place in a pot with the sugar and boil for 5 minutes; then add 4 slices of pineapple, cut into small pieces. Remove from the heat and cool. When cool, add the Kirsch. Using the serrated knife, cut the Génoise into 2 equal layers. Place one layer on top of the cardboard disk and, using the spatula, spread on the apricot and pineapple mixture. Cover with the second layer of cake.

Decorating: Cut the candied cherries in half and quarter the remaining slices of pineapple. Place the cherries and pineapple pieces in a circle on top of the cake.

Place the slivered almonds on the baking sheet and broil for 3 minutes or until golden brown. Brush the whole cake with the hot apricot jam and sprinkle with the slivered almonds.

To Store: This cake will keep 2 or 3 days in the refrigerator.

92

Almond Succès (Succès Praliné)

(Photo page 95)

This beautiful white-topped cake can either be decorated with crushed caramelized almonds or simply wrapped in a gold-colored ribbon to give it a more festive air before serving.

PREPARATION 20 minutes

BAKING TIME	1 hour
INGREDIENTS	*For 1 cake, 6 servings* 4 cups (750 g) almond butter cream (Recipe 23) 2 baked Succès circles 8″ (20 cm) (Recipe 5) Confectioners' sugar ⅓ cup (50 g) crushed caramelized almonds [optional]
UTENSILS	8″ (20 cm) cardboard disk Flexible blade-spatula Sugar dredger Gold ribbon

Assembling the Cake: If the almond butter cream was prepared in advance, then take it out of the refrigerator 1 hour before you intend to use it. Place one of the Succès circles on the cardboard disk and cover it with 3¼ cups (600 g) of the cream. Press, very lightly, when you cover the cream with the second Succès circle. Cover the entire cake with the remaining butter cream, using a spatula. Dust the top of the cake generously with confectioners' sugar. Refrigerate for 1 hour, then press the crushed caramelized almonds, if using, around the sides of the cake or tie a large, decorative, golden ribbon around the cake. Serve cold.

To Store: The cake will keep 3 to 4 days in the refrigerator.

Chapter 5

PIES AND TARTS

RECIPES

93. Fruit Flan (Clafoutis Tutti Frutti)
94. Apple Dartois (Dartois aux Pommes)
95. Prune or Raisin Cake (Far aux Pruneaux ou aux Raisins)
96. Cheese Brioche (La Chantellée)
97. Royal Brioche Pudding (Pudding Royal)
98. Apricot Tart (Tarte aux Abricots)
99. Pineapple Tart (Tarte Feuilletée à l'Ananas)
100. Banana Tart (Tarte Antillaise aux Bananes)
101. Lemon Meringue Pie (Tarte au Citron Meringuée)
102. Eleanor's Apple Tart (Tarte Eléonore)
103. Mirabelle Plum Tart (Tarte aux Mirabelles)
104. Normandy Tart with Royal Icing (Tarte Normande Glace Royale)
105. St. Nicholas' Apple Tart (Tarte Normande Saint-Nicolas)
106. Candied Orange Tart (Tarte aux Oranges Confites)

107. Country Style Apple Tart (Tarte Paysanne)
108. Pear or Peach Tart with Almonds (Tarte aux Poires [or aux Pêches] aux Amandes)
109. Tarte Tatin

93

Fruit Flan (Clafoutis Tutti Frutti)

(*Photo page 97*)

This flan is usually made in early summer with ripe red cherries but it can also be prepared all year round with fresh or stewed peaches, pears or cherries.

PREPARATION 10 minutes

RESTING TIME 1 hour

BAKING TIME 25 to 30 minutes

INGREDIENTS *For 2 flans, 6 servings*
10½ ounces (300 g) short pastry dough (Recipe 10)
1 cup (¼ l) milk
1 vanilla bean, split lengthwise
6½ tablespoons (100 g) crème fraîche *or* heavy cream
4 eggs
¾ cup, generous (200 g), granulated sugar
4 drops orange-flower water
1 pound (450 g) fresh fruit *or*
2½ cups (450 g) stewed fruit (if using stewed fruit, use only ½ cup, scant [100 g], sugar)

UTENSILS Saucepan
2 disposable aluminum pie pans, 8″ (20 cm) or 2 fireproof porcelain dishes
Mixing bowl
Parchment paper and lentils for the mold

Making the Filling: Roll out the dough and use it to line two lightly buttered pie pans. Refrigerate for at least 1 hour before baking (this can be done a day ahead).

Preheat the oven to 400°F (200°C).

Boil the milk with the vanilla bean for about one minute, then add the cream. In the mixing bowl, beat the eggs and the sugar together, then add the milk-cream mixture a little at a time, beating constantly. Stir in the orange-flower water. Place the bowl in cold water to cool the mixture while you beat it. Beat until the mixture is smooth and cold.

Baking: Bake the two pie shells without the filling by lining them with parchment paper, then filling the paper with lentils. Place in a 400°F (200°C) oven for 5 to 10 minutes, then carefully lift out the paper and the lentils.

Fill the half-cooked pie shells with the fruit, dicing the fruit if too large. Pour the creamy filling prepared earlier over the fruit. The pie pan should be no more than ¾ full. Bake in a 400°F (200°C) oven for 20 minutes. Serve warm or cold.

To Freeze: The flans can be frozen before baking. They can be baked without defrosting them but then add 5 to 10 minutes to the baking time.

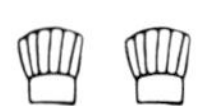

94

Apple Dartois (Dartois aux Pommes)

(Photo page 97)

PREPARATION	15 minutes
BAKING TIME	30 minutes
INGREDIENTS	*For 8 servings* 12 ounces (350 g) apples, peeled, cored, and diced 1 cup, generous (300 g), apple sauce (Recipe 179) ¾ teaspoon vanilla powder *or* extract 3 tablespoons (40 g) granulated sugar 1 pound 1½ ounces (500 g) classic *or* quick flaky pastry dough (Recipe 3 *or* 4) 1 egg, beaten
UTENSILS	Mixing bowl Baking sheet Rolling pin Pastry brush Fork

Assembling the Cake: Preheat the oven to 475°F (240°C).

In a bowl, mix the diced apples, apple sauce, vanilla powder, and sugar. Divide the dough into 2 equal parts, roll each piece into a 1/16″ (2 mm) thick

Pear Tart with Almonds, Recipe 108

PARIS·DEAUVILLE·NEW YOR

rectangle. Both rectangles should be the same size and shape. Place the first rectangle on a baking sheet and prick with a fork. Wet with a pastry brush 1¼″ (3 cm) all around the edges, then spread the apple filling evenly over the surface without touching the wet border.

Prick the second rectangle of dough, then lay it on top of the first one, pressing the edges together to seal them.

Baking: Brush the entire surface with a beaten egg and, with a knife, draw lines to form a diamond-shaped pattern on the top of the cake. Bake in a 475°F (240°C) oven for 5 minutes, reduce the heat to 425°F (220°C), and bake for 25 minutes more.

95

Prune or Raisin Cake (Far aux Pruneaux ou aux Raisins)

Easy to prepare and very nourishing, this dessert is often prepared on cold winter nights.

PREPARATION — 10 minutes

BAKING TIME — 35 minutes

INGREDIENTS — *For 8 servings*
6 tablespoons (60 g) flour
⅔ cup (150 g) granulated sugar
5 eggs
2 cups (½ l) warm milk
1½ tablespoons rum
A few drops vanilla extract
1 cup, generous (200 g), pitted prunes or raisins

UTENSILS — Mixing bowl
Wire whisk
1 round cake pan 9½″ (24 cm) wide and 2″ (5 cm) high *or*
2 round cake pans 6″ (16 cm) wide

Assembling the Cake: Preheat oven to 450°F (230°C).

In a mixing bowl, beat together the flour, the sugar, and the eggs with a wire whisk. Still beating, add the milk little by little, then add the rum and the vanilla extract. Gently stir the prunes or raisins into the batter, then pour it into a well-buttered cake pan.

Baking: Bake in a 450°F (230°C) oven for 10 minutes, then reduce the heat to 350°F (180°C) and cook for another 25 minutes.

Turn out while still warm or serve in the pan it cooked in.

96
Cheese Brioche (La Chantellée)

This is a brioche with a light cheese filling.

PREPARATION	15 minutes
BAKING TIME	50 minutes
INGREDIENTS	*For 6 servings* 7 ounces (200 g) brioche dough (Recipe 9) 1 cup (350 g) vanilla pastry cream (Recipe 24) 1 cup, generous (250 g), farmer's cheese 2 whole eggs 2 egg yolks 2 tablespoons (20 g) cornstarch ⅓ cup (80 g) granulated sugar A pinch of salt 1 lemon peel, finely chopped ¼ cup (60 g) melted butter
UTENSILS	Round cake pan 8½″ (22 cm) wide and 2″ (5 cm) high Mixing bowl Wire whisk

Assembling the Cake: Preheat the oven to 350°F (180°C).

Line the mold with the brioche dough, rolled very thin. Do not let the dough

rise. In a large bowl, mix all the ingredients listed above, except the butter, very rapidly with a wire whisk, then add the melted butter. Fill the mold containing the brioche dough up to the top with the batter.

Bake in a 350°F (180°C) oven for 50 minutes. Turn out when cold.

97

Royal Brioche Pudding (Pudding Royal)

This dessert is a favorite with children because of the colorful candied fruit in it. It can be served with either a vanilla or a chocolate sauce, or simply by itself.

PREPARATION 20 minutes

BAKING TIME 50 minutes

INGREDIENTS *For 12 servings*
3 cups (¾ l) milk
1 vanilla bean, split lengthwise
5 whole eggs
8 egg yolks
2 cups (450 g) granulated sugar
9 ounces (250 g) leftover baked brioche (or egg bread)
2 cups (300 g) mixture of whole candied cherries, raisins, dried currants and finely chopped candied fruits of your choice

For the sauces [*optional*]
2 cups (½ l) vanilla sauce (Recipe 32)
2 cups (½ l) chocolate sauce (Recipe 31)

UTENSILS 2 round molds, either fireproof porcelain or metal, 9″ (23 cm) wide and 1½″ (4 cm) high
Mixing bowl
Electric mixer

Tarte Tatin, Recipe 109

Assembling the Cake: Preheat the oven to 400°F (200°C).

Boil the milk with the split vanilla bean for one minute. In a bowl, beat the whole eggs, the yolks, and the sugar for one minute. Add slowly, while still beating, the hot milk. Generously butter the molds and coat the insides with granulated sugar. Slice the brioche into ⅝″ (1.5 cm) thick slices. Line the bottom of the molds with the brioche slices and cover with the candied fruits and raisins, then place the remaining brioche slices on top and fill the molds with the batter.

Baking: Bake in a bain-marie in the oven at 400°F (200°C) for about 50 minutes or until golden brown. If the pudding browns too quickly, cover it either with buttered waxed paper or with aluminum foil.

Turn out when cold. Serve cold, either as is, or with vanilla or chocolate sauce.

98

Apricot Tart (Tarte aux Abricots)

PREPARATION 15 minutes

BAKING TIME 40 minutes

INGREDIENTS *For 8 servings*

10½ ounces (300 g) sweet short pastry dough (Recipe 12)
2½ tablespoons (25 g) crushed vanilla wafers *or* bread crumbs
2¼ pounds (1 kg) fresh, very ripe apricots, *or* canned apricot halves
¼ cup apricot jam (to glaze)
Slivered almonds (to decorate)

UTENSILS

1 round cake mold 10½″ (26 cm) wide and 1½″ (4 cm) high
Pastry brush
Rolling pin
Cake rack

Assembling the Cake: Preheat the oven to 425°F (220°C).

Roll out the dough. Butter the mold and line it with the dough. Let stand for 1 hour if possible.

Crush the cookies or use bread crumbs to sprinkle over the bottom of the pie crust. Pit the apricots and cut them in half; if canned fruit is used, drain before using. Cover the bottom of the pie crust with fruit.

Baking: Bake the tart in a 425°F (220°C) oven for about 10 minutes, then lower the temperature to 400°F (200°C) and bake for 30 minutes more. Turn out while still warm and place the tart on a rack to cool. With a pastry brush, decorate with the warm apricot jelly, then sprinkle the tart with some slivered almonds just before serving.

99

Pineapple Tart (Tarte Feuilletée à l'Ananas)

Pineapple slices and pastry cream are placed on top of a flaky pastry square and served cold.

PREPARATION	20 minutes
BAKING TIME	30 minutes
INGREDIENTS	*For 8 servings* 7 ounces (200 g) flaky pastry dough (Recipe 3 *or* 4) ½ cup, scant (100 g), vanilla pastry cream (Recipe 24) ½ teaspoon Kirsch 12 slices canned pineapple *or* one 1¾ pound (800 g) fresh pineapple 4 tablespoons (80 g) apricot jam 8 candied cherries [optional]
UTENSILS	Rolling pin Knife Fork Pastry brush Baking sheet

Baking: Preheat oven to 450°F (240°C).

Roll out the dough until it forms a 10″ by 10″ square (25 cm x 25 cm) and is 1/16″ (2 mm) thick. Place it on a slightly damp baking sheet. Prick the dough with a fork. With a ruler, cut a strip of dough ⅝″ (1.5 cm) wide from each side of the square. Wet the edges of the square using a pastry brush dipped in water and place the cut out strips on the edges of the dough to form a border. With the back of a knife, lightly press down the top of this border, so that it will stick to the square.

Bake in a 450°F (240°C) oven for about 10 minutes, then lower the temperature to 400°F (200°C) and bake for 20 minutes more. Cool.

Making the Filling: While the dough is baking, prepare the pastry cream and flavor it with the Kirsch.

If you are using fresh pineapple, peel, core and slice it.

A few minutes before serving, garnish the cooked dough with the cold pastry cream, then place the pineapple on top. Brush on the apricot jelly and decorate with the candied cherries.

Note: If the flaky pastry dough is not rolled out until it is only 1/16″ (2 mm) thick, it will puff up too much during baking and the cake will look more like a "Millefeuille" than a tart.

100

Banana Tart (Tarte Antillaise aux Bananes)

(Photo page 120)

PREPARATION 20 minutes

BAKING TIME 20 to 25 minutes

INGREDIENTS *For 8 servings*
10½ ounces (300 g) sweet short pastry dough (Recipe 12)
⅔ cup (150 g) granulated sugar
⅔ cup (1½ dl) water

6½ tablespoons (1 dl) rum
5 ripe bananas
1½ cups, generous (400 g), vanilla pastry cream (Recipe 24)

For the sauce
2¾ cups (500 g) canned pineapple (drained) *or*
1 fresh pineapple, weighing 1¾ pounds (800 g), cored and sliced, plus ½ cup, scant (100 g), granulated sugar

UTENSILS

Pie pan 10½″ (26 cm)
Rolling pin
Large frying pan
Parchment paper, lentils to line the dough

Assembling the Tart: Prepare the dough a day ahead. Roll it out and line the pie pan the day you make the tart. Refrigerate it for an hour in the pie pan.

Preheat the oven to 425°F (220°C). In a large frying pan, mix the sugar, water and rum. Bring to a boil.

Peel the bananas and cut them in ½″ (1 cm) thick slices. Place the banana slices into the frying pan with the liquid and simmer very slowly for 10 minutes.

Meanwhile, prick the dough with a fork, line it with parchment paper, and fill the paper with lentils. Bake for 25 minutes in a 425°F (220°C) oven. Remove the paper and lentils when the dough is cooked. During the baking, prepare the pastry cream and let it cool. Fill the cooked pie crust with the pastry cream, then cover the cream with the drained banana slices, placed neatly close together.

Prepare a pineapple sauce in a blender, using either canned pineapple or fresh pineapple and sugar. Blend until the sauce is smooth. Cover the whole cake with a little of this sauce and serve the remaining sauce in a sauce boat. Serve immediately.

Note: The tart can be glazed with apricot jam instead of being coated with the pineapple sauce and other fruits (i.e., peaches, strawberries, etc.) can be used instead of pineapple to make the sauce.

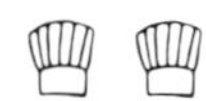

101

Lemon Meringue Pie (Tarte au Citron Meringuée)

(Photo page 181)

This tart's exquisite lemon filling is decorated with Italian meringue which is browned quickly under the broiler.

PREPARATION 40 minutes

BAKING TIME 25 minutes

INGREDIENTS *For 8 servings*
10½ ounces (300 g) sweet short pastry dough (Recipe 12)

For the pastry cream
1 cup (¼ l) milk
¼ vanilla bean, split lengthwise
3 egg yolks
2 tablespoons (30 g) granulated sugar
3 tablespoons (30 g) cornstarch
Juice of 3 lemons
Rind of 1½ lemons, finely grated

For the Italian meringue
3 egg whites
¾ cup, generous (180 g), granulated sugar
Confectioners' sugar, to glaze

UTENSILS
Mixing bowl
Electric mixer
Rolling pin
Small saucepan
Pie pan 8″ (20 cm)
Lentils
Parchment paper to line the dough
Wooden spatula
Pastry bag with ⅝″ (1.5 cm) star-shaped nozzle
Sugar dredger
Candy thermometer [optional]

Baking: Prepare the dough a day ahead. The next day, roll it out and line the pie pan with the dough. Cover the dough with the parchment paper and fill the paper with lentils. Bake for 25 minutes in a 425°F (220°C) oven. Remove and allow to cool. Remove the lentils and the paper.

Making the Filling: Prepare the pastry cream following the instructions given in Recipe 24 but using the ingredients given above. Once the cream is cooked and before it has cooled, stir in the lemon juice and grated rind.

To prepare the meringue, beat the egg whites until very firm, adding halfway through 1 tablespoon granulated sugar. Meanwhile, place the remaining sugar and 3 tablespoons of water in a saucepan; bring to a boil; boil the mixture until it reaches the hard ball stage (248°F = 120°C) on a candy thermometer (to test, dip a spoon in the sugar and drop a little bit of sugar in a glass of cold water; if the drop forms a ball on the bottom of the glass, the sugar is ready). Cooking the sugar will take about 5 minutes. Begin beating the egg whites again and pour the cooked sugar into them. Add the sugar quickly and try to pour it between the side of the bowl and the beaters. Continue beating at a low speed until the mixture has cooled (about 5 minutes). Take ⅓ of the meringue and carefully fold it into the lemon pastry cream with a wooden spatula. Spread this mixture onto the pie crust. Place the remaining meringue in a pastry bag fitted with a star-shaped nozzle and squeeze it out into little peaks that cover the whole tart. Sprinkle with confectioners' sugar and place under the broiler for 2 minutes or until golden brown.

Note: To simplify preparing this tart, French meringue (Recipe 7) can be used instead of Italian meringue. Boil the milk with a little lemon peel and add more lemon juice to the pastry cream if you want a stronger-flavored filling.

102

Eleanor's Apple Tart (Tarte Eléonore)

(Photo page 142)

This tart is made with flaky pastry topped with apples. Some people like serving a bowl of heavy cream with the tart, but it is delicious alone as well.

PREPARATION	15 minutes
BAKING TIME	20 minutes
INGREDIENTS	*For 6 servings, or 3 tarts 7" (18 cm) wide* 7 ounces (200 g) flaky pastry dough (Recipe 3 *or* 4) 6 tablespoons (100 g) apple sauce (Recipe 179) 5 cooking apples, peeled, cored, quartered Confectioners sugar to sprinkle on tarts 4 tablespoons (60 g) butter 3 tablespoons créme fraîche *or* heavy cream [optional]

UTENSILS

Rolling pin
Baking sheet
Sugar dredger

Baking: Preheat the oven to 450°F (240°C).

Roll out the flaky pastry until it is ⅛″ (3 mm) thick. Cut the dough into three circles, placing the excess dough in the center of each circle. Roll out each circle until it is 7″ (18 cm) wide, then place the three circles on a baking sheet.

In the center of each circle of dough, place a thin layer (2 tablespoons) of apple sauce (leave a border 1½″ wide uncovered around the edges).

Cut the quartered apples in half and place these pieces of apple in a circle on top of the apple sauce on top of each tart (see photo, page 142). Sprinkle each tart generously with confectioners' sugar and place small dabs of butter on top of the sugar.

Bake the tarts in a 450°F (240°C) oven for about 20 minutes. Five minutes before the end of baking, sprinkle each tart again with confectioners' sugar to glaze the fruit. Serve while warm, either as is or with a tablespoon of cream on each tart.

103

Mirabelle Plum Tart (Tarte aux Mirabelles)

The mirabelles are small, yellow plums common in France. Any other sweet, firm plum could be used in making this recipe.

PREPARATION

20 minutes

BAKING TIME

35 minutes

INGREDIENTS

For 8 servings
1 pound (450 g) short pastry dough (Recipe 10)
1 pound 5 ounces (600 g) fresh mirabelles *or*
3⅓ cups (600 g) canned mirabelles
3½ tablespoons (50 g) butter
¼ cup (60 g) granulated sugar
2 tablespoons mirabelle-flavored brandy (*or* plum brandy)
2 cups (350 g) almond cream (Recipe 17)
1 egg, beaten

UTENSILS

Pie pan 10½″ (26 cm) wide
Knife

Lemon Meringue Pie, Recipe 101

Pastry brush
Rolling pin
Frying pan

Assembling the Tart: Set aside a little more than 1/5 of the dough, then roll out the remaining dough and use it to line the pie pan. Refrigerate the dough in the pie pan while preparing the fruit.

Pit the fresh mirabelles or drain them if they are canned. In a frying pan, melt the butter and the sugar; add the fruit and cook for 5 minutes, then add the mirabelle brandy and ignite. Remove from the heat and allow to cool.

Preheat the oven to 425°F (220°C).

Place the almond cream on top of the pie crust, then lay the mirabelles on top of it, placing them very close together. Roll out the dough put aside in the beginning and cut it into long strips.

Decorate the top of the tart with the strips of dough, forming a criss-cross pattern and sticking the ends of each strip to the edges of the tart by wetting them slightly. Brush the top of the tart with beaten egg.

Bake at 425°F (220°C) for about 35 minutes, or until golden brown. Turn out while still warm and serve immediately.

Note: If canned fruit is used, use only 2 tablespoons of sugar.

104

Normandy Tart with Royal Icing (Tarte Normande Glace Royale)

Under a crunchy royal icing, you will find a creamy layer of apples.

PREPARATION 30 minutes + ½ hour to cool apples

BAKING TIME 40 minutes

INGREDIENTS *For 8 servings*
4 tart cooking apples
3½ tablespoons (50 g) butter
⅓ cup (80 g) vanilla sugar
12 ounces (350 g) short pastry dough (Recipe 10)

For the royal icing
½ egg white = 4 teaspoons
¾ cup (125 g) confectioners' sugar
3 drops lemon juice

UTENSILS Pie pan 10½″ (26 cm) wide and 1½″ (4 cm) high
Frying pan
Knife
Rolling pin
Spoon
Flexible blade-spatula

Preparing the Apples: Peel the apples and cut them into thick slices. Melt the butter in a frying pan and add the vanilla sugar. Fry the apples in the vanilla butter for about 5 minutes. Allow to cool.

Baking: Roll out half the dough and line the pie pan. Prick the dough with a fork. Cover the dough with the apples. Roll out the remaining dough in a circle 10″ (26 cm) and cover the apples; make this cover stick to the edges of the tart by pressing the two together with your fingers.

Preheat the oven to 400°F (200°C).

Preparing the Royal Icing: In a bowl, mix the egg white and the confectioners' sugar with a spoon for 2 minutes. Add the lemon juice, then spread this icing over the surface of the tart using a flexible blade-spatula. Bake in a 400°F (200°C) oven for 40 minutes. The royal icing will turn light brown. As soon as the icing is dry, cover the tart with aluminum foil to prevent it from browning too much. Turn out while the tart is still warm and serve right away.

105

St. Nicholas' Apple Tart (Tarte Normande Saint-Nicolas)

This is an apple and raisin tart flavored with cinnamon. It should be eaten warm, but the filling may be made a few hours in advance.

PREPARATION	45 minutes + ½ hour to cool apples
BAKING TIME	30 minutes
INGREDIENTS	*For 8 servings* ⅔ cup (150 g) butter 12 ounces (350 g) short pastry dough (Recipe 10) 1½ pounds (750 g) golden apples, peeled and cored 1 large cooking apple, peeled, cored, and quartered 1 cup (230 g) granulated sugar 1½ teaspoons (5 g) cinnamon 1½ teaspoons (8 g) vanilla sugar 2 eggs ½ cup, generous (80 g), flour 1½ teaspoons (5 g) baking powder 2 tablespoons (50 g) apricot jam ¼ cup (50 g) raisins
UTENSILS	Mold or flan ring 10″ (26 cm) wide and 1½″ (4 cm) high Pastry bag with ½″ (1 cm) nozzle 1 medium-size saucepan Mixing bowl Wire whisk Frying pan

Making the Filling: Take the butter out of the refrigerator to soften it. Roll out the dough and line the mold or the flan ring with it. Make apple sauce by simmering the large cooking apple with 2½ tablespoons (40 g) sugar, 2 tablespoons of water, and the cinnamon. Dice the golden apples and sauté in a frying pan with 2½ tablespoons butter, 5 tablespoons of sugar, and the vanilla sugar. Cook for 10 minutes on low heat, then allow to cool. Beat the remaining butter with the remaining sugar until creamy. Add the eggs, one after another, then add the apple sauce, the sifted flour, and the baking powder.

Baking: Preheat the oven to 400°F (200°C).

Spread the jam over the dough, then place the raisins on top. Cover with the diced apples. Fill a pastry bag with the apple sauce-egg mixture and squeeze it in a spiral to completely cover the diced apples.

Bake for 30 minutes. Remove from the oven and allow to cool for 15 to 20 minutes. While still warm, take out of the mold and serve.

106

Orange Tart (Tarte aux Oranges)

This is a tart decorated with oranges and filled with a very light Chantilly cream.

PREPARATION — 20 minutes a day ahead,
35 minutes the next day

BAKING TIME — 20 minutes

INGREDIENTS — *For 8 servings*
¾ cup water
⅔ cup, generous (160 g), granulated sugar
2 oranges
10½ ounces (350 g) sweet short pastry dough (Recipe 12)
1½ cups, generous (400 g), vanilla pastry cream (Recipe 24)
Juice of 1 orange
⅔ cup (100 g) Chantilly cream (Recipe 13)
Granulated sugar

UTENSILS — Small saucepan
Bowl
Pie pan 10″ (26 cm)
Parchment paper
Lentils
Knife
Rolling pin
Wooden spatula
Flat iron rod or kitchen knife

Preparing the Filling: A day ahead, prepare the syrup. Bring the water and granulated sugar to a boil, add the unpeeled oranges, sliced very thin, and simmer for 15 minutes. Remove from the heat and let cool. Cover and keep till the next day.

Baking: Preheat the oven to 400°F (200°C).

Roll out the dough and line the pie pan. Line the dough with the parchment paper and fill with lentils. Bake for 20 minutes. Remove the lentils and the paper.

Assembling the Tart: Prepare the pastry cream as described in Recipe 24 but add the orange juice to the cream while it is still warm. Take a little less than a quarter of the macerated oranges and chop them into very small pieces. With a wooden spatula, carefully fold the Chantilly into the pastry cream, then add the chopped oranges.

Spread this mixture on the baked pie crust and decorate with the remaining orange slices. To complete the decoration, dust the surface with granulated sugar and with a red hot iron rod or kitchen knife, burn a checkerboard pattern into the sugar. Refrigerate until ready to serve.

107

Country Style Apple Tart (Tarte Paysanne)

This is a small, rich, country style tart made with apples and currants covered with a creamy batter.

PREPARATION	15 minutes
BAKING TIME	30 minutes
INGREDIENTS	*For 2 to 3 servings* 1 egg 5 tablespoons (75 g) sugar 3 tablespoons (30 g) flour 6 tablespoons (1 dl) heavy cream 2 tablespoons (20 g) dried currants 2 medium (300 g) cooking apples, peeled, cored, and thinly sliced 3 tablespoons (40 g) butter, melted

UTENSILS
2 bowls
Wire whisk
Wooden spoon
Pie pan 8″ (20 cm) wide

Preparing the Filling: Preheat the oven to 400°F (200°C).

In a bowl, beat the egg and sugar with the whisk until the mixture whitens. Stir in the flour and cream. Beat until completely smooth. Mix the currants and apples together in another bowl, then pour over them a little more than half of the batter prepared above. Stir well, with a wooden spoon. Spread the apple-currant mixture evenly over the bottom of a buttered pie pan.

Baking: Place the pan in the oven and cook for 15 minutes. Meanwhile, add the melted butter, little by little, to the remaining batter, beating the mixture until smooth with the wire whisk. Remove the tart from the oven and raise the oven heat to 475°F (245°C). Spread the remaining batter over the half-cooked tart; replace the tart in the oven and cook for another 15 minutes. (Adding half of the batter in the beginning, and half at this time makes the tart creamier than if all the batter were added at once.)

Remove the tart from the oven and allow to cool for 10 minutes. Serve warm in the pan it cooked in.

108
Pear or Peach Tart with Almonds
(Tarte aux Poires ou aux Pêches aux Amandes)

(Photo page 169)

PREPARATION 15 minutes

BAKING TIME 30 minutes

INGREDIENTS
For 8 servings
12 ounces (350 g) short pastry dough (Recipe 10)
2 cups (350 g) almond cream (Recipe 17)

4 large canned pears *or* canned peaches
Apricot jam, to glaze

UTENSILS

Flan ring or pie pan 10½″ (26 cm)
Rolling pin
Pastry brush
Knife

Baking: Preheat the oven to 425°F (220°C).

Roll out the dough and line the mold; fill with the cold almond cream. Cut each half-fruit in thin slices, crosswise, then make a star with the fruit on top of the cream (see photo, page 169). Bake 30 minutes at 425°F (220°C). Remove from the pan while still warm. When the tart is cold, brush on the jam.

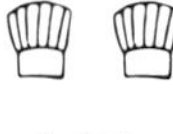

109

Tarte Tatin

(Photo page 172)

Caramelized apples characterize this tart which is cooked "upside down" with a flaky pie crust.

PREPARATION — 10 minutes

COOKING TIME — 20 minutes

BAKING TIME — 25 minutes

INGREDIENTS

For 8 servings
6¼ ounces (180 g) flaky pastry dough (Recipe 3 *or* 4)
½ cup (120 g) butter
1¼ cups, scant (270 g), granulated sugar
2¾ pounds (1.250 kg) tart cooking apples, peeled, cored, and halved

UTENSILS

Cake pan or preferably a round cast-iron enameled dish 9½″ (24 cm) wide and 2″ (5 cm) high
Fork
Rolling pin

Assembling the Tart: On a floured table, roll out the dough 1/16″ (2 mm) thick into a 10″ (26 cm) circle. Place the dough on a plate and prick it with a fork. Refrigerate, while you prepare the apples.

Preheat the oven to 400°F (200°C).

In the pie pan or dish, melt the butter and the sugar on top of the stove, then place the apples in the dish very close together. Continue cooking very slowly until the sugar begins to caramelize. This should take about 20 minutes and the apples should soften considerably. The caramel should be very light in color.

Baking: Put the dish in the oven for 5 minutes, then cover the apples with the rolled out flaky dough. Raise the oven temperature to 450°F (240°C) and continue baking for 20 minutes or until the pie crust looks done.

Once cooked, turn the dish over on a serving platter. Serve the tart warm.

Chapter 6

LITTLE PASTRIES

RECIPES

110. Chocolatines
111. Cream Puffs flavored with Almonds (Choux Pralinés)
112. Almond Butter Cream Pastries (Colisées)
113. Coffee or Chocolate Eclairs (Eclairs au Café ou au Chocolat)
114. Large Eclairs with Chantilly Cream (Gros Eclairs à la Chantilly)
115. Pineapple Eclairs (Eclairs Martiniquais)
116. Meringues with Chantilly Cream (Meringues à la Chantilly)
117. Chocolate Heads (Meringues Tête de Nègre)
118. Mont-Blanc
119. Hazelnut Cream Cakes (Noisettines)
120. Paris-Brest
121. Wells of Love (Puits d'Amour)
122. Individual Saint-Honoré Cakes (Saint-Honoré)
123. Salambo Cream Puffs (Salambos)
124. Individual Savarin Cakes (Savarins)
125. Individual Succès (Succès)

126. Fruit Tartlets (basic recipe) (Tartelettes aux Fruits)
127. Cherry Tartlets (Tartelettes aux Cerises)
128. Mirabelle Plum Tartlets (Tartelettes aux Mirabelles)
129. Blueberry Tartlets (Tartelettes aux Myrtilles)
130. Pear Tartlets (Tartelettes aux Poires)
131. Apricot Tartlets (Tartelettes aux Abricots)
132. Pineapple Tartlets (Tartelettes à l'Ananas)
133. Sunshine Tartlets (Tartelettes Coup de Soleil)
134. Walnut Tartlets (Val d'Isère)

110
Chocolatines

(*Photo page 193*)

In this recipe, Succès pastry shells are filled with chocolate mousse and sprinkled with chocolate flavored confectioners' sugar.

PREPARATION	30 minutes
BAKING TIME	1 hour
INGREDIENTS	*For 10 small cakes* 20 baked Succès shells 2½" (6 cm) (Recipe 5) 2 cups (300 g) chocolate mousse (Recipe 30) ⅓ cup (50 g) confectioners' sugar 2 tablespoons (20 g) cocoa powder
UTENSILS	10 metal circles 2½" (6 cm) wide and 1" (3 cm) high Sponge

Assembling the Cake: In each metal ring, place a Succès shell. Cover with chocolate mousse, then put a second Succès shell on top and cover with chocolate mousse. Refrigerate for 1 hour.

Remove from the refrigerator and rub a sponge dipped in hot water around each metal ring. Remove the rings. Mix the confectioners' sugar with the cocoa powder and sprinkle over the top of each cake. Serve the cakes the day they are prepared or, at the latest, the following day.

Note: A one-inch high band of cardboard can be used to form a ring and used instead of the metal ring. This cardboard ring is simply cut off after the cake has been refrigerated.

111
Almond Cream Puffs (Choux Pralinés)

(*Photo page 196*)

These are made with cream puff pastry filled with pastry cream, sweetened with powdered candied almonds. The cream puffs can also be filled with pastry cream flavored with rum, Kirsch or Grand Marnier; in this case, they are called salambos (see page 208).

PREPARATION	30 minutes
BAKING TIME	30 minutes
INGREDIENTS	*For 10 cream puffs* ⅔ cup (300 g) cream puff dough (Recipe 11) ½ cup (80 g) chopped, *or* 1 cup, scant (80 g), slivered almonds ¾ cup (200 g) vanilla pastry cream (Recipe 24), cooled ⅓ cup (50 g) powdered caramelized almonds 6½ tablespoons (100 g) soft butter Confectioners' sugar
UTENSILS	2 pastry bags, one with ⅝″ nozzle (1.5 cm) and one with ½″ (1 cm) nozzle Parchment paper Sugar dredger Serrated knife Baking sheet Wire whisk Bowl

Baking: Preheat the oven to 425°F (220°C). Prepare the cream puff pastry dough.

On a buttered baking sheet (or one covered with parchment paper), squeeze out 10 round puffs 1½″ (4 cm) using the pastry bag with the ⅝″ (1.5 cm) nozzle. Sprinkle the top of each cream puff with the chopped or slivered almonds

Bake at 425°F (220°C) for 30 minutes, keeping the oven door slightly ajar with a wooden spoon. Meanwhile, place the pastry cream in a bowl and while beating with a wire whisk, add the powdered caramelized almonds and butter until you have a light and homogenous mixture.

Filling the Cream Puffs: To fill the puffs, cut open one side using a serrated knife. Place the pastry cream mixture in the pastry bag with the ½″ (1 cm) nozzle, and fill the puffs with the cream.

Dust the cream puffs with confectioners' sugar and refrigerate. Serve them the same day they are prepared.

Hazelnut Cream Cakes, Recipe 119; Almond Butter Cream Pastries, Recipe 112; Chocolatines, Recipe 110
Meringues with Chantilly Cream, Recipe 116; Chocolate Heads, Recipe 117

112

Almond Butter Cream Pastries (Colisées)

(Photo page 193)

These little cakes are made of Succès pastry shells filled with rum and almond-flavored butter cream.

PREPARATION 30 minutes

RESTING TIME 1 hour and 30 minutes, minimum

INGREDIENTS *For 10 small pastries*
20 small oval Succès shells (Recipe 5)
1¾ cups (350 g) almond butter cream (Recipe 23)
½ cup, generous (100 g), raisins
1½ tablespoons rum

For the chocolate icing (Recipe 27)
4½ ounces (125 g) chocolate
3½ tablespoons (50 g) butter
⅔ cup (100 g) confectioners' sugar
3 tablespoons water

UTENSILS 10 metal circles 2½" (6 cm) wide and 1¼" (3 cm) high
Spatula

Assembling the Cakes: Prepare the Succès shells a day ahead.

The next day, prepare the almond butter cream. Soak the raisins in the rum while preparing the butter cream. In each metal circle place one Succès shell. Drain the raisins, add them to the almond cream, then cover the Succès shell with a layer of cream.

Place a second pastry shell on top of the cream and cover with more cream up to the rim. Refrigerate for 1 hour.

To remove from the mold, wipe the metal circle with a sponge dipped in hot water. Prepare the chocolate icing following the directions given in Recipe 27 but using the ingredients listed above.

Cover each cake with the icing and refrigerate for at least ½ hour. Serve the cakes the same day they are made or keep refrigerated and serve a day later at most.

Note: Strips of cardboard can be used to make rings the same size as the metal rings used in this recipe. If cardboard rings are used, they are simply cut away from each pastry after being refrigerated.

113

Coffee or Chocolate Eclairs (Eclairs au Café ou au Chocolat)

(Photo page 196)

PREPARATION 30 minutes

BAKING TIME 30 minutes

INGREDIENTS *For 10 éclairs*
⅔ cup (300 g) cream puff pastry (Recipe 11)
1½ cups (400 g) coffee pastry cream (Recipe 25) *or* chocolate pastry cream (Recipe 26) *or* a mixture of ¾ cup (200 g) of each cream
¾ cup (225 g) chocolate icing (Recipe 27) *or* 1 cup (350 g) coffee fondant icing (Recipe 28)

UTENSILS 2 pastry bags, one with ⅝″ (1.5 cm) nozzle and one with ¼″ (0.6 cm) nozzle
Waxed paper
Serrated knife
Baking sheet

Baking: Preheat the oven to 425°F (220°C).

Using the pastry bag with the ⅝″ (1.5 cm) nozzle, form 10 éclairs 4″ (10 cm) long on a buttered or waxed paper-lined baking sheet.

Bake at 425°F (220°C) for 15 minutes and then lower the temperature to 400°F (200°C) and bake for 15 minutes more, keeping the oven door ajar with a spoon. When done, remove from the oven and allow to cool.

Filling and Decorating the Eclairs: When the éclairs are cold, cut them open along the side with a serrated knife and using the pastry bag with the ¼″ (0.6 cm) nozzle, fill them with the pastry cream of your choice.

Glaze the éclairs with an icing the same flavor as the pastry cream filling. Refrigerate. Serve the same day they are prepared. Keep the éclairs refrigerated until ready to serve.

114

Large Eclairs with Chantilly Cream
(Gros Eclairs à la Chantilly)

(Photo page 196)

PREPARATION 30 minutes

BAKING TIME About 35 minutes

INGREDIENTS *For 8 éclairs*
⅔ cup (300 g) cream puff pastry (Recipe 11)
2 tablespoons (20 g) chopped almonds
2 cups, generous (300 g), Chantilly cream (Recipe 13)

For the caramel
3 tablespoons water
¾ cup, generous (200 g), granulated sugar
3 drops lemon juice

UTENSILS 2 pastry bags—one with a ⅝″ (1.5 cm) nozzle and one with a star-shaped nozzle
Fork
Serrated knife
Baking sheet
Parchment paper
Frying pan

Baking: On a buttered or parchment paper-lined baking sheet, form eight 6″ (15 cm) long éclairs, using a pastry bag with a ⅝″ (1.5 cm) nozzle. With a fork dipped in milk, draw lines on the top of each éclair. Sprinkle the éclairs with chopped almonds.

Bake in a 425°F (220°C) oven for 15 minutes, then lower the temperature to 400°F (200°C) and bake for 20 minutes more, keeping the door ajar with a spoon. Allow to cool.

Filling and Decorating the Eclairs: Prepare the Chantilly cream; chill. Prepare a caramel by boiling the water with the sugar and lemon juice in the frying pan until a cinnamon-colored caramel is formed. Dip the top of each éclair into the caramel and place them (caramel side down) on a cold baking sheet until cool (dip them in the caramel twice if necessary). Cut open one side of each éclair with a serrated knife; using a pastry bag with a star-shaped nozzle, fill the éclairs with the Chantilly. Refrigerate. Serve the éclairs as soon as possible (no more than 2 hours after being filled).

Coffee and Chocolate Eclairs, Recipe 113; Large Eclairs with Chantilly Cream, Recipe 114; Salambo Cream Puffs, Recipe 123; Almond Cream Puffs, Recipe 111

115

Pineapple Eclairs (Eclairs Martiniquais)

PREPARATION 30 minutes

BAKING TIME 30 minutes

INGREDIENTS *For 10 éclairs*
⅔ cup (300 g) cream puff pastry (Recipe 11)
1½ cups (350 g) vanilla pastry cream (Recipe 24)
1½ tablespoons Kirsch [optional]
½ cup (80 g) pineapple, finely chopped
1 cup (350 g) unflavored fondant icing (Recipe 28)
2 slices of pineapple cut into chunks

UTENSILS 2 pastry bags—one with a ⅝″ (1.5 cm) nozzle and one with a ½″ (1 cm) nozzle
Baking sheet
Parchment paper
Serrated knife

Baking: On a buttered or parchment paper-lined baking sheet, form ten 4″ (10 cm) long éclairs using the pastry bag with the ⅝″ (1.5 cm) nozzle. Bake in a 425°F (220°C) oven for 15 minutes; then lower the temperature to 400°F (200°C) and bake for 15 minutes more, keeping the oven door ajar with a spoon; cool.

Filling and Decorating the Eclairs: Meanwhile, prepare the pastry cream flavored with Kirsch or any other flavoring of your choice. Mix the finely chopped pineapple with the pastry cream.

When the éclairs are cold, cut open one side with a serrated knife and, using the pastry bag with the ½″ (1 cm) nozzle, fill the éclairs with the cream. Prepare the white fondant and dip the top of the éclairs in the warm fondant icing. Place the éclairs on a platter and decorate the top of each éclair with two small pieces of pineapple.

Serve the éclairs the same day they are made. Keep them refrigerated until ready to serve.

116

Meringues with Chantilly Cream (Meringues à la Chantilly)

(*Photo page 193*)

If you prepare the meringue shells in advance, you can make this dessert very quickly.

PREPARATION 20 minutes

INGREDIENTS *For 10 servings*
20 baked French meringue shells (Recipe 7)
3 cups, generous (450 g), Chantilly cream (Recipe 13)

UTENSILS 10 decorative paper containers
1 pastry bag with ¾″ (2 cm) star-shaped nozzle

Filling the Meringues: Place 2 meringue shells in each paper container (the flat sides should be facing each other), then fill the space in between the two meringues with Chantilly cream using a pastry bag with a ¾″ (2 cm) nozzle. Refrigerate until ready to serve. Serve them as soon as possible. Once filled, the meringue shells will not keep more than 2 hours.

Note: You can make paper containers by cutting doilies into oval shapes large enough to hold two meringues and folding up the edges to form a border.

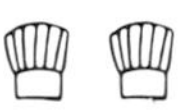

117

Chocolate Heads (Meringues Tête de Nègre)

(*Photo page 193*)

These meringue shells are filled with either chocolate-flavored butter cream or chocolate mousse, then rolled in grated chocolate. This dessert can be prepared up to three days in advance.

PREPARATION 20 minutes

RESTING TIME — 1 hour

INGREDIENTS — *For 10 servings*
20 baked French meringue shells (Recipe 7)
2⅔ cups (500 g) chocolate-flavored butter cream (Recipe 22) *or* 3⅓ cups (500 g) chocolate mousse (Recipe 30)
7 ounces (200 g) grated semi-sweet chocolate

UTENSILS — 10 paper containers (see note, Recipe 116)
Flexible blade-spatula

Assembling and Decorating: Set aside a little more than a third of the butter cream or chocolate mousse. Cover the flat side of a baked meringue with a thick layer of the remaining butter cream or chocolate mousse and press the flat side of a second meringue into the cream. Continue assembling the other meringue shells in this way. Refrigerate for 30 minutes.

Take the meringues out of the refrigerator and, using the spatula, spread each meringue with a thin coat of the butter cream or chocolate mousse reserved earlier. Roll the meringues in the grated chocolate. Place each Chocolate Head in a paper container and refrigerate for 30 minutes before serving.

118

Mont-Blanc

These small cakes are made with a Chantilly cream filling and decorated with chestnut cream.

PREPARATION — 30 minutes

BAKING TIME — 12 minutes

INGREDIENTS — *For 10 cakes*
9 ounces (250 g) sweet short pastry dough (Recipe 12)
4 cups (570 g) Chantilly cream (Recipe 13)
⅔ cup (200 g) chestnut cream
1½ tablespoons rum *or* milk [optional]

UTENSILS

2 pastry bags—one with a star-shaped nozzle, one with a 1/16″ (2 mm) nozzle
Cookie cutter 3″ (8 cm)
Fork
Baking sheet
Rolling pin

Baking: Preheat the oven to 400°F (200°C).

On a lightly floured table, roll out the dough and cut it into circles 3″ (8 cm). Prick the dough with a fork and place on a baking sheet. Bake for 12 minutes or until golden brown. Remove from the oven and cool.

Making the Filling: The baked circles must be cold; if necessary refrigerate 10 minutes before filling them. Using a pastry bag with a star-shaped nozzle, fill the crust with Chantilly cream, forming large, pointed roses, making them look like small mountain peaks.

Fill another pastry bag with the 1/16″ (2 mm) nozzle with chestnut cream (either rum or milk can be stirred into the cream if it is very stiff). Squeeze out the chestnut cream into very thin lines all over the top of the cake. Refrigerate for several hours before serving.

Note: Mont-Blancs can also be prepared by using two oval meringue shells. If this is done, fill the meringue shells with Chantilly cream as in Recipe 116 and cover them with the chestnut cream, using a pastry bag with a 1/16″ (2 mm) nozzle.

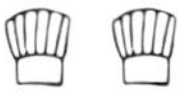

119

Hazelnut Cream Cakes (Noisettines)

(Photo page 193)

PREPARATION

30 minutes

RESTING TIME

1 hour

INGREDIENTS

For 10 Noisettines
20 small oval Succès shells (Recipe 5)
2 cups (350 g) almond butter cream (Recipe 23)
⅔ cup (100 g) finely chopped hazelnuts
Confectioners' sugar

UTENSILS

10 metal circles 2¼″ (6 cm) (see note, Recipe 110)
Spatula
Sponge
Sugar dredger

Assembling the Cakes: In each metal circle, place a Succès shell. Cover with the almond cream and sprinkle with chopped hazelnuts. Place a second Succès shell on top and cover with cream up to the rim of the metal circle. Refrigerate for 1 hour.

To serve, rub the circles with a sponge dipped in hot water and remove the ring. Sprinkle each cake with confectioners' sugar. Refrigerate before serving.

120

Paris-Brest

(Photo page 74)

The cream puff circles can be prepared a day ahead; they will keep fresh if kept in a sealed plastic bag. Any one of three different fillings can be used when making this cake. Choose from among three different kinds of fillings.

PREPARATION

30 minutes

BAKING TIME

30 minutes

INGREDIENTS

For 10 individual Paris-Brest
½ cup (200 g) cream puff dough (Recipe 11)
½ cup (80 g) chopped almonds

For the pastry cream filling
6½ tablespoons butter
⅓ cup (50 g) powdered caramelized almonds
¾ cup (200 g) vanilla pastry cream (Recipe 24), cold
Confectioners' sugar

For the Chantilly cream filling
2 cups, generous (300 g), Chantilly cream (Recipe 13), flavored with 2 teaspoons strong coffee
Confectioners' sugar

For the Chiboust cream filling
4 cups (300 g) Chiboust cream (Recipe 19)
Confectioners' sugar

UTENSILS — Pastry bag with ⅝″ (1.5 cm) nozzle, either round or star-shaped
Parchment paper
Serrated knife
Baking sheet
Wire whisk
Sugar dredger

Baking: Preheat the oven to 425°F (220°C). On a buttered or parchment paper-lined baking sheet, squeeze out six 2¼″ (6 cm) circles of cream puff pastry, using a pastry bag with a ⅝″ (1.5 cm) nozzle. Sprinkle the circles of dough with the chopped almonds. Bake for 30 minutes in a 425°F (220°C) oven, keeping the oven door ajar with a spoon. If, after 15 minutes, the cream puffs are too brown, lower the temperature of the oven to 400°F (200°C) for the remainder of the baking time. Remove from the oven and allow the puffs to cool.

Filling the Puffs: Using a serated knife, cut each puff in half and fill with one of the following:

With the pastry cream: With a wire whisk, beat the butter and powdered caramelized almonds until a light creamy mixture is formed. Add the cold pastry cream and beat for another minute. Using a pastry bag with a ⅝″ (1.5 cm) round or star-shaped nozzle, fill the bottom half of the cream puff circles with this cream. Place the other half on top and dust with confectioners' sugar.

With the Chantilly cream-flavored with coffee: Fill the cakes and sprinkle with sugar as described above.

With the Chiboust cream: Fill the cakes and sprinkle with sugar as described above.

Refrigerate until ready to serve. These cakes should be eaten the day they are made.

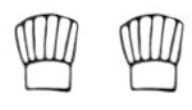

121

Wells of Love (Puits d'Amour)

These are small tartlets made with cream puff pastry, caramelized and filled with pastry cream.

PREPARATION — 30 minutes

BAKING TIME 20 minutes

INGREDIENTS

For 10 Puits d'Amour
½ cup, scant (200 g), cream puff pastry (Recipe 11)
1⅔ cups (450 g) vanilla pastry cream, cooled (Recipe 24)
or 2 cups (150 g) Chiboust cream (Recipe 19)

For the caramel
¾ cup, generous (200 g), granulated sugar
3 drops lemon juice
3 tablespoons water
Granulated sugar for glazing

UTENSILS

10 small tartlet pans 3″ (8 cm) wide and 1″ (2½ cm) in height
Pastry bag with ½″ (1 cm) star-shaped nozzle
Spoon
Pastry brush
Baking sheet
Saucepan

Baking: Use tartlet pans with smooth, high sides. Butter the pans lightly. Preheat the oven to 425°F (220°C).

Prepare the cream puff pastry and when the batter is cold, place a spoonful in each tartlet pan, then with your finger, spread the dough evenly on the bottom and the sides of the pans. Bake in a 425°F (220°C) oven for 20 minutes, keeping the oven door ajar with a spoon. Lower the temperature to 400°F (200°C) if the tartlets brown too fast.

Filling and Decorating the Tartlets: Turn out the tartlets while they are still warm and allow to cool. Prepare the caramel by cooking the sugar, lemon juice, and water in a saucepan until the mixture is cinnamon-colored. Dip the tops of the pastries in the caramel, then set aside (right side up) to cool.

Fill the tartlets with the pastry cream, using a pastry bag with a star-shaped nozzle. Sprinkle the surface with granulated sugar and place the tartlets under the broiler for 1 minute or until golden brown.

Serve cold the day they are prepared. Refrigerate until ready to serve.

122

Individual St-Honoré Cakes

PREPARATION 30 minutes

BAKING TIME 30 minutes

INGREDIENTS

For 10 cakes
3½ ounces (100 g) flaky pastry dough (Recipe 3 or 4)
⅔ cup (300 g) cream puff pastry dough (Recipe 11)

For the caramel
¾ cup, generous (200 g), granulated sugar
3 drops lemon juice
3 tablespoons water
2¾ cups (400 g) Chantilly cream (Recipe 13) *or*
3 cups (225 g)Chiboust cream (Recipe 18)

UTENSILS

2 pastry bags—one with 1½″ (1 cm) nozzle and one with ⅛″ (0.3 cm) nozzle
Rolling pin
Round cookie cutter 3″ (8 cm)
Pastry brush
Parchment paper

Baking: Preheat the oven to 425°F (220°C). On a lightly floured board, roll out the cold flaky pastry until it is extremely thin. With a cookie cutter, cut out 3″ (8 cm) circles and prick them with a fork; place them on a buttered or parchment paper-lined baking sheet. Use a pastry brush dipped in a little water to lightly wet the top (around the rim) of each circle of pastry.

Using the pastry bag with the ½″ (1 cm) nozzle, make a circle of cream puff dough ¼″ (½ cm) from the edge of each piece of flaky pastry. On the baking sheet, next to these circular pastries, make 30 very small cream puffs. Bake at 425°F (220°C), keeping the oven door ajar with a spoon. The small puffs should bake in 10 to 15 minutes, the circular pastries need 10 minutes more. Remove from the oven and allow to cool.

Filling and Decorating the Puffs: Prepare the caramel; boil the sugar, lemon juice, and water together until cinnamon colored. Stick each small cream puff on the point of a knife, then dip the top of the puff into the caramel. Place the cream puffs, caramelized side down,on a baking sheet to cool (dip them twice if not well coated). A few minutes later, dip the other side of the cream puffs into the caramel and stick 3 cream puffs onto each circle of dough. Fill the

Individual Savarin Cakes, Recipe 124

A variety of Tartlets: Cherry, Recipe 127; Pear, Recipe 130; Apricot, Recipe 131; Sunshine, Recipe 133

center of each circular pastry with either Chantilly cream or Chiboust cream and refrigerate before serving.

Serve the same day they are prepared.

Note: Each cream puff can be filled with pastry cream before being dipped in caramel (see Recipe 90).

123

Salambo Cream Puffs (Salambos)

(Photo page 196)

These are small caramelized cream puffs, filled with pastry cream flavored with rum, Kirsch, or Grand Marnier.

PREPARATION 30 minutes

BAKING TIME 20 minutes

INGREDIENTS

For 10 Salambos
⅔ cup (300 g) cream puff pastry (Recipe 11)
1½ cups (400 g) vanilla pastry cream (Recipe 24) cooled and flavored with 1½ tablespoons either rum, Kirsch, *or* Grand Marnier

For the caramel
⅔ cup (125 g) granulated sugar
2 tablespoons water
3 drops lemon juice

For the glaze
¾ cup, generous (300 g), pink *or* green fondant icing (Recipe 28)

UTENSILS

2 pastry bags—one with a ⅝″ (1.5 cm) nozzle and one with a ⅛″ (0.3 cm) nozzle
Saucepan
Baking sheet
Parchment paper

Baking: Butter a baking sheet or line it with parchment paper; using the pastry bag with the ⅝" (1.5 cm) nozzle, make 10 ovals 1¼" by 2¾" (3 × 7 cm) with the cream puff pastry. Bake in a 425°F (220°C) oven for 20 minutes, then cool.

Filling and Decorating: When the puffs are cold, make a small hole in the bottom of each puff and, using the pastry bag with the ⅛" (0.3 cm) nozzle, fill them with pastry cream. Glaze the top of each pastry either with caramel or fondant icing. To make the caramel, cook the sugar, lemon juice, and water until golden brown. Dip the top of each puff in the hot caramel, then place caramel side down on the baking sheet to cool. A few minutes later, place the puffs on a plate to serve. Otherwise, glaze the puffs with fondant icing. Dip the top of the already filled puffs in the lukewarm fondant and turn them over to cool.

Refrigerate and serve the same day.

Note: When the puffs are filled with rum-flavored cream, they are usually glazed with caramel; when Grand Marnier cream is used, they are glazed with pink fondant icing; and when filled with Kirsch-flavored cream, green fondant icing is used.

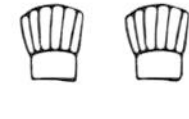

124

Individual Savarin Cakes (Savarins)

(Photo page 206)

There are three possible fillings for a Savarin: Chantilly cream, pastry cream and fruit salad.

PREPARATION	30 minutes
BAKING TIME	15 minutes
INGREDIENTS	*For 10 Savarins* 9 ounces (250 g) baba dough (Recipe 62) *For the syrup* 1½ cups (350 g) granulated sugar 1½ tablespoons rum *or* ¾ teaspoon vanilla extract 2 cups (5 dl) water

126

Fruit Tartlets - Basic Recipe (Tartelettes aux Fruits)

PREPARATION 10 minutes

BAKING TIME 20 minutes

INGREDIENTS *For 10 tartlets*
10½ ounces (300 g) of sweet short pastry dough (Recipe 12)
2 cups, generous (400 g), almond cream (Recipe 17)
1⅓ to 2 cups (250-400 g) fresh *or* stewed fruit
⅓ cup (100 g) apricot jam, warm

UTENSILS 10 metal circles 3″ (8 cm) or 10 small rectangular tartlet pans
Baking sheet
Pastry brush
Rolling pin

Preparing the Tartlets: Roll the cold dough out on a lightly floured table. Line the pans or the circles and place them on a baking sheet; refrigerate for 1 hour.

Preheat the oven to 425°F (220°C).

Fill each tartlet with almond cream, then add the fruit (or fill the tartlets with fruit, then add the cream—see recipes that follow) and bake for 15 minutes.

Turn out while still warm. Glaze the tarts right away with the warm apricot jam.

127

Cherry Tartlets (Tartelettes aux Cerises)

(Photo page 207)

PREPARATION 10 minutes

BAKING TIME	20 minutes
INGREDIENTS	*For 10 tartlets* ½ pound (250 g) cherries Ingredients and utensils used in Recipe 126

Preparing the Tartlets: Follow basic Recipe 126. Before baking, cover the almond cream with the fresh pitted cherries. Finish as described earlier.

128

Mirabelle Plum Tartlets (Tartelettes aux Mirabelles)

(Photo page 294)

PREPARATION	10 minutes
BAKING TIME	20 minutes
INGREDIENTS	*For 10 mirabelle tartlets* 10½ ounces (300 g) mirabelles, *or* small plums of your choice (fresh *or* stewed) Ingredients and utensils used in Recipe 126

Preparing the Tartlets: Follow the basic Recipe 126. Cover the almond cream with the drained fruit before baking. Finish as described earlier.

129

Blueberry Tartlets (Tartelettes aux Myrtilles)

(Photo page 294)

PREPARATION 10 minutes

BAKING TIME 20 minutes

INGREDIENTS *For 10 blueberry tartlets*
14 ounces (400 g) stewed blueberries
Ingredients and utensils used in the Recipe 126

Preparing the Tartlets: Follow the basic Recipe 126. Bake the tarts with the almond cream and cool. Garnish with the drained cooked blueberries.

130

Pear Tartlets (Tartelettes aux Poires)

(Photo page 207)

PREPARATION 10 minutes

BAKING TIME 20 minutes

INGREDIENTS *For 10 pear tartlets*
½ pound (250 g) pears
Ingredients and utensils used in Recipe 126

Preparing the Tartlets: Follow Recipe 126. Before baking the tarts, fill them with almond cream and garnish them with thin slices of pears.

Note: The tartlets can be garnished after they are cooked if you are using stewed fruit.

131

Apricot Tartlets (Tartelettes aux Abricots)

(Photo page 207)

PREPARATION	10 minutes
BAKING TIME	25 minutes
INGREDIENTS	*For 10 apricot tartlets* 10½ ounces (300 g) short pastry dough (Recipe 10) *or* 10½ ounces (300 g) sweet short pastry dough (Recipe 12) ⅔ cup (100 g) cookie crumbs 30 to 40 fresh or canned apricot halves ¾ cup, generous (200 g), granulated sugar (only if you use fresh fruit) ⅓ cup (100 g) apricot jam
UTENSILS	Same as Recipe 126

Preparing the Tartlets: Preheat oven to 400°F (200°C).

Line the tartlet pans or circles with the short pastry or the sweet short pastry. Sprinkle cookie crumbs over the bottom of each tartlet (they will absorb the fruit juices during baking). Place the apricot halves into each tartlet (the apricots should overlap each other). If you use fresh fruit, sprinkle the fruit with granulated sugar. Bake for 25 minutes and turn out while still hot. Using a pastry brush, glaze the tarts with warm apricot jam.

132

Pineapple Tartlets (Tartelettes à l'Ananas)

(Photo page 294)

PREPARATION	45 minutes
BAKING TIME	20 minutes
INGREDIENTS	*For 10 pineapple tartlets* 12 ounces (350 g) flaky pastry dough (Recipe 3 *or* 4) 1 cup (250 g) pastry cream (Recipe 24), flavored with 2 teaspoons rum 10 slices canned pineapple, drained 5 large candied cherries ⅓ cup (100 g) apricot jam, warm
UTENSILS	Knife Rolling pin Fork Pastry brush Baking sheet

Preparing the Tartlets: Preheat the oven to 425°F (220°C).

On a lightly floured table, roll out the flaky pastry very thin. To prepare square tartlets, cut the dough into squares 3″ (8 cm) on each side. Fold each square in half (forming a triangle) and cut around the two short sides making a band ½″ (1 cm) wide—but do not detach this band or cut all the way to the end. Open the square, fold over the cut ends, crossing each one to the opposite side (see photo, page 294 and photo 5, page 35). Prick the bottom of each tartlet with a fork and lightly wet the edges so that the border will stick to the bottom. Place the unfilled tartlets on a baking sheet and bake in a 425°F (220°C) oven for 20 minutes or until golden brown, then remove and allow to cool.

Filling and Decorating: The baked and cooled tartlets are filled with a layer of rum-flavored pastry cream, then decorated with the pineapple. Place half a candied cherry on each tartlet and brush with the apricot jam to glaze.

Serve as soon as possible since flaky pastry gets soggy after being filled.

Caramel Custard, Recipe 161

133

Sunshine Tartlets (Tartelettes Coup de Soleil)

(Photo page 207)

These are tartlets filled with pastry cream and pears.

PREPARATION	25 minutes
BAKING TIME	15 minutes
INGREDIENTS	*For 10 tartlets* 10½ ounces (350 g) sweet short pastry dough (Recipe 12) 2 cups (500 g) pastry cream (Recipe 24) 7 ounces (200 g) fresh or stewed pears Granulated sugar, for glazing
UTENSILS	10 tartlet pans or metal flan circles 3″ (8 cm) wide Rolling pin Parchment paper Lentils Flexible blade-spatula Baking sheet

Baking: On a lightly floured board, roll out the dough very thin. Line the pans or the circles with the dough and place them on a baking sheet. Prick the bottom of the dough and let it stand for 1 hour.

Preheat the oven to 400°F (200°C). Line the tartlets with parchment paper and fill them with lentils. Bake the tartlets 15 minutes, then remove from the oven and allow to cool. Remove the lentils and the paper. Turn out the pastry.

Filling and Decorating: Peel the pears and slice very thin. Spread a little pastry cream on the bottom of each pastry shell and put the sliced pears on top. Spread another layer of pastry cream on top of the pears, smoothing it over the top in a dome-like mound. Sprinkle generously with granulated sugar and caramelize the sugar by placing the tartlets under the broiler for a minute. The tartlets should only be assembled and caramelized at the last minute. Serve immediately.

Note: This recipe can also be prepared with fresh or stewed peaches, pineapple, bananas, strawberries, cherries, raspberries, or with stewed gooseberries or apricots.

134

Walnut Tartlets (Val d'Isère)

This is a very nice winter dessert made with a light almond paste flavored with Kirsch, surrounding a ladyfinger filling and topped with chocolate icing and walnuts.

PREPARATION	30 minutes a day ahead, 30 minutes the next day
RESTING TIME	1 hour
BAKING TIME	15 minutes
INGREDIENTS	*For 12 cakes* 9 ounces (250 g) sweet short pastry dough (Recipe 12) *For the syrup* ½ cup, scant (100 g), granulated sugar 3 tablespoons water 3 tablespoons Kirsch 14 ounces (400 g) almond paste (Recipe 18) 3 tablespoons (½ dl) Kirsch 6½ tablespoons (100 g) butter ⅔ cup, generous (100 g), powdered walnuts 6 ladyfingers (Recipe 1) 1½ cups (450 g) chocolate icing (Recipe 27) 36 walnut halves
UTENSILS	12 metal flan circles or tartlet pans 3″ (8 cm) wide and ⅝″ (1.5 cm) high Electric mixer with dough hook or paddle Mixing bowl Spoon Baking sheet Lentils Parchment paper

Baking: Roll out the dough on a lightly floured table. Line the pans or metal circles with the dough and place them on a baking sheet. Prick the bottom of the dough with a fork. Refrigerate for an hour.

LIQVOR
CORDON ROUGE
Triple Orange
Triple Orange
Grand Marnier
LIQVOR

Preheat the oven to 400°F (200°C).

Line the tartlets with parchment paper and fill them with lentils. Bake the tartlets about 15 minutes or until light brown, then allow to cool. Remove the lentils and the paper. Turn out the pastries.

Filling and Decorating: Prepare the Kirsch-flavored syrup, mixing together the sugar, water, and Kirsch. Bring to a boil, then remove from the heat. Place the almond paste in a mixing bowl and, using a low speed, mix in the Kirsch. Add the butter, which should be fairly hard, and beat for 2 minutes more at low speed so as to obtain a very light and creamy batter. Toward the end, add the powdered walnuts and continue to beat for about one minute more. Fill the bottom of each tartlet with a thin layer of batter, then place on top of each tartlet half a ladyfinger which has been dipped in Kirsch syrup. Cover with the remaining batter piled high and smoothed into a dome-like mound. Refrigerate for 15 minutes.

Meanwhile, prepare the chocolate icing. Dip all the tartlets in the chocolate icing, smooth the icing with a spoon, and top each tartlet with 3 walnut halves. Serve cold.

To Store: Walnut tartlets will keep 3 or 4 days in the refrigerator.

Crêpes Suzette, Recipe 136

Chapter 7

HOT DESSERTS–OMELETTES AND SOUFFLÉS

RECIPES

135. Fruit Fritters (Beignets Mille Fruits)
136. Crêpes Suzette
137. Waffles (Gaufres)
138. Dessert Omelette with Rum (Omelette Flambée au Rhum)
139. Almond Soufflé (Soufflé aux Amandes)
140. Lemon Soufflé (Soufflé au Citron Etoilé)
141. Chocolate Soufflé (Soufflé au Chocolat)
142. Soufflé au Grand Marnier
143. Chestnut Soufflé (Soufflé aux Marrons)
144. Pistachio Soufflé (Soufflé aux Pistaches)
145. Caramel Almond Soufflé (Soufflé Praliné)
146. Coconut Soufflé (Soufflé à la Noix de Coco)
147. Apple Soufflé with Calvados (Soufflé aux Pommes)
148. Vanilla Soufflé (Soufflé à la Vanille)

135

Fruit Fritters (Beignets Mille Fruits)

PREPARATION 30 minutes

RESTING TIME 2 hours

COOKING TIME 8 minutes per batch

INGREDIENTS *For 10 servings*
1⅔ cups (240 g) flour
½ cup, generous (13 cl), milk
6½ tablespoons (1 dl) beer
2 egg yolks
½ cake (10 g) compressed baker's yeast, diluted in 2 teaspoons milk
2 tablespoons oil
1¾ pounds (800 g) mixed fresh fruit or drained stewed fruit, (e.g., bananas, apples, pears, apricots, peaches, etc.)
6½ tablespoons (1 dl) rum
½ cup, scant (100 g), granulated sugar
2 egg whites
⅓ cup, scant (70 g), granulated sugar
Oil for deep frying

UTENSILS Deep fryer
Mixing bowl
Wire whisk or electric mixer
Vegetable peeler
Knife

The Batter: In a bowl, mix the flour, a third of the milk, the beer, egg yolks, and yeast. When the batter is smooth, add the remaining milk and the oil. Let the batter stand for 2 hours.

The Fruit: Meanwhile, peel and cut the fruit. Slice the bananas into ¾″ (2 cm) slices; the apples, pears, and pineapple should be sliced in ½″ (1 cm) thick slices, after being peeled and cored. Pit the apricots, peaches, and plums; cut them in half. Quarter the oranges. Marinate all the fruit for 1 hour with the rum and ½ cup (100 g) sugar.

Frying: Beat the egg whites until stiff, halfway through adding ⅓ cup (70 g) sugar. Fold the whites into the batter just before frying. Heat the oil for deep frying. Cook the fruit in small batches; don't crowd the pot. Dip the fruit in the batter, then lift it out with a fork and drop into the hot oil; the fruit will sink to the bottom, then rise to the top. Cook until golden brown (about 8 minutes). Be careful not to overheat the oil, the fritters would be too greasy. When the fritters are done, drain on a towel. Sprinkle with granulated sugar while still hot. Serve with red current jelly.

Note: If you have some leftover batter, mix it with fruit cut in large pieces. Butter an ovenproof dish and fill with the batter and fruit mixture, adding 2 tablespoons of rum-flavored dessert syrup. Bake for 15 to 30 minutes. This will make a very fine fruit flan.

136

Crêpes Suzette

(Photo page 220)

These crêpes are filled with an orange-flavored pastry cream and flamed with Grand Marnier.

PREPARATION	1 hour, 30 minutes
COOKING TIME	(with two crêpe pans): 20 minutes, plus 10 minutes when serving
INGREDIENTS	*For 30 crêpes, 6" (15 cm)* 5½ tablespoons (80 g) butter 1¾ cups (250 g) flour ⅓ cup (80 g) oil ¼ cup (60 g) granulated sugar 6 eggs 2 teaspoons Grand Marnier 1 orange peel, finely chopped 3 cups, generous (¾ l), milk 3⅔ cups (900 g) vanilla pastry cream (Recipe 24), flavored with 2 teaspoons Grand Marnier, juice of one orange, and 2 orange peels, finely chopped

For the syrup
⅔ cup (150 g) butter
⅔ cup (150 g) granulated sugar
Juice of 2 oranges
⅔ cup (1½ dl) Grand Marnier

UTENSILS

2 platters, 16″ (40 cm) long
Aluminum foil
2 crêpe pans 6″ (15 cm) wide at the bottom
Saucepan
Wire whisk or electric mixer
Bowl
Spatula
Saucepan
Bowl and soup ladle
Very large frying pan, if possible

The Batter: Cook the butter until it is barely light brown and has a slightly nutty smell. In a mixing bowl, mix the flour, oil, sugar, eggs, Grand Marnier, rum, orange peel, melted butter, and 1 cup of milk. Beat until the mixture is smooth and continue adding all but 1 cup of the milk. Save this cup of milk for later. Flavor the pastry cream with the Grand Marnier, orange juice, and chopped orange peel.

Cooking and Serving: Make the crêpes in two crêpe pans, cooking them for about 1 minute on each side. Keep the crêpes warm once they are cooked. Prepare the syrup with the Grand Marnier; in a saucepan, melt the butter, add the sugar and the juice of 2 oranges and half the Grand Marnier (keep the other half warm in a small saucepan). Bring this mixture to a boil and remove from heat. Spoon a little of this syrup over the serving platter. Fill each crêpe with 1 generous tablespoon of pastry cream, roll, and keep warm on the serving platter, covered with aluminum foil. Just before serving, heat the remaining syrup in a large frying pan and place the rolled crêpes in the syrup. When the crêpes are hot, pour the remaining Grand Marnier into the skillet as well and light with a match. Serve the crêpes very quickly. (This last step should be done in front of guests because the crêpes will not flame for a very long time).

Note: It is advisable to mix either cognac or rum with the Grand Marnier used to flame the crêpes. This recipe can be simplified by not filling the crêpes with pastry cream. Simply fold the crêpes in four, place them in the skillet and pour the Grand Marnier syrup over them. Heat and pour a tablespoon of hot Grand Marnier over them, light and serve.

137

Waffles (Gaufres)

(Photo page 229)

PREPARATION	15 minutes
COOKING TIME	4 minutes per waffle
INGREDIENTS	*For 20 small waffles* 1½ cups (35 cl) milk 1 pinch salt 6½ tablespoons (100 g) butter 1¾ cups (250 g) flour 8 eggs 1 cup (¼ l) milk mixed with 1 cup (¼ l) heavy cream *or* 1⅓ cups (3 dl) milk mixed with ¾ cup (2 dl) crème fraîche Confectioners' sugar, jam, Chantilly cream (Recipe 13), *or* chocolate sauce (Recipe 31)
UTENSILS	Waffle iron Saucepan Mixing bowl Electric mixer Sugar dredger Wooden spoon

The Batter: Heat the milk with the salt, add the butter and bring to a boil. Away from the heat, add the flour all at once and mix in with a wooden spoon. Put the batter back on the fire for a few seconds, stirring constantly until it comes away from the sides in a smooth mass and no longer sticks to the spoon. Pour into a mixing bowl and with an electric beater set at low speed, beat in the eggs two by two.

Still beating at low speed, add one of the milk-cream mixtures listed above.

Cooking: Heat the waffle iron and butter it lightly. With a ladle, fill the waffle iron and cook two minutes on each side, if using a hand held iron, or approximately four minutes total in an electric waffle iron.

Serve the waffles hot, sprinkled with confectioners' sugar or spread with jam, Chantilly cream, or chocolate sauce.

Waffles, Recipe 137

138

Dessert Omelette with Rum (Omelette Flambée au Rhum)

Dessert omelettes are easy to prepare and can be made at the last minute.

PREPARATION — 15 minutes

COOKING TIME — 5 minutes

INGREDIENTS — *For 5 servings*
6 eggs
5 tablespoons (70 g) granulated sugar
1½ tablespoons rum
1½ tablespoons granulated sugar
2 tablespoons (30 g) butter
Granulated sugar
2 tablespoons rum

UTENSILS — Omelette pan or frying pan
Wooden spatula
Small saucepan
Mixing bowl
Electric mixer
Serving platter

Preparing and Serving: Separate the yolks from the whites. Beat the egg yolks with sugar until they begin to whiten, then add the rum. Beat the egg whites until stiff, adding 1½ tablespoons of sugar halfway through. With a wooden spatula, fold the egg whites into the egg yolks and sugar. Heat the butter in a frying pan, then pour the omelette into the pan. When the bottom of the omelette is cooked but the top is still creamy, fold it in two and slide it onto a warm serving platter (or serve it in the pan it cooked in). Sprinkle the omelette generously with sugar. Heat the rum and pour it over the omelette, then light a match and serve the flaming omelette.

Note: Try the following variation with fruit filling:

INGREDIENTS — ½ pound (250 g) fresh apples or bananas
3½ tablespoons (50 g) butter
2 tablespoons granulated sugar

Peel and slice the fruit. Cook the fruit for 5 minutes with the butter and sugar. When the omelette is cooked, just before folding it in two, fill the omelette with the fruit and finish as described above.

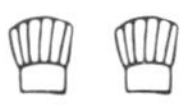

139

Almond Soufflé (Soufflé aux Amandes)

PREPARATION 20 minutes

BAKING TIME 20 minutes

INGREDIENTS *For 3 to 4 servings*
⅔ cup (1½ dl) milk
2½ tablespoons (35 g) granulated sugar
1½ tablespoons (15 g) flour
1½ tablespoons (20 g) butter
3 egg yolks
⅓ cup (50 g) coarsely chopped almonds
1½ tablespoons Kirsch
3 egg whites
1½ tablespoons (20 g) granulated sugar
Confectioners' sugar

UTENSILS 1 soufflé dish 6″ (16 cm)
Mixing bowl
Wooden spatula
Sugar dredger
Electric mixer

Preparing the Soufflé: Follow the instructions given in Recipe 35 but use the ingredients listed above. Add the almonds and then the Kirsch after adding the egg yolks.

140
Lemon Soufflé (Soufflé au Citron Etoilé)

PREPARATION 30 minutes

BAKING TIME 20 minutes

INGREDIENTS
For 3 to 4 servings
1 lemon
6½ tablespoons (1 dl) water
⅓ cup (75 g) granulated sugar
Ingredients given in basic Recipe 35
Confectioners' sugar

UTENSILS
Soufflé dish 6″ (16 cm)
Vegetable peeler
Knife
Sugar dredger
Mixing bowl
Wooden spatula
Electric mixer
Small saucepan

Preparing the Lemon: Use a vegetable peeler to cut six strips of lemon peel. Then cut the lemon in half and cut one half of the lemon into thin slices. Simmer for 15 minutes the water, sugar, lemon peel, and lemon slices, then allow to cool. Remove the lemon peels (which will be used for decorating). Drain the lemon slices and chop very fine.

Making the Soufflé: Prepare the soufflé as described in Recipe 35, flavoring it with the chopped lemon. Before baking, decorate the top of the soufflé with the lemon peel and sprinkle with confectioners' sugar.

Chocolate Soufflé, Recipe 141; Caramel Almond Soufflé, Recipe 145

141

Chocolate Soufflé (Soufflé au Chocolat)

(Photo page 232)

This chocolate soufflé can be served with a chocolate sauce.

PREPARATION	20 minutes
BAKING TIME	20 minutes
INGREDIENTS	*For 3 to 4 servings* 3 ounces (90 g) chocolate ¼ cup (60 g) granulated sugar 3 tablespoons milk 2 egg yolks 3 egg whites 1½ tablespoons (20 g) granulated sugar Confectioners' sugar ¾ cup (2 dl) chocolate sauce (Recipe 31)
UTENSILS	Soufflé dish 6″ (16 cm) Bowl Electric mixer Wooden spoon Sugar dispenser Knife Double-boiler Saucepan

Preparing the Soufflé: Preheat the oven to 350°F (180°C).

In a double-boiler, melt the chocolate, then add the sugar and the milk and beat until well mixed. Remove from the heat. Allow the mixture to cool for 5 minutes, then add the egg yolks, beating constantly. Whip the egg whites until very stiff, adding 1½ tablespoons (20 g) sugar halfway through. Fold the egg whites into the chocolate mixture.

Pour the mixture into a buttered and sugared soufflé mold. Bake 20 minutes at 350°F (180°C). Test for doneness by inserting a knife blade: if blade comes out dry, the soufflé is ready. Serve immediately, sprinkled with confectioners' sugar.

Note: If you serve the soufflé with a chocolate sauce, the sauce should be cool and served alongside in a sauce boat.

142
Soufflé au Grand Marnier

PREPARATION	5 minutes a day ahead, 20 minutes the next day
BAKING TIME	20 minutes
INGREDIENTS	*For 3 to 4 servings for the syrup* 6½ tablespoons (1 dl) water ⅓ cup (80 g) granulated sugar ½ orange, thinly sliced 2 teaspoons Grand Marnier *For the soufflé* ⅓ cup (45 g) flour ¼ cup (60 g) granulated sugar 1 cup (¼ l) milk 2 tablespoons (30 g) butter 3 egg yolks 1½ tablespoons Grand Marnier 3 egg whites 1½ tablespoons (20 g) granulated sugar 2 ladyfingers (Recipe 1)
UTENSILS	Soufflé mold 6″ (16 cm) wide Large saucepan Mixing bowl Electric mixer Wooden spatula

Preparing the Soufflé: Prepare the syrup a day ahead: boil the water with the sugar, add orange slices and boil for 5 minutes. Remove from the heat and leave overnight.

The next day, drain the oranges and chop them fine. Add 2 teaspoons of Grand Marnier to the syrup, then dip the ladyfingers in the syrup and cut them into small pieces.

Follow Recipe 35 using the ingredients listed above. After adding the egg yolks, add the chopped oranges and the remaining Grand Marnier to the soufflé. Pour half this batter in the soufflé mold. Sprinkle on the batter the diced ladyfingers and finish filling the mold with the remaining batter. Bake the soufflé as described in Recipe 35.

143

Chestnut Soufflé (Soufflé aux Marrons)

PREPARATION	20 minutes
BAKING TIME	25 minutes
INGREDIENTS	*For 6 servings* ¾ cup (180 g) milk 2 tablespoons (30 g) granulated sugar 3 tablespoons (30 g) cornstarch 1½ tablespoons (20 g) butter 3 egg yolks 2 teaspoons rum ⅔ cup (200 g) chestnut cream ⅔ cup (100 g) diced candied chestnuts 4 egg whites 1½ tablespoons (20 g) sugar
UTENSILS	1 soufflé mold 8″ (20 cm) wide or 2 molds 6″ (16 cm) wide Mixing bowl Electric mixer Wooden spatula

Preparing the Soufflé: Follow the instructions given in Recipe 35 but use the ingredients listed above. After the egg yolks, add the rum and the chestnut cream. Pour half the batter into the mold, then sprinkle on top the diced candied chestnuts; fill the mold with remaining batter. Bake following the instructions in Recipe 35.

144

Pistachio Soufflé (Soufflé aux Pistaches)

PREPARATION	20 minutes
BAKING TIME	25 minutes

INGREDIENTS

For 3 to 4 servings
⅔ cup (1½ dl) milk
2½ tablespoons (35 g) granulated sugar
1½ tablespoons (15 g) cornstarch
1½ tablespoons (20 g) butter
3 egg yolks
3 tablespoons (30 g) powdered almonds
6 tablespoons (60 g) chopped pistachio nuts
1½ tablespoons Kirsch
4 egg whites
1½ tablespoons (20 g) granulated sugar
Confectioners' sugar

UTENSILS

Soufflé mold 7″ (18 cm) wide
Rolling pin
Sugar dredger
Mixing bowl
Electric mixer
Wooden spatula

Preparing the Soufflé: Follow the instructions given in Recipe 35 using the ingredients given above. After the egg yolks, add the almonds, pistachios, then the Kirsch.

145

Caramel Almond Soufflé (Soufflé Praliné)

(Photo page 232)

PREPARATION

20 minutes

BAKING TIME

20 minutes

INGREDIENTS

For 3 to 4 servings
1 cup (¼ l) milk
2½ tablespoons (40 g) granulated sugar
¼ cup (40 g) flour
1½ tablespoons (20 g) butter

3 egg yolks
⅔ cup (100 g) powdered caramelized almonds
2 teaspoons rum
4 egg whites
1½ tablespoons (20 g) granulated sugar
⅓ cup, generous (80 g), sugared almonds, coarsely crushed

UTENSILS

Soufflé mold 7″ (18 cm) wide
Wire whisk
Whip
Spatula

Preparing the Soufflé: Follow the instructions given in Recipe 35 using the ingredients listed above. After adding the egg yolks, add the powdered caramelized almonds, then the rum. Pour half the batter into the mold, sprinkle on top the coarsely crushed sugared almonds. Then pour in the remaining batter and bake following as described in Recipe 35.

146

Coconut Soufflé (Soufflé à la Noix de Coco)

PREPARATION

20 minutes

BAKING TIME

25 minutes

INGREDIENTS

For 3 to 4 servings
¾ cup (2 dl) milk
2½ tablespoons (35 g) granulated sugar
1½ tablespoons (15 g) cornstarch
1½ tablespoons (20 g) butter
3 egg yolks
⅔ cup, scant (90 g), grated coconut
1½ tablespoons Kirsch
4 egg whites
1½ tablespoons (20 g) granulated sugar
Confectioners' sugar (to decorate)

UTENSILS

Soufflé mold 7″ (18 cm) wide
Sugar dredger
Mixing bowl
Electric mixer
Wooden spatula

Preparing the Soufflé: Follow the instructions given in Recipe 35 using the ingredients listed above. After adding the egg yolks, add the grated coconut and the Kirsch, then continue as described in Recipe 35.

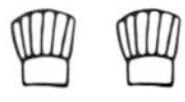

147

Apple Soufflé with Calvados (Soufflé aux Pommes - parfumé au Calvados)

PREPARATION 20 minutes

BAKING TIME 25 minutes

INGREDIENTS *For 4 servings or 4 individual soufflés*
1 cup (¼ l) milk
¼ vanilla bean
¼ cup (65 g) sugar
¼ cup (40 g) flour
1½ tablespoons (20 g) butter
1½ tablespoons Calvados (apple brandy)
3 egg yolks
2 apples
3 egg whites
1½ tablespoons (20 g) granulated sugar
1½ tablespoons Calvados for flaming

UTENSILS Soufflé mold 7″ (18 cm) wide or 4 individual soufflé molds
Electric mixer
Mixing bowl
Wooden spatula
2 saucepans

The Batter: Boil all but 3 tablespoons of the milk with the vanilla bean. In a mixing bowl, mix the sugar, the flour and 3 tablespoons of milk. Then add, stirring with a spatula, half the boiling milk, mix well; add the remaining boiling milk beating all the while. Pour back into the sauce pan and boil for 2 minutes more.

Away from the heat, stir in the butter and the Calvados, cover and allow to cool. When the batter has cooled, but is still warm, add the egg yolks.

Baking: Preheat the oven to 350°F (180°C).

Peel and cut the apples into very thin slices. Beat the egg whites until very stiff. Halfway through, add 1½ tablespoons (20 g) sugar, then fold the stiff egg whites into the batter prepared earlier. Butter and sugar the mold. Fill the mold with a third of the batter, then place a layer of apples on top of the batter. Add another third of the batter and a layer of apples. Finish filling the mold and place apple slices on top. Sprinkle the surface with confectioners' sugar. Bake the soufflé at 350°F (180°C) for 25 minutes.

Just before removing it from the oven, heat 1½ tablespoons of Calvados in a small saucepan and light. Pour the Calvados over the soufflé and serve immediately.

148

Vanilla Soufflé (Soufflé à la Vanille)

PREPARATION 20 minutes

BAKING TIME 20 minutes

INGREDIENTS *For 3 to 4 servings*
1 cup (¼ l) milk
1 vanilla bean
¼ cup, generous (65 g), granulated sugar
⅓ cup, scant (45 g), flour
1½ tablespoons (20 g) butter
3 egg yolks
3 egg whites
1½ tablespoons (20 g) granulated sugar

UTENSILS Soufflé mold 7″ (18 cm) wide
Mixing bowl
Electric mixer
Wooden spatula

Preparing the Soufflé: Follow the instructions given in Recipe 35 using the ingredients listed above. Boil the milk with the vanilla bean split lengthwise. Finish as described in Recipe 35.

Chapter 8

COLD DESSERTS— CHARLOTTES AND STEWED FRUIT

RECIPES

149. Fruit-Flavored Bavarian Cream (Bavarois sans Alcool)
150. Bread and Butter Pudding
151. Filled Brioches (General Comments)
152. Brioche with Bavarian Cream (Brioche Estelle au Bavarois)
153. Brioche Filled with Chocolate Mousse (Brioche Estelle à la Mousse au Chocolat)
154. Brioche Filled with Fruit Salad (Salpicon de Fruits en Brioche)
155. Brioche Polonaise
156. Chocolate-Vanilla Charlotte (Charlotte Cécile)
157. Strawberry or Raspberry Charlotte (Charlotte aux Fraises ou aux Framboises)
158. Chestnut Charlotte (Charlotte aux Marrons)
159. Peach or Pear Charlotte (Charlotte aux Pêches ou aux Poires)
160. Apple Charlotte (Charlotte aux Pommes)
161. Caramel Custard (Crème à la Vanille Caramelisée)

162. Semolina Cake with Raisins (Gâteau de Semoule aux Raisins)
163. Floating Island (Ile Flottante)
164. Snow Eggs (Oeufs à la Neige)
165. Chocolate Rice Pudding (Riz au Chocolat pour Géraldine)
166. Rice Pudding with Eight Treasures (Riz Impératrice aux Huit Trésors)
167. Stewed Fruit (General Comments)
168. Stewed Apricots (Abricots au Sirop)
169. Stewed Whole Apricots (Abricots Frais avec leurs noyaux)
170. Stewed Bananas (Bananes au Sirop)
171. Dried Figs Stewed in Wine (Figues au Sirop)
172. Stewed Strawberries (Fraises au Sirop)
173. Mixed Fruit Stewed in Wine (Fruits Panachés au Sirop)
174. Stewed Lichees (Letchis au Sirop)
175. Peaches Stewed in Wine (Pêches au Sirop)
176. Stewed Pears with Honey (Poires au Sirop)
177. Stewed Prunes in Wine (Pruneaux au Sirop)
178. Stewed Muskmelon or Cantaloupe (Compote de Melons Verts)
179. Apple Sauce (Compote de Pommes)
180. Stewed Rhubarb (Compote de Rubarbe)
181. Oranges with Grenadine Syrup (Oranges à la Grenadine)
182. Red Currant Jelly (Gelée de Groseille)

149

Fruit-Flavored Bavarian Cream
(Bavarois sans Alcool)

(Photo page 245)

This light vanilla-flavored dessert can be made in a ring mold or any other shaped mold of your choice.

PREPARATION 15 minutes

RESTING TIME 2 hours, minimum

INGREDIENTS *For 4 to 6 servings*
2 cups (285 g) Chantilly cream (Recipe 13)
2¾ cups (650 g) Bavarian cream (Recipe 33), cooled
1 cup (¼ l) raspberry sauce (Recipe 15) [optional]
1 pound 1½ ounces (500 g) mixed fresh fruit, to make a fruit salad

UTENSILS 1½-quart ring mold
Pastry bag with star-shaped nozzle
Bowl
Wire whisk

Preparing the Cream: Set aside half of the Chantilly cream for decorating and refrigerate.

When the Bavarian cream (Recipe 33) is completely cool (but not too cold) very delicately fold in the Chantilly. Slightly dampen the mold, then sprinkle the bottom and sides with granulated sugar (this will help when turning out the Bavarian cream). Cover the bottom of the mold with a thin layer of raspberry sauce [optional]. Then fill the mold up to the rim with the batter and refrigerate for at least 2 hours.

To turn out, dip the mold in hot water for a few seconds, then turn out onto a serving platter. Using a pastry bag with a star-shaped nozzle, decorate the Bavarian cream with the Chantilly cream reserved earlier. Serve the raspberry sauce in a sauce boat and fresh fruit salad at the same time.

Note: When using a ring mold, you can fill the center with fruit salad.

150

Bread and Butter Pudding

(Photo page 255)

PREPARATION	20 minutes
BAKING TIME	30 minutes
INGREDIENTS	*For 6 servings* 7 ounces (200 g) fresh sandwich bread, uncut Butter for bread 2 cups, generous (½ l), milk 1 vanilla bean 3 eggs 2 egg yolks ½ cup, generous (125 g), granulated sugar
UTENSILS	Wire whisk Mixing bowl Oval baking dish 13″ (32 cm) long Baking dish large enough to contain oval baking dish Spoon Knife

Preparing and Baking: Remove the crust from the bread and slice very thin. Lightly butter these slices and cut them in half, from corner to corner, so that each piece forms 2 triangles. Brown the buttered side under the broiler for about 3 minutes. Cover the bottom of the oval baking dish with the bread, toasted side up in overlapping pieces.

Preheat the oven to 425°F (220°C). Boil the milk with the vanilla bean. Beat the eggs and the egg yolks with the sugar for a few minutes until the mixture whitens. Then, slowly pour the hot milk (not boiling) into the egg mixture, stirring all the while. Pour the mixture carefully over the bread, holding the bread slices in place with a spatula, so that they will not float up. Place the smaller baking dish into the large one; pour boiling water into the large dish until it comes halfway up the side of the smaller dish. Bake for 30 minutes in a 425°F (220°C) oven. In the beginning, push down the slices of bread that rise to the surface. When baked, remove from the oven and allow to cool, then refrigerate the pudding until ready to serve.

This pudding can be served with vanilla sauce (Recipe 32) or a raspberry sauce (Recipe 15).

Fruit-Flavored Bavarian Cream, Recipe 149

151

Filled Brioches (General Comments)

The following four recipes are all made either with a mousseline brioche or a Parisian brioche prepared in advance. Often, you will have to hollow out the brioches; this is easier to do with a Parisian brioche than with a mousseline brioche. In any case, save what you hollow out and use this for other desserts such as Royal Pudding (Recipe 97) or Brioche Almond Slices (Recipe 60).

Hollowing out the Brioches: Remove the top or "head" of the brioche. Stick a serrated knife straight down into the brioche, ½" (1 cm) from the crust (without completely reaching the bottom). Cut all around the inside of the brioche to detach the middle from the sides. Make a slit ¾" (2 cm) wide in the side, just above the bottom of the brioche, push the blade of the knife through this opening and carefully cut until the central core of the brioche is completely detached. Remove it. It is important to damage the crust as little as possible (see photo Brioche Filled with Fruit Salad, page 258).

152

Brioche Filled with Bavarian Cream
(Brioche Estelle au Bavarois)

PREPARATION 20 minutes

RESTING TIME 5 hours

INGREDIENTS *For 8 servings*
1 baked brioche (Recipe 41 or 43)
¾ cup (2 dl) dessert syrup flavored with Kirsch *or* vanilla (Recipe 29), cooled
2¾ cups (650 g) Bavarian cream (Recipe 33), cooled

UTENSILS Knife
Pastry brush

Assembling the Brioche: Hollow out the brioche (see Recipe 151). Brush the inside of the brioche with the cooled dessert syrup. Brush the top (or head) of the brioche with syrup as well. Fill the brioche with Bavarian cream (if there is not enough Bavarian cream to fill the whole brioche, dice the inside of the brioche and mix it with Bavarian cream to fill the brioche to the top). Cover the brioche with its top. Refrigerate for 5 hours. Take the brioche out of the refrigerator half an hour before serving.

Note: This brioche can be served as is or with a fruit sauce (Recipe 15), a chocolate sauce (Recipe 31), a caramel sauce (Recipe 16) or a fresh fruit salad.

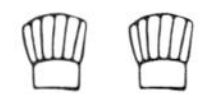

153

Brioche Filled with Chocolate Mousse (Brioche Estelle à la Mousse au Chocolat)

PREPARATION 15 minutes

RESTING TIME 1 hour

INGREDIENTS *For 8 servings*
1 baked brioche (Recipe 41 or 43)
2 cups (300 g) chocolate mousse (Recipe 30)
2⅔ cups (6 dl) vanilla sauce (Recipe 32)

Assembling the Brioche: Hollow out the brioche (Recipe 151). Set aside the inside of the brioche.

Fill the brioche with the chocolate mousse and cover with the top or head. Refrigerate for at least one hour. Half an hour before serving, remove the brioche from the refrigerator. Serve cold vanilla sauce in a sauce boat, alongside the brioche.

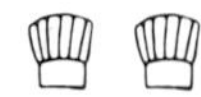

154

Brioche Filled with Fruit Salad (Salpicon de Fruits en Brioche)

(Photo page 258)

If Bavarian cream and the chocolate mousse are too rich for your taste, a brioche can be filled with fresh fruit salad.

PREPARATION	15 minutes
RESTING TIME	2 to 3 hours
INGREDIENTS	*For 8 servings* 1 brioche prepared a day ahead (Recipe 41 or 43) 2 cups, generous (300 g), fresh fruit salad seasoned with granulated sugar and lemon juice to taste Cold butter
UTENSILS	Serrated knife

Assembling the Brioche: Prepare the fresh fruit salad two or three hours ahead of time, using whatever fruit is in season. For instance, fruit salad in the wintertime: oranges, bananas, apples, pears, prunes, and raisins. Fruit salad in the summertime: strawberries, raspberries, gooseberries, peaches, and very ripe apricots. Exotic fruit salad: lichees, mangoes, guavas, mangosteens (this is a tropical fruit from Malaysia). Sugar the fruit salad to your taste and pour a little lemon juice over it to bring out the flavor of the fruit (it will also prevent the fruit from turning black). Refrigerate.

Hollow out the brioche (see Recipe 151). Close the bottom hole with a dab of cold butter. Just before serving, fill the brioche with the fruit salad. If you have extra fruit salad, serve it in a bowl alongside the brioche.

Note: Fruit salad will taste and look better when a fruit sauce is poured over it. For example, in winter, use a pear sauce; in the summer, use a raspberry or an apricot sauce.

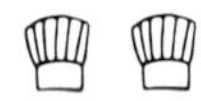

155

Brioche Polonaise

(Photo page 259)

This is another inventive dessert with a brioche as its main ingredient.

PREPARATION — 45 minutes

BAKING TIME — 10 minutes

INGREDIENTS

For 8 servings
1 Parisian brioche (Recipe 43)
⅔ cup (1½ dl) rum-flavored syrup (Recipe 29)
1¾ cups, generous (450 g), vanilla pastry cream (Recipe 24) flavored with ½ teaspoon rum
½ cup (100 g) chopped candied fruit
⅓ cup (50 g) whole candied cherries

For the Italian meringue
4 egg whites = ⅔ cup (120 g)
1 cup, generous (250 g), granulated sugar
3 tablespoons water

For the decoration
Slivered almonds
Confectioners' sugar

UTENSILS

1 cake pan (wider than the brioche)
Spatula
Pastry brush
Mixing bowl
Electric mixer
Sugar dredger
Thermometer [optional]

Preparing the Brioche: Cut off the top of the brioche and cut the brioche in four equal slices horizontally (see photo, page 259). (You can lightly toast each slice [optional].)

Brush the bottom slice of the brioche with the syrup. Place that slice on the bottom of the cake pan. Spread a layer of pastry cream on this first slice, then some chopped candied fruit and candied cherries, then place another slice of brioche on top, brush with syrup, and cover as described above. Continue in this way with all the layers. Then, replace the top of the brioche (brush the inside of the top with syrup before putting it into place).

Making the Meringue: To prepare the Italian meringue, beat the egg whites until very stiff, adding 2 teaspoons of sugar halfway through. Mix the remaining sugar with the water, boil until it reaches the hard ball stage—248°F (120°C)—on the candy thermometer or until one drop of sugar holds its shape when dropped into a glass of cold water. Still beating at low speed, pour the boiling sugar into the egg whites, between the beaters and the sides of the mixing bowl. Keep on beating at low speed until the mixture is cool (about 5 minutes).

Baking: Preheat the oven to 475°F (240°C).

Using a spatula, completely cover the brioche with a ½″ (1 cm) layer of meringue. Sprinkle with slivered almonds and confectioners' sugar.

Bake for about 10 minutes or until the meringue hardens and begins to brown. Turn off the oven after 5 minutes if the meringue browns too quickly, but leave the brioche for 5 minutes more in the oven to finish cooking.

Note: You can replace the rum by Kirsch when making the dessert syrup and pastry cream.

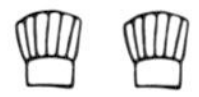

156

Chocolate-Vanilla Charlotte (Charlotte Cécile)

(*Photo page 269*)

This is a charlotte made with vanilla sauce, Chantilly, and chocolate mousse.

PREPARATION	45 minutes
RESTING TIME	1 hour, 30 minutes
INGREDIENTS	*For 4 to 6 servings* 1⅓ cups (3 dl) vanilla sauce (Recipe 32) 1½ teaspoons (2 sheets) gelatin, softened in 1½ tablespoons cold water 14 ladyfingers (Recipe 1) 2 cups (300 g) chocolate mousse (Recipe 29) 2¼ cups (325 g) Chantilly cream (Recipe 13) Shaved or grated chocolate [optional]

UTENSILS

Ribbed brioche mold 8½″ (22 cm) wide or straight-sided charlotte mold 6¼″ (16 cm)
Mixing bowl
Electric beater
Vegetable peeler
Pastry bag with star-shaped nozzle

Assembling the Charlotte: Make the vanilla sauce as described in Recipe 32. Add the softened gelatin to the vanilla sauce while the sauce is still warm. Cool the sauce by placing the pot it cooked in into ice water. Stir the sauce frequently until the sauce is cold and quite thick. Meanwhile, lightly butter the sides of the mold and garnish with the ladyfingers, cutting them off at the rim of the mold. Fill the mold halfway with chocolate mousse. Refrigerate for 30 minutes.

Set aside ¾ cup (100 g) of Chantilly cream for later use. Fold the remaining Chantilly cream into the cold vanilla sauce. Pour this batter on top of the chocolate mousse and fill the mold completely. Refrigerate for at least 1 hour.

To turn out, dip the mold for a few seconds into hot water and turn it upside down on a platter. Decorate the top of the charlotte with the Chantilly cream reserved earlier. Using a pastry bag with a star-shaped nozzle, make a decoration with the Chantilly or, using a vegetable peeler, shave some chocolate and place it on top of the charlotte.

Note: When using ladyfingers to line a mold, it is easiest to bake them close together in a straight line—they will stick together after baking and be easier to handle while lining the mold. Individual ladyfingers may also be used.

157

Strawberry or Raspberry Charlotte (Charlotte aux Fraises ou au Framboises)

PREPARATION

20 minutes

RESTING TIME

2 hours

INGREDIENTS

For 4 to 6 servings
1⅓ cups (3 dl) vanilla sauce (Recipe 32)
1½ teaspoons (2 sheets) gelatin, softened in 1½ tablespoons cold water

1½ cups, scant (200 g), Chantilly cream (Recipe 13)
14 ladyfingers (Recipe 1)—see note, Recipe 156
1¾ cups (200 g) strawberries or raspberries
3½ tablespoons (50 g) granulated sugar
2 cups, generous (½ l), strawberry or raspberry sauce

UTENSILS

Ribbed brioche mold 8½″ (22 cm) wide or straight-sided charlotte mold 6¼″ (16 cm)
Mixing bowl
Spoon
Wooden spatula
Electric mixer

Assembling the Charlotte: Prepare the vanilla sauce (Recipe 32). Add the softened gelatin to the hot sauce. Mix well, then place the pot into a bowl of ice water. Stir the sauce frequently until it is cold and quite thick. Fold the Chantilly cream into the cold, thick vanilla sauce. Lightly butter the sides of the mold and line it with the ladyfingers (cut off the ladyfingers at the rim of the mold).

Sprinkle the bottom of the mold with sugar and pour a third of the cold batter into the mold, then place on top a layer of fresh fruit (strawberries or raspberries) rolled in sugar. Continue filling the mold with alternate layers of batter and fruit. Finish with a layer of batter. If you don't have enough batter to completely fill the mold, chop up some ladyfingers and mix them with the batter to increase its volume. Refrigerate for 2 hours.

Turn out the charlotte onto a deep platter, dipping it first in hot water for a few seconds. Decorate with a raspberry or strawberry fruit sauce. Spoon the sauce carefully over the charlotte so that the sauce will not cover the ladyfingers, but will run down between them.

Serve the remaining sauce in a sauce boat.

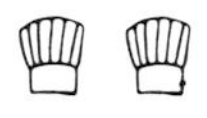

158

Chestnut Charlotte (Charlotte aux Marrons)

This charlotte is made with chestnut cream, flavored with Scotch.

PREPARATION 20 minutes

RESTING TIME 3 hours

INGREDIENTS *For 4 to 6 servings*

14 ladyfingers (Recipe 1)—see note, Recipe 156
2½ cups, generous (500 g), chestnut cream
3 tablespoons (½ dl) Scotch whiskey
3½ cups (500 g) Chantilly cream (Recipe 13)
1½ teaspoons (2 sheets) gelatin, softened in 1½ tablespoons cold water
3 tablespoons (50 g) chopped candied chestnuts
¾ cup, generous (2 dl), chocolate sauce (Recipe 31)
¾ cup, scant (100 g), Chantilly cream

UTENSILS Ribbed brioche mold 8½″ (22 cm) wide or straight-sided charlotte mold 6¼″ (16 cm)
Pastry bag with star-shaped nozzle
Paper circle (to set in bottom of mold)
Wire whisk
Mixing bowl
Double boiler

Assembling the Charlotte: Lightly butter the sides of the mold and line the bottom of the mold with the paper circle. Line the sides with the ladyfingers placed very close together. Cut off the ladyfingers at the rim of the mold.

In a mixing bowl, whip the chestnut cream until smooth, then add the Scotch.

In a double boiler, beat 2 tablespoons of Chantilly cream with the softened gelatin (this keeps the gelatin from setting too fast). Then pour this mixture into the chestnut cream and fold in the rest of the Chantilly. Mix well. Fill the mold with alternate layers of this batter and chopped candied chestnuts. Refrigerate for 3 hours.

To turn out, dip the mold for a few seconds in warm water and turn out onto a platter. Remove the paper on top, then pour a little bit of chocolate sauce over the charlotte or, using a pastry bag with a star-shaped nozzle, press out small roses of Chantilly. Decorate the top of the charlotte with the whole glazed chestnuts and serve.

159

Peach or Pear Charlotte
(Charlotte aux Pêches ou aux Poires)

PREPARATION — 20 minutes

RESTING TIME — 2½ hours

INGREDIENTS — *For 4 to 6 servings*
14 ladyfingers (Recipe 1)—see note, Recipe 156
1⅓ cups (3 dl) vanilla sauce (Recipe 32)
2 teaspoons (2½ sheets) gelatin, softened in 2 tablespoons cold water
2 cups (300 g) stewed peaches *or* pears, drained
2 cups, generous (300 g), Chantilly cream (Recipe 13)

UTENSILS — Ribbed brioche mold 8½″ (22 cm) or straight-sided charlotte mold 6¼″ (16 cm)
Pastry bag with star-shaped nozzle
Paper circle to set in bottom of mold
Wire whisk
Mixing bowl
Pastry brush
Saucepan
Knife

Assembling the Charlotte: Lightly butter the sides of the mold with a pastry brush. Line the bottom of the mold with the paper circle. Line the sides with the ladyfingers, placed close together, then cut them off at the rim of the mold.

Warm the vanilla sauce, and add the softened gelatin to it. Place the pot containing the sauce into a bowl of ice water. Stir frequently until the sauce is cold and quite thick. Leave ⅓ of the fruit whole for decorating and reserve; cut the rest into quarters. Save ¾ cup (100 g) of the Chantilly for decorating as well, then mix the remaining Chantilly with the cold vanilla sauce.

Fill the mold with alternate layers of charlotte batter and quartered fruit, ending with the batter. Refrigerate for 2½ hours.

To turn out, dip the mold in hot water and turn it over onto a serving platter. Remove the paper. Using the pastry bag with a star-shaped nozzle, decorate the charlotte with the remaining Chantilly and the remaining whole fruit.

Note: This charlotte can be served with cold vanilla sauce or a peach or pear sauce (Recipe 15).

Bread and Butter Pudding, Recipe 150

160

Apple Charlotte (Charlotte aux Pommes)

(Photo page 272)

Use tart cooking apples and fresh white bread when making this dessert.

PREPARATION	30 minutes
BAKING TIME	25 minutes
INGREDIENTS	*For 4 to 6 servings* 7 ounces (200 g) fresh white bread Butter for bread 2¼ pounds (1 kg) tart cooking apples ⅔ cup (150 g) granulated sugar 1 vanilla bean 1 lemon peel, finely chopped [optional] 2 cups (½ l) apricot sauce (Recipe 15) *or* vanilla sauce (Recipe 32) Confectioners' sugar
UTENSILS	Straight-sided charlotte mold 6¼″ (16 cm) Saucepan Electric mixer

Assembling the Charlotte: Slice the bread into thin slices; butter one side of each slice. Toast the buttered sides under the broiler. Cut each slice into a rectangle 3″ by 1¼″ (8 cm × 3 cm). Line the mold with the slices of bread (the buttered side against the mold), overlapping the slices.

Preheat the oven to 450°F (240°C).

Peel, core, and quarter the apples. Prepare an apple sauce by stewing the apples with the sugar and the vanilla bean until they are soft (the lemon peel can be added if the apples are too sweet). Pass the softened apples through a sieve to make apple sauce. Fill the mold with the apple sauce.

Baking: Bake in 450°F (240°C) oven for about 10 minutes, then lower the heat to 425°F (220°C) and bake for 15 minutes more. Cool the charlotte before turning it out. Cover the top of the charlotte with an apricot sauce or a vanilla sauce. Sprinkle the sides with confectioners' sugar and serve.

161

Caramel Custard (Crème à la Vanille Caramelisée)

(Photo page 217)

This caramel custard is served with vanilla sauce.

PREPARATION 15 minutes

BAKING TIME 40 minutes

INGREDIENTS

For 8 servings of the caramel
¾ cup, generous (200 g), granulated sugar
1½ tablespoons water
3 drops lemon juice

For the custard
4⅓ cups (1 l) milk
1 vanilla bean
4 eggs
8 egg yolks
¾ cup, generous (200 g), granulated sugar
1⅓ cups (3 dl) vanilla sauce (Recipe 32)

UTENSILS

Soufflé mold 8½" (22 cm) wide or charlotte mold 7" (18 cm) wide
Mixing bowl
Wire whisk
Small saucepan

Assembling and Baking: Make the caramel in a small saucepan by heating the sugar, water, and lemon juice until the mixture is golden brown (about 8 to 10 minutes). Pour the caramel into the mold, turning the mold so that the caramel covers both the bottom and the sides.

Preheat the oven to 400°F (200°C).

Boil the milk with the vanilla bean. In a mixing bowl, beat the eggs, the egg yolks, and the sugar. Stirring constantly, stir the hot milk into the egg mixture. Pour this custard into the mold and bake in a bain-marie for 40 minutes at 400°F (200°C). To be sure the cream is cooked, insert a knife blade into the cream; if the blade comes out clean, the cream is done. Remove from the oven and cool. Turn out the caramel custard onto a platter and serve with a vanilla sauce on the side.

Brioche Filled with Fruit Salad, Recipe 154
Brioche Polonaise, Recipe 155

Note: Try the following variations: instead of pouring the caramel into the mold, pour it into the boiling milk, mixing it gently. In this case, butter the mold and sprinkle some sugar into it before adding the custard. Or you might want to butter the mold and sprinkle with sugar, then fill the mold with the custard. Prepare the caramel as described above and pour it over the top of the custard before baking.

162

Semolina Cake with Raisins (Gâteau de Semoule aux Raisins)

This is a classic dessert which can be served with either an apricot, strawberry, or raspberry sauce.

PREPARATION	15 minutes
RESTING TIME	2 hours
COOKING TIME	20 minutes
INGREDIENTS	*For 4 to 6 servings* ½ cup, generous (100 g), raisins 3 tablespoons rum 3 cups, generous (¾ l), milk Half a lemon peel, finely chopped A pinch of salt ½ cup, scant (100 g), granulated sugar ⅔ cup (125 g) fine semolina (farina) 5 tablespoons (75 g) butter 2 eggs Fruit sauce (Recipe 15) [optional] 8 large candied cherries *or* 2 stewed or canned fruit halves, (e.g., apricots, peaches, etc.) [optional]
UTENSILS	Straight-sided charlotte mold 6¼″ (16 cm) or ribbed brioche mold 8½″ (22 cm) Saucepan with cover Knife Spoon

Preparing and Baking: Soak the raisins in the rum for one hour. Place the milk, the chopped lemon peel, sugar, and salt in a saucepan and bring to a boil. Sprinkle the semolina into the milk stirring constantly until all the semolina has been added. Cover the pot and cook very slowly for 20 minutes. At the end of this time, stir with a spoon; if all the milk has not been absorbed, continue cooking several minutes more. Remove from the heat and stir in the butter, eggs and the drained raisins; mix well.

Butter the mold lightly and line the sides with sliced candied cherries or stewed fruit. Fill the mold with the semolina and refrigerate for 2 hours. Dip the mold into hot water and turn out ½ hour before serving. Refrigerate. Just before serving, some fruit sauce may be poured over the cake. Serve the rest of the sauce in a sauce boat.

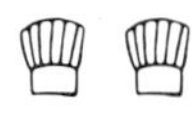

163

Floating Island (Ile Flottante)

In this dessert, an "island" made of egg whites floats on a lake of vanilla sauce.

PREPARATION	15 minutes
RESTING TIME	1 hour
COOKING TIME	30 minutes
INGREDIENTS	*For 4 to 6 servings* 6 egg whites = ¾ cup, generous (180 g) ¾ cup (180 g) granulated sugar ⅔ cup (120 g) coarsely crushed sugared almonds (white) 2⅔ cups (6 dl) vanilla sauce (Recipe 32)
UTENSILS	Straight-sided charlotte mold 6¼″ (16 cm) or ribbed brioche mold 8½″ (22 cm) Electric mixer Aluminum foil Mixing bowl

Preparing and Baking: Preheat the oven to 350°F (180°C).

Beat the egg whites very stiff, adding 3½ tablespoons (50 g) granulated sugar halfway through. Once the whites are stiff, add the rest of the sugar and beat lightly for 30 seconds more. Stir in the crushed sugared almonds.

Butter the mold and sprinkle with sugar. Fill the mold with the beaten egg whites and bake in a bain-marie for 30 minutes, covering the mold with a piece of lightly buttered aluminum foil to prevent the egg whites from browning.

Remove from the oven and allow to cool. Pour the cold vanilla sauce onto a serving platter. Turn out the cold "floating island" onto the vanilla sauce and chill for at least 1 hour before serving.

164
Snow Eggs (Oeufs à la Neige)

(Photo page 284)

Elegant rose-shaped pieces of egg white are served on a vanilla sauce in this dessert.

PREPARATION	10 minutes
COOKING TIME	10 minutes per batch
INGREDIENTS	*For 6 servings* 6 egg whites ¾ cup, generous (200 g), granulated sugar 2⅔ cups (6 dl) vanilla sauce (Recipe 32)
UTENSILS	Pastry bag with star-shaped nozzle ¾″ (2 cm) Clean dish towel Large frying pan Large sheet of waxed paper Slotted spoon or spatula

Poaching the "Eggs": Simmer 2 quarts of water in a large frying pan. Do not let the water boil. Meanwhile, beat the egg whites until very stiff, then add the sugar and continue beating slowly for 30 seconds. Place a large sheet of waxed paper next to the frying pan. Dampen the paper lightly. Fill the pastry bag with the egg whites, and squeeze out large rose-shaped designs onto the paper (about 20 of them). Lift them one at a time very carefully with a spatula and slide them into the simmering water. Poach for 7 minutes on one side without allowing the water to boil; then, turn them over and poach again for 3 more minutes. Remove and drain on a dish towel. The "roses" should not touch one another while poaching. Poach in several batches and do not crowd the pan. When the "roses" are drained, place them on top of the cold vanilla sauce in a serving dish. Chill for at least 1 hour before serving. Don't place them on top of one another, since they might break.

165

Chocolate Rice Pudding
(Riz au Chocolat pour Géraldine)

This is a chocolate-flavored rice pudding decorated with a Chantilly cream.

PREPARATION	20 minutes
RESTING TIME	1 hour and 30 minutes
COOKING TIME	25 minutes
INGREDIENTS	*For 4 to 6 servings* ½ cup, generous (125 g), rice 2 cups (½ l) water 2 cups (½ l) milk ⅔ cup (150 g) granulated sugar ½ vanilla bean, split lengthwise 7 ounces (200 g) semi-sweet chocolate 3½ tablespoons (50 g) butter 1½ teaspoons (2 sheets) gelatin, softened in 1½ tablespoons cold water 1½ cups (200 g) Chantilly cream (Recipe 13) 1⅓ cups (3 dl) vanilla sauce (Recipe 32) Grated chocolate
UTENSILS	Ribbed brioche mold 8½" (22 cm) 2 pots Pastry bag with star-shaped nozzle

Cooking the Rice: Boil the rice for 2 minutes in the boiling water. Drain and rinse under cold water to remove the starch. Meanwhile, bring the milk to a boil with the sugar, vanilla bean, chocolate, and butter stirring frequently.

Add the rice and cook very slowly for 25 minutes. If the rice has not absorbed all the milk at the end of this time, continue cooking several minutes more. Once cooked, add the softened gelatin, then allow to cool until barely lukewarm, stirring occasionally.

Assembling and Decorating: Fold delicately all but ⅓ cup (50 g) of the Chantilly cream into the rice. Slightly dampen the mold and sprinkle with sugar. Fill the mold with the rice mixture and refrigerate for at least 1 hour, 30 minutes. Turn out onto a deep platter and decorate with the reserved Chantilly cream using a pastry bag with a star-shaped nozzle to form roselike designs. Sprinkle the top of the dessert with grated chocolate. Serve with a vanilla sauce in a sauce boat.

Note: Do not beat the Chantilly cream too stiff or else it won't mix easily with the rice.

166

Rice Pudding with Eight Treasures (Riz Impératrice aux Huit Trésors)

(Photo page 284)

The eight treasures are eight different candied fruits: dates, prunes, raisins, ginger, etc. (or others of your choice).

PREPARATION	1 hour
RESTING TIME	3 hours
COOKING TIME	35 minutes
INGREDIENTS	*For 8 to 10 servings* 1 cup (200 g) rice 3 cups, generous (¾ l), water 3 cups, generous (¾ l), milk 1 vanilla bean 3½ tablespoons (50 g) granulated sugar 1 piece candied ginger, 1½″ (4 cm) long 2⅔ cups (6 dl) vanilla sauce (Recipe 32)

2¼ teaspoons (3 sheets) gelatin, softened in 2 tablespoons cold water
1¾ cups (250 g) Chantilly cream (Recipe 13)
1½ cups (300 g) candied fruits (8 different kinds), diced very small
1 orange peel, diced
½ lemon peel, diced
1 cup (150 g) candied cherries
⅔ cup (100 g) stewed peaches
2 cups, generous (½ l), raspberry sauce (Recipe 15)

UTENSILS

1 ring mold 11″ (28 cm)
Pastry bag with star-shaped nozzle
Mixing bowl
Wire whisk
Spatula
Grater
Large saucepan

Cooking the Rice: Boil the rice for 2 minutes in the boiling water. Drain and rinse the rice under cold water to remove the starch. Meanwhile, in a heavy-bottomed saucepan, bring the milk to a boil with the vanilla bean split in two lengthwise. As soon as the milk boils, pour in the rice, the sugar and the ginger. Cover and cook for 25 minutes or until the rice has absorbed all the liquid. Remove the vanilla bean and the ginger and allow the rice to cool.

Assembling and Decorating: Set aside half the vanilla sauce in a sauce boat. Add the softened gelatin to the remaining warm vanilla sauce. Cool the vanilla sauce by placing the pot it cooked in into a bowl of ice water. Stir frequently, until the sauce is cold and quite thick. Set aside ¾ cup (100 g) of Chantilly cream and refrigerate. Add the remaining Chantilly cream to the cold vanilla sauce. When the boiled rice is cold, stir in the diced candied fruit, the orange peel, and the lemon peel. Fold this mixture very delicately into the Chantilly-vanilla sauce mixture. Slightly dampen the mold and sprinkle with sugar. Fill the bottom with candied cherries cut in half, then pour in the rice mixture. Refrigerate for 3 hours.

To turn out, dip the mold for a few seconds in warm water and turn it over onto a serving platter. Decorate with sliced peaches. Using a pastry bag with a star-shaped nozzle, decorate the center with rose shape designs made with the Chantilly reserved earlier.

167

Stewed Fruit (General Comments)

Pears, apricots, quinces, peaches, plums, strawberries, raspberries, and oranges can be stewed to make delicious desserts. The recipes that follow are for making stewed fruit. Any fresh fruit may be stewed according to the general directions given here.

INGREDIENTS

For a typical syrup
2¾ cups to 3½ cups (600 to 800 g) granulated sugar
4⅓ cups (1 l) water
1 vanilla bean

Preparing the Fruit: The amount of sugar used depends upon individual taste. There should be enough liquid to cover the fruit when it is added. Most fruits cook 15 to 20 minutes (the syrup must never boil) over low heat. The fruit is done when it is completely soft; i.e., a knife enters the fruit with no resistance. The fruit should be left in the syrup in a covered bowl, for several hours, or even overnight, before serving.

The flavorings used in some of the following recipes may surprise some people. They were chosen because they complement the taste of the fruit they are stewed with and add variety to this kind of dessert cooking.

168

Stewed Apricots in Wine (Abricots au Sirop)

PREPARATION — 10 minutes

COOKING TIME — 15 minutes

RESTING TIME — 3 hours, minimum

INGREDIENTS

2 pounds (1 kg) fresh apricots *or*
  1 pound (500 g) dried apricots
Approximately 1 bottle dry white wine *or* sweet white wine; e.g., Sauterne
1¾ cups (400 g) granulated sugar
1 lemon, sliced

UTENSILS

Knife
Pot
Serving bowl with cover

Preparing the Fruit: If dried apricots are used, they have to be soaked for 2 hours in lukewarm water before cooking.

Cut fresh apricots in two and remove the pit. Poach the apricots for 15 minutes in a pot with the white wine, sugar, and sliced lemon (there should be just enough liquid to cover the fruit at the start of cooking). When cooked, place in a covered bowl at least 3 hours before serving. Serve cold.

169

Stewed Whole Apricots
(Abricots Frais avec leurs Noyaux)

PREPARATION

10 minutes

COOKING TIME

15 to 20 minutes

RESTING TIME

Several hours

INGREDIENTS

4⅓ cups (1 l) water
1⅓ cups (300 g) granulated sugar
1 cup (300 g) honey
A few pieces candied ginger
3¼ pounds (1.5 kg) fresh whole apricots

UTENSILS

Large pot
Serving bowl with cover

Preparing the Fruit: Place all the ingredients except the apricots into a pot and bring to a boil, then add the apricots and simmer (do not boil) for about 15 minutes. Pour the apricots and their syrup into a bowl and allow to sit, covered, for several hours before serving. Serve cold.

170

Stewed Bananas (Bananes au Sirop)

PREPARATION	10 minutes
COOKING TIME	15 minutes
RESTING TIME	2 to 3 hours
INGREDIENTS	2 cups (½ l) water 3 tablespoons (½ dl) rum 1⅓ cups (300 g) granulated sugar 1½ teaspoons (8 g) vanilla sugar 2¼ pounds (1 kg) bananas, peeled and thickly sliced
UTENSILS	2 large pots Serving bowl with cover

Preparing the Fruit: Place all the ingredients except the bananas in a pot and bring to a boil. Place the bananas in another pot and pour the boiling liquid over them. Poach over low heat for about 15 minutes. Place the bananas and syrup in a bowl and cover while allowing to cool. Serve cold.

To Store: This dessert can be kept refrigerated for 3 days

171

Dried Figs Stewed in Wine (Figues au Sirop)

PREPARATION	10 minutes
COOKING TIME	15 minutes
RESTING TIME	48 hours

Chocolate-Vanilla Charlotte, Recipe 156

LENOTRE
Traiteur
PARIS-DEAUVILLE-NEW YORK

INGREDIENTS	1 bottle of red wine 1 cup, generous (250 g), granulated sugar 4 whole bay leaves 2¼ pounds (1 kg) dried figs
UTENSILS	Knife Large pot Serving bowl with cover

Preparing the Fruit: With the point of a sharp knife, cut an X on each fig (this will split them in a star-shaped fashion when cooking). Place all the ingredients, except the figs, in a large pot and bring to a boil. Add the figs, lower the heat and cook slowly for 10 to 15 minutes. Pour into a bowl to cool, then cover the bowl and place in the refrigerator. Allow the figs to sit for 48 hours before serving them.

To Store: The stewed figs can be kept refrigerated for 8 days.

172
Stewed Strawberries (Fraises au Sirop)

PREPARATION	15 minutes
RESTING TIME	30 minutes
COOKING TIME	5 minutes
INGREDIENTS	2 cups (½ l) water *or* 1 cup (¼ l) water and 1 cup (¼ l) sweet white wine 1¾ cups (400 g) granulated sugar 1 vanilla bean, split lengthwise Juice of 1 or 2 lemons 2¼ pounds (1 kg) fresh strawberries
UTENSILS	Large pot Bowl

Preparing the Fruit: Place the strawberries in a bowl; pour over them the lemon juice and ¾ cup of sugar (the amount of lemon juice and sugar can be varied according to taste). Leave for 30 minutes before cooking. Place the remaining sugar and the other ingredients into a pot (if you are using wine, use ½ cup (100 g) less sugar than stated above). Add the strawberries and poach for 5 minutes on a very low flame. Allow to cool before serving. Serve cold no more than 12 hours after being prepared.

173

Mixed Fruit Stewed in Wine (Fruits Panachés au Sirop)

PREPARATION	20 minutes
COOKING TIME	About 20 minutes
RESTING TIME	24 hours
INGREDIENTS	Red wine (to cover fruit) 2¾ cups (600 g) sugar per bottle of wine 4 whole bay leaves 1 cinnamon stick 3¼ pounds (1.5 kg) pears, preferably small wild pears 1 pound 1½ ounces (500 g) prunes 1½ cups (150 g) shelled walnuts
UTENSILS	Large pot Serving bowl with cover

Preparing the Fruit: Place the fruit and the walnuts in a large pot with the wine. Add the sugar, cinnamon, and bay leaves. Simmer slowly over low heat until cooked. The fruit is cooked when a knife enters it with no resistance. Remove from the heat, place in a covered bowl and leave 24 hours before serving. Serve cold.

To Store: The stewed fruit will keep 4 to 5 days refrigerated.

174

Stewed Lichees (Letchis au Sirop)

PREPARATION 5 to 10 minutes

COOKING TIME 15 minutes

RESTING TIME 24 hours

INGREDIENTS
Juice of 3 limes, plus their peels
2¾ cups (600 g) granulated sugar per
4⅓ cups (1 l) water
Approximately 4⅓ cups (1 l) water
2¼ pounds (1 kg) peeled fresh lichees

Or 5½ cups (1 kg) drained canned lichees
Juice of 3 limes, plus their peels
The juice from the can
1 cup, generous (250 g), granulated sugar

UTENSILS
Large pot
Serving bowl and cover

Preparing the Fruit: *For fresh fruit*: Place all the ingredients, except the lichees, into a pot and bring to a boil. Add the lichees and simmer slowly for 15 minutes. Pour the fruit with the syrup into a bowl, cover and leave for 24 hours before serving.

For canned fruit: Prepare as described above using the juice from the can instead of water.

175

Peaches Stewed in Wine (Pêches au Sirop)

White-fleshed peaches are best in this dessert.

PREPARATION 15 minutes

Apple Charlotte, Recipe 160

COOKING TIME	15 minutes
RESTING TIME	Several hours
INGREDIENTS	Red wine 6 tablespoons (1 dl) Madeira ¾ teaspoon black peppercorns 2¾ cups (600 g) granulated sugar per bottle of wine 2¼ pounds (1 kg) peaches
UTENSILS	2 large pots Serving bowl

Preparing the Fruit: Peel the peaches by dipping them for a few seconds into boiling water, then into cold water. Leave the fruit whole since the pit adds flavor to the syrup. Place all the ingredients, except the peaches, into a large pot and bring to a boil. Add the peaches and simmer over low heat for 15 minutes. Pour into a bowl and allow to sit for several hours before serving.

176

Stewed Pears with Honey (Poires au Sirop)

PREPARATION	15 minutes
COOKING TIME	15 minutes
RESTING TIME	Overnight
INGREDIENTS	4⅓ cups (1 l) water 1¾ cups (400 g) sugar ⅔ cup (200 g) honey 3 whole bay leaves 2 cloves ¾ teaspoon black peppercorns 2¼ pounds (1 kg) pears, peeled, cored, and quartered
UTENSILS	Pot Serving bowl with cover

Preparing the Fruit: Place all the ingredients, except the pears, in a pot and bring to a boil. Add the fruit and simmer for 15 minutes. Don't overcook. Place the pears and the syrup in a bowl, cover, and allow to sit overnight before serving.

177

Stewed Prunes in Wine (Pruneaux au Sirop)

PREPARATION	15 minutes
COOKING TIME	20 minutes
RESTING TIME	Several hours
INGREDIENTS	1 bottle Sauterne, plus ¾ cup, generous (200 g), sugar *or* 1 bottle red wine, plus 1⅓ cups (300 g) sugar 10 orange slices 5 lemon slices 2¼ pounds (1 kg) prunes, unpitted
UTENSILS	Pot Serving bowl

Preparing the Fruit: Place all the ingredients except the prunes in a pot and bring to a boil. Add the prunes and simmer over very low heat for about 20 minutes. Pour into a bowl and allow to cool for several hours before serving.

178

Stewed Muskmelon or Cantaloupe (Compote de Melons Verts)

PREPARATION 15 minutes

COOKING TIME 20 minutes

INGREDIENTS
3 medium-sized melons
1½ cups (350 g) granulated sugar
3 tablespoons vinegar
The zest of 1 lemon

UTENSILS
Potato peeler
Knife
Pot (preferably copper)
Bowl

Preparing the Fruit: Peel the melons with a potato peeler; cut open and remove the seeds. Cut the melon into small pieces. Place the fruit in a pot with the other ingredients and cook over low heat for about 20 minutes or until soft. Pour into a bowl and chill before serving.

179

Apple Sauce (Compote de Pommes)

PREPARATION 15 minutes

COOKING TIME 20 minutes

INGREDIENTS
For 2 to 3 servings
1 pound 1½ ounces (500 g) cooking apples, peeled, cored, and quartered
⅔ cup (150 g) granulated sugar

½ vanilla bean, split lengthwise
6½ tablespoons (1 dl) water
Juice of ½ lemon, plus the peel, finely chopped [optional]

UTENSILS

Pot (preferably copper)
Sieve or food mill

Preparing the Fruit: Place the apples in a pot with the sugar, vanilla bean, and water. (Add the lemon peel and juice if the apples are too sweet.) Cook over low heat for about 20 minutes. Remove the vanilla bean and work the apples through a sieve or food mill to make a purée.

To Store: Apple sauce will keep for 8 days in the refrigerator.

180

Stewed Rhubarb (Compote de Rubarbe)

PREPARATION

15 minutes

COOKING TIME

30 minutes

INGREDIENTS

For 2 to 3 servings
1½ pounds (700 g) rhubarb
¾ cup, generous (200 g), granulated sugar
1 vanilla bean, split lengthwise

UTENSILS

Pot
Knife
Bowl

Preparing the Fruit: Peel the rhubarb and cut into 1″ (2.5 cm) pieces. In a pot, place a layer of rhubarb and cover with a layer of sugar. Continue filling the pot in this manner until all the fruit and sugar are used. Add the vanilla bean, bring quickly to a boil, then lower the heat. Cook over very low heat for 30 minutes (longer if you intend to keep the rhubarb several days). Pour into a bowl and allow to cool before serving.

Note: If you like the stewed rhubarb sweeter, blanch it first, then drain before cooking it with the sugar.

181

Oranges with Grenadine Syrup (Oranges à la Grenadine)

PREPARATION	20 minutes
COOKING TIME	45 minutes
RESTING TIME	Several hours
INGREDIENTS	*For 4 servings* 4 oranges 1⅓ cups, scant (3 dl), Grenadine syrup
UTENSILS	Vegetable peeler 2 pots Paring knife Serving bowl with cover

Preparing the Fruit: Wash the fruit and remove the skin of 2 oranges with a vegetable peeler. Cook the orange skins in the Grenadine syrup for about 30 minutes. Cut off the remaining white part of the skin from the first two oranges, as well as the entire skin from the remaining two oranges, with a knife. Discard these skins. Cut out all the orange sections, place them in a pot, and pour the hot Grenadine-orange skin mixture over them. Cook for about 15 minutes. Pour into a bowl and cover. Allow to cool for several hours before serving.

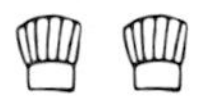

182
Red Currant Jelly (Gelée de Groseilles)

PREPARATION	15 minutes
COOKING TIME	15 minutes
INGREDIENTS	Juice of 2¼ pounds (1 kg) red currants 1 cup granulated sugar for every cup of juice 1 cup (2½ dl) water
UTENSILS	1 preserving pan Candy thermometer [optional] Wooden spoon Large jars with lids (sterilized)

Preparing the Jelly: Boil the sugar in the water until it reaches 276.8°F (136°C) on the candy thermometer. If you do not have a thermometer, cook until one drop of sugar in a bowl of cold water forms a ball that's hard and slightly sticky. Pour the red currant juice into the sugar and bring to a boil (the temperature should be 170°F (95°C) on the sugar thermometer). Remove from the heat immediately and stir with a wooden spoon without stopping for 15 minutes. Pour the jelly into the jars and close the lids immediately.

Note: Red currant juice is made by grinding the fresh currants through a sieve or food mill.

To Store: The jelly can be kept easily for a month at room temperature and several months refrigerated.

Chapter 9
PETITS FOURS AND COOKIES

RECIPES

183. Petits Fours made with Cream Puff Dough (General Comments)
184. Miniature Eclairs (Carolines)
185. Cream Puffs with Grand Marnier or Kirsch Filling (Choux au Grand Marnier ou au Kirsch)
186. Rum-Flavored Salombos (Salombos au Rhum)
187. Caramel Almond Puffs (Choux Pralinés)
188. Miniature Fruit Tartlets (Mini-Tartelettes aux Fruits)
189. Glazed Match Sticks (Allumettes Glacées)
190. Orange Cream Tartlets (Caissettes Oranges)
191. Diamond-Studded Circles (Diamants)
192. Sacristains
193. Raisin Cookies (Palets aux Raisins)
194. Palmiers
195. Congolese Cookies (Rochers Congolais)
196. Arlesian Cookies (Sablés Arlésiens)
197. Little Cornflower's Cookies (Sablés Corn Flower)
198. Teddybear's Cookies (Sablés Nounours)

199. Hazelnut Cookies (Sablés Noisettes)
200. Financiers
201. Rolled Almond Cookies (Tuiles aux Amandes)

Miniature Fruit Tartlets, Recipe 188; Cream Puffs with Grand Marnier and Kirsch, Recipe 185; Rum-Flavored Salambos, Recipe 186; Caramel Almond Puffs, Recipe 187; Miniature Eclairs, Recipe 184

PARIS DEAUVILLE

183

Petits Fours Made with Cream Puff Dough (General Comments)

Filling the Pastries: The quantities given in the following recipes are for 40 to 50 petits fours. With ⅔ cup (300 g) of cream puff dough, you can prepare 3 different kinds of cream puffs; ⅓ of the dough can be used for making small éclairs, ⅓ for small cream puffs, and ⅓ for small salambos. They can all be placed on the same baking sheet although they are garnished differently.

It is advisable to prepare a large amount of pastry cream for filling the choux pastries. Divide the cream into 3 or 4 equal parts and flavor each one differently while the cream is cooling.

Note: If you have trouble using a pastry bag, make small cream puffs instead of éclairs or salambos (which are harder to form).

To Store: The baked, unfilled cream puffs can be kept at least 8 days in the refrigerator in a tightly closed plastic bag or bowl, or they can be kept frozen for one month. The filled cream puffs should be eaten the same day they are prepared.

184

Miniature Eclairs (Carolines)

(Photo page 283)

PREPARATION 20 minutes

BAKING TIME 20 minutes

INGREDIENTS *For 40 to 50 small éclairs*
⅔ cup (300 g) cream puff pastry (Recipe 11)
2 cups (500 g) coffee or chocolate pastry cream (Recipe 25 *or* 26)
1½ cups (450 g) chocolate icing (Recipe 27) *or* coffee-flavored fondant icing (Recipe 28)

Snow Eggs, Recipe 164
Rice Pudding with Eight Treasures, Recipe 166

UTENSILS	2 pastry bags—one with ½″ (1 cm) nozzle and one with ⅛″ (0.3 cm) nozzle Parchment paper [optional] Baking sheet Knife

Baking: Preheat the oven to 425°F (220°C). On a buttered or parchment paper-lined baking sheet, squeeze out 1½″ (4 cm) long sticks of cream puff pastry, using the pastry bag with the ½″ (1 cm) nozzle. Bake for 10 minutes in a 425°F (220°C) oven; lower the heat to 400°F (200°C) and bake for another 10 minutes, keeping the oven door ajar with a spoon. Remove and allow to cool.

Filling the Pastries: Fill the miniature éclairs by making an opening in the bottom of each pastry with the tip of a knife and filling them with pastry cream using a pastry bag with a ⅛″ (0.3 cm) nozzle. Prepare the fondant or chocolate icing and dip the top of each éclair in the icing. Let the icing dry, then refrigerate the éclairs. Serve cold.

185

Cream Puffs with Grand Marnier or Kirsch Filling (Choux au Grand Marnier ou au Kirsch)

(Photo page 283)

PREPARATION	20 minutes
BAKING TIME	20 minutes
INGREDIENTS	*For 40 to 50 cream puffs* ⅔ cup (300 g) cream puff pastry (Recipe 11) 2 cups (500 g) vanilla pastry cream (Recipe 24) 2 tablespoons Grand Marnier or Kirsch 1½ cups (450 g) pink or green fondant icing (Recipe 28) *or* confectioners' sugar

UTENSILS

2 pastry bags—one with a ½″ (1 cm) nozzle and one with a ⅛″ (0.3 cm) nozzle
Knife
Baking sheet
Sugar dredger
Parchment paper [optional]

Baking: Preheat the oven to 425°F (220°C). On a buttered or parchment paper-lined baking sheet, squeeze out the puff pastry into 40 to 50 cream puffs 1″ (2.5 cm) using a pastry bag with a ½″ (1 cm) nozzle. Bake in a 425°F (220°C) oven for 10 minutes; lower the heat to 400°F (200°C) and bake for another 10 minutes, keeping the oven door ajar with a spoon. Remove from the oven and allow to cool.

Filling the Pastries: To fill the cream puffs, make a small opening in the bottom of each one with the point of a knife. Using a pastry bag with a ⅛″ (0.3 cm) nozzle, fill the puffs with the pastry cream of your choice. Dip the top of each cream puff into fondant icing or simply sprinkle the cream puffs with confectioners' sugar and refrigerate before serving.

186

Rum-Flavored Salambos (Salambos au Rhum)

(Photo page 283)

PREPARATION 10 minutes

BAKING TIME 20 minutes

INGREDIENTS

For 40 to 50 salambos
⅔ cup (300 g) cream puff pastry (Recipe 11)
2 cups (500 g) vanilla pastry cream (Recipe 24), flavored with 2 tablespoons rum
¾ cup, generous (200 g), granulated sugar
3 tablespoons water
3 drops lemon juice

UTENSILS

Baking sheet
Parchment paper [optional]
Knife
2 pastry bags—one with a ½″ (1 cm) nozzle and one with ⅛″ (0.3 cm) nozzle

Baking: Preheat the oven to 425°F (220°C). On a buttered or parchment paper-lined baking sheet, squeeze out 40 to 50 ovals of cream puff pastry 1¼″ (3 cm) in length using a pastry bag with a ½″ (1 cm) nozzle.

Bake in a 425°F (220°C) oven for 10 minutes; lower the heat to 400°F (200°C) and bake for another 10 minutes more, keeping the oven door ajar with a spoon. Remove and allow to cool.

Filling the Pastries: Prepare some caramel by cooking the sugar, water, and lemon juice until it turns a cinnamon color. Dip the top of each cream puff in the caramel. Place the cream puffs, caramel side down, on a baking sheet to cool. Once cool, make a small opening with a knife underneath each puff and then fill them with the pastry cream, using a pastry bag with a ⅛″ (0.3 cm) nozzle. Refrigerate before serving.

187
Caramel Almond Puffs (Choux Pralinés)

(Photo page 283)

PREPARATION: 20 minutes

BAKING TIME: 20 minutes

INGREDIENTS

For 40 to 50 almond puffs
⅔ cup (300 g) cream puff pastry (Recipe 11)
2½ tablespoons (25 g) chopped almonds
1 cup (250 g) vanilla pastry cream (Recipe 24)
½ cup (75 g) powdered caramelized almonds
3½ tablespoons (50 g) butter, softened
Confectioners' sugar

UTENSILS

Wire whisk
Knife
2 pastry bags—one with a ½″ (1 cm) nozzle and one with a ⅛″ (0.3 cm) nozzle
Sugar dredger
Parchment paper [optional]

Baking: Preheat the oven to 425°F (220°C). On a buttered or parchment paper-lined baking sheet, squeeze out 40 to 50 cream puffs 1″ (2.5 cm) using a pastry bag with a ½″ (1 cm) nozzle. Sprinkle the chopped almonds on top. Bake in a 425°F (220°C) oven for 10 minutes. Lower the heat to 400°F (200°C) and bake for 10 minutes more, keeping the oven door ajar with a spoon. Remove and allow to cool.

Filling the Pastries: Prepare the pastry cream and while the cream is cooling, stir in the powdered caramelized almonds and the softened butter. Beat the mixture until you have a smooth, light cream.

Fill the cream puffs with the pastry cream, using a pastry bag with a ⅛″ (0.3 cm) nozzle. Make a small hole in the bottom of each cream puff with the point of a knife, insert the nozzle and fill the cream puffs with pastry cream.

Sprinkle the cream puffs with confectioners' sugar and refrigerate before serving.

188

Miniature Fruit Tartlets (Mini-Tartelettes aux Fruits)

(Photos pages 283 and 294)

PREPARATION

20 minutes

BAKING TIME

8 to 10 minutes

INGREDIENTS

For 20 tartlets
8½ ounces (240 g) short pastry dough (Recipe 10)
1 cup (200 g) almond cream (Recipe 17)
10 apricots *or* 40 cherries *or* 5 pears *or* 20 wedges of pineapple
⅓ cup (100 g) apricot jam, warm

UTENSILS 20 small tartlet pans or circles
Pastry brush
Cookie cutter (a little larger than the pans or circles)
Fork
Rolling pin

Assembling the Tart: On a lightly floured table, roll out the cold dough and cut it with a cookie cutter slightly larger than the circles or tartlet pans.

Line the molds with the dough and prick the bottom with a fork. Fill each tartlet with almond cream.

Filling and Baking: Preheat the oven to 400°F (200°C). Choose one of the following two procedures:

I. Place on top of the cream in each tartlet either half an apricot, 2 or 3 cherries, or a quarter of a pear, sliced very thin. Push the fruit slightly into the cream. Bake in a 400°F (200°C) oven for 8 to 10 minutes. Turn out and allow to cool, then brush each tartlet with apricot jam and refrigerate before serving.

II. Bake the dough filled with the almond cream (without the fruit) for 8 to 10 minutes in a 400°F (200°C) oven. Turn out and allow to cool, then place on top of the cream a wedge of pineapple. Brush each tartlet with a little apricot jam and refrigerate before serving.

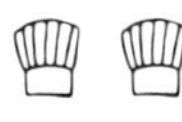

189

Glazed Match Sticks (Allumettes Glacées)

(Photo page 295)

PREPARATION 15 minutes

BAKING TIME 10 minutes

INGREDIENTS *For 36 pastries*
1 cup (150 g) confectioners' sugar
1 egg white
3 drops lemon juice
7 ounces (200 g) classic flaky pastry dough (Recipe 3)

UTENSILS

Spoon
Bowl
Knife
Rolling pin
4 tartlet rings ¾″ (2 cm) high
Cake rack
Ruler
Baking sheet

Making the Icing: Make an icing by beating the confectioners' sugar with the egg white for about 2 minutes, using a spoon, until the mixture is light and homogenous. Then stir in the lemon.

Baking: Preheat the oven to 400°F (200°C). On a lightly floured table, roll out the dough into a rectangle 16″ by 8″ (40 × 20 cm). Using a ruler and a knife, cut the dough in three 16″ (40 cm) long pieces. Fold two of these pieces and refrigerate while preparing the third piece of dough. Place this piece of dough on a slightly damp baking sheet. Cover the dough with the icing (spreading it evenly about 1/16″ [1.5mm] thick). Cut the dough into about 12 strips (using a damp knife). Ice and cut the two remaining pieces of dough the same way. Place all the sticks on the same baking sheet. Before baking, place on each corner of the baking sheet a small ¾″ (2 cm) high tartlet ring on top of which you place a cake rack so that the dough will rise evenly and each pastry will be the same height.

Bake in a 400°F (200°C) oven for 10 minutes, keeping the oven door ajar with a spoon. Bake until golden brown. During the baking, the sticks shrink a little in width and will detach themselves from each other. If you used too much icing and the pastry sticks together, cut the sticks apart with a knife while they are baking.

To Store: These little pastries will keep 10 days in a tightly closed container, but be sure the sticks are completely cool before storing them.

190

Orange Cream Tartlets (Caissettes Oranges)

PREPARATION 20 minutes

BAKING TIME 15 to 16 minutes

INGREDIENTS	*For 70 tartlets* 1 cup (125 g) powdered almonds ¾ cup (125 g) confectioners' sugar Peel of ½ orange, finely chopped 5 tablespoons (75 g) butter, melted 3 egg whites = ½ cup, scant (90 g) ½ teaspoon sugar Confectioners' sugar
UTENSILS	2 bowls Wire whisk 70 small paper cupcake molds 1⅜″ (3.5 cm) Pastry bag with a ¼″ (0.6 cm) nozzle *or* teaspoon Sugar dredger Baking sheet

The Batter: In a bowl, beat the powdered almonds and confectioners' sugar until the mixture is homogenous, then add the orange peel, the melted butter, and half the egg whites. Stir well. Beat the remaining egg whites until they are very stiff, adding ½ teaspoon of sugar halfway through. Fold the beaten egg whites delicately into the sugar-almond mixture. Fill the paper cups with this batter, using a teaspoon or a pastry bag with a ¼″ (0.6 cm) nozzle. Sprinkle with confectioners' sugar.

Baking: Preheat the oven to 400°F (200°C). Bake the orange cream tartlets for 15 to 16 minutes, then remove and allow to cool.

To Store: Orange cream tartlets will keep two weeks in a tightly closed container in the refrigerator. Serve cold.

191

Diamond Studded Circles (Diamants)

(*Photo page 295*)

It is important in this recipe not to work the dough too much; just mix the ingredients rapidly together. This dough can be made one day ahead.

PREPARATION 30 minutes

RESTING TIME 45 minutes

BAKING TIME 13 minutes

INGREDIENTS *For 60 pastries*
½ cup, scant (100 g), granulated sugar
¾ cup (190 g) butter, soft
½ teaspoon vanilla extract
1¾ cups (250 g) flour
A pinch of salt
1 egg yolk
Broken rock candy (to roll pastries in)

UTENSILS Electric mixer with dough hook
Bowl
Baking sheet
Parchment paper [optional]
Pastry brush
Sheet of paper
Knife

Making the Dough: In a mixing bowl, at low speed, beat the granulated sugar, butter, and vanilla. Then, all at once, add the flour and salt. Beat the dough until very smooth; this step should not take more than 2 minutes. Place the dough in the refrigerator for 30 minutes.

Divide the dough into 3 equal parts; roll each piece in the shape of a sausage 1¼″ (3 cm). Refrigerate again for 15 minutes.

Baking: Beat the egg yolk. Place the broken rock candy on a sheet of paper. Brush each roll of dough with the egg yolk, then roll in the rock candy (pressing lightly so that the sugar will stick to the dough).

Preheat the oven to 400°F (200°C). Cut each roll of dough into ½″ (1 cm) slices and place on a lightly buttered or parchment paper-lined baking sheet. Bake in a 400°F (200°C) oven for about 13 minutes or until a light golden brown.

Note: Granulated sugar can be used instead of broken rock candy.

To Store: These pastries will keep 10 days in a tightly closed container; allow to cool completely before storing.

Mirabelle Plum Tartlets, Recipe 128; Blueberry Tartlets, Recipe 129; Pineapple Tartlets, Recipe 132

Glazed Match Sticks, Recipe 189; Diamond-Studded Circles, Recipe 191; Palmiers, Recipe 194

Sacristains, Recipe 192

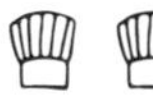 

192

Sacristains

(Photo page 296)

PREPARATION	15 minutes
BAKING TIME	30 minutes per sheet
INGREDIENTS	*For 80 cookies* 1 pound (450 g) classic flaky pastry dough (Recipe 3) *or* quick flaky pastry dough (Recipe 4) 1 cup, generous (160 g), broken rock candy 1 cup (160 g) chopped almonds 1 egg, beaten

UTENSILS	Pastry brush Rolling pin Knife 2 baking sheets

Shaping the Dough: Work quickly. On a lightly floured table, roll out the cold dough into a rectangle 5½″ × 15″ (14 × 40 cm), 1/16″ (2 mm) thick. Cut the dough lengthwise into 2 equal strips. Fold one of the strips in half and refrigerate. Brush the other strip with a little beaten egg. Sprinkle with ¼ of the rock candy and ¼ of the chopped almonds. Press the almonds and sugar into the dough lightly with a rolling pin. Turn the dough upside down and brush the other side with a little beaten egg, then sprinkle with chopped almonds and sugar as just described.

Cut this strip of dough into rectangles ¾″ by 2¾″ (2 cm × 7 cm); twist each rectangle slightly to form the cookies (see photo, page 295).

Baking: Preheat the oven to 400°F (200°C). Place the cookies on a baking sheet (about 40 per sheet). Bake for 10 minutes in a 400°F (200°C) oven, then lower the heat to 325°F (160°C) and bake for another 20 minutes. The cookies will puff up and shorten during baking. Meanwhile, remove the second strip of dough from the refrigerator and prepare and bake as described above.

To Store: In a tightly sealed container, these cookies will keep for 6 days

193

Raisin Cookies (Palets aux Raisins)

PREPARATION	20 minutes
BAKING TIME	20 minutes total
INGREDIENTS	*For 60 cookies* ½ cup, generous (100 g), raisins 6½ tablespoons (1 dl) rum, warmed 6½ tablespoons (100 g) butter, softened ½ cup, generous (80 g), confectioners' sugar 1 egg 3 drops of vanilla extract 1¼ cups (160 g) flour ⅓ cup (50 g) powdered almonds

UTENSILS	Pastry bag with ¾″ (2 cm) nozzle Bowl Electric mixer Wooden spoon 2 baking sheets

The Batter: Soak the raisins in the warm rum for 1 hour. Using the mixer, beat the butter and the sugar until smooth, then beat in the egg and the vanilla extract. Continue beating for about one minute; then with the wooden spoon, carefully fold the flour and the almonds into the batter. The batter should be soft. Stir in the raisins and the rum.

Baking: Preheat the oven to 400°F (200°C). On buttered baking sheets, squeeze out half the batter, using a pastry bag with a ¾″ (2 cm) nozzle. Make 30 cookies the size of a walnut. Prepare one baking sheet at a time; refrigerate the remaining batter while baking the first batch. Bake for 10 minutes. Halfway through the baking of the first batch, prepare the second batch for baking. Bake the second batch as soon as the first is done. These cookies are delicious when eaten warm, but they can also be stored and eaten cold.

To Store: Raisin cookies will keep 10 days in a tightly sealed container. Allow to cool completely before storing.

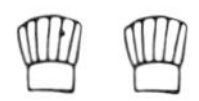

194

Palmiers

(*Photo page 295*)

PREPARATION	15 minutes
RESTING TIME	10 minutes
BAKING TIME	10 minutes per sheet
INGREDIENTS	*For 60 palmiers* 7 ounces (200 g) flaky pastry dough with 4 turns (Recipe 3) ½ cup, generous (80 g), confectioners' sugar, plus 1 teaspoon powdered vanilla

UTENSILS

Rolling pin
Knife
Parchment paper [optional]
2 baking sheets
Pastry brush

Shaping the Dough: On a table, sprinkled heavily with confectioners' sugar, give the dough the last 2 turns; then freeze for 5 minutes. Roll the dough out again in the confectioners' sugar into 2 strips 6″ by 12″ (15 × 30 cm). Moisten the dough lightly with a damp pastry brush. Fold in the sides of the dough until they touch in the center (fold lengthwise). Fold again lengthwise, this time in half, pressing down lightly. The dough will now be 4 layers thick (see photo, page 295). Place these strips in the freezer for 3 to 5 minutes. When the dough has hardened, slice each strip into ¼″ (½ cm) thick slices. Place each slice on a buttered or parchment paper-lined baking sheet. Do not place the palmiers too close to one another as they spread while baking.

Baking: Preheat the oven to 400°F (200°C). Bake one sheet at a time; leave the remaining dough in the freezer until ready to use. Bake in a 400°F (200°C) oven for 10 minutes, then remove and allow to cool. Do not place the palmiers on top of each other until they are completely cold or else they will stick together.

To Store: Palmiers will keep 8 days in a tightly sealed container.

195

Congolese Cookies (Rochers Congolais)

PREPARATION

15 minutes

BAKING TIME

20 minutes

INGREDIENTS

For 30 Congolese cookies
4 egg whites
1⅓ cups (300 g) granulated sugar
1 tablespoon apple sauce *or* jam
4 cups (300 g) grated coconut

UTENSILS

Large double boiler, or mixing bowl and large pot of boiling water
Wire whisk
Baking sheet

The Batter: In a double boiler, beat the egg whites and the sugar until the mixture is hot to the touch (almost burns). Away from the heat, stir in the apple sauce or jam and the coconut. Beat for 3 minutes.

Baking: Preheat the oven to 350°F (180°C). Spoon the batter onto a buttered baking sheet making balls the size of a small egg. With damp fingers, shape the balls into little pyramids. Bake in a 350°F (180°C) oven for 20 minutes. The cookies should be moist inside and barely browned outside when done.

To Store: Congolese cookies will keep 10 days refrigerated in a tightly sealed container.

196

Arlesian Cookies (Sablés Arlésiens)

These are delicious cookies lightly flavored with lemon and almonds.

PREPARATION — 30 minutes

RESTING TIME — 1½ hours, minimum

BAKING TIME — 10 minutes per sheet

INGREDIENTS

For 140 cookies
⅓ cup, generous (60 g), confectioners' sugar
½ cup (60 g) powdered almonds
⅔ cup (150 g) butter, soft
½ egg, beaten
2½ tablespoons (25 g) confectioners' sugar
A pinch of salt
Peel of 1 lemon, finely chopped
1 cup, generous (150 g), flour

UTENSILS — Small-toothed pastry wheel or knife
Rolling pin
2 baking sheets
Electric mixer with dough hook
Parchment paper [optional]
Flexible blade-spatula

The Batter: It is preferable to prepare the dough a day ahead of time. Mix the larger amount of confectioners' sugar with the powdered almonds; in another bowl, using an electric mixer, beat the soft butter with the egg, the smaller amount of sugar, the salt, and the lemon peel. Add the sugar-almond mixture and finally the flour. Do not work this dough too long. Refrigerate for at least one hour or overnight before baking. Before baking, roll out the dough ¼″ (½ cm) thick, then refrigerate for ½ hour more.

Baking: Preheat the oven to 350°F (180°C). With the pastry wheel or knife, cut the dough into 1¼″ (3 cm) squares. Using a spatula, place these squares on a buttered or parchment paper-lined baking sheet. Refrigerate the remaining cookies while the first batch is baking. Bake in a 350°F (180°C) oven for 10 minutes. Bake one sheet at a time. These cookies are very fragile when cooked so be careful when handling them.

To Store: Arlesian cookies keep for 10 days in a tightly sealed container. Allow to cool completely before storing.

197

Little Cornflower's Cookies (Sablés Corn Flower)

These cookies always delight children. Try and cut the dough into as many amusing shapes as possible.

PREPARATION — 15 minutes

RESTING TIME — 2 hours, minimum

BAKING TIME — 25 minutes per sheet

INGREDIENTS	*For 40 cookies*
	⅔ cup (100 g) confectioners' sugar
	⅓ cup (50 g) powdered almonds
	¾ cup, generous (200 g), butter
	2 eggs
	1¾ cups (250 g) flour
	1½ teaspoons (8 g) vanilla sugar
	A pinch of salt
	1½ tablespoons water
	Beaten egg to brush on top
UTENSILS	2 bowls
	Electric mixer with dough hook
	Cookie cutters (animal, star shapes, etc.)
	Spoon
	Baking sheet
	Parchment paper [optional]
	Rolling pin
	Pastry brush

The Batter: Mix half of the confectioners' sugar [⅓ cup (50 g)] with the powdered almonds. In another bowl, with the electric mixer on low speed, mix together the butter and the remaining sugar. When the mixture is smooth, add the eggs. Then add the sugar-almond mixture, the flour, vanilla sugar, and salt all at once. Beat well, then add the water. Form the dough quickly into a ball, cover and refrigerate for 2 hours or overnight.

Baking: Preheat the oven to 350°F (180°C). On a lightly floured table, roll out the dough until it is ¼" (½ cm) thick. Using cookie cutters in the shapes of stars, hearts, animals, etc., cut the dough into cookies.

Brush each cookie with a little beaten egg. Place a third of the cookies on a buttered or parchment paper-lined baking sheet. Bake for 15 minutes; then turn off the oven and leave the cookies inside to bake for 10 minutes more. Bake the remaining cookies in the same way.

To Store: These little cookies will keep 10 days in a tightly sealed container.

198

Teddybear's Cookies (Sablés Nounours)

PREPARATION	20 minutes
RESTING TIME	2 hours, minimum

BAKING TIME	15 minutes per sheet
INGREDIENTS	Same ingredients as for the preceding recipe, plus 2 tablespoons (20 g) bitter cocoa powder 10½ ounces (300 g) semi-sweet chocolate, melted

The Batter: Follow the instructions in the preceding recipe, but mix the bitter cocoa powder with the flour before adding it. When the cookies are cold, cover them with a thin layer of warm melted chocolate. Refrigerate the cookies on a piece of waxed paper (chocolate side up) for 15 minutes to obtain a shiny icing.

To Store: These cookies will keep 10 days refrigerated in a tightly sealed container.

199

Hazelnut Cookies (Sablés aux Noisettes)

PREPARATION	15 minutes
BAKING TIME	8 to 10 minutes
INGREDIENTS	*For 60 cookies* 6½ tablespoons (100 g) butter, soft ½ cup, scant (100 g), granulated sugar 3 eggs 1½ teaspoons (8 g) vanilla sugar ¾ cup (100 g) flour ¼ cup (40 g) powdered hazelnuts ½ cup, scant (75 g), coarsely chopped hazelnuts
UTENSILS	Pastry bag with a ½″ (1 cm) nozzle Wire whisk Bowl Spoon Double boiler Baking sheet

The Batter: In a double boiler, beat the softened butter with the sugar, then add the eggs one at a time and finally add the vanilla sugar. In a bowl, mix the flour with the powdered hazelnuts, then add this mixture to the above ingredients working them as little as possible until well mixed.

Baking: Preheat the oven to 400°F (200°C). On a buttered baking sheet, squeeze out the batter using a pastry bag. Make small balls as big as a walnut or shape the cookies like question marks. Sprinkle each cookie with chopped hazelnuts. Bake 8 to 10 minutes, turning around the baking sheet halfway through to ensure even browning.

Note: Do not crowd the cookies. Cook them on two baking sheets if necessary.

To Store: The cookies will keep 10 days stored in a tightly sealed container.

200
Financiers

PREPARATION	15 minutes
BAKING TIME	15 minutes
INGREDIENTS	*For 50 financiers* ¾ cup, scant (170 g), butter 1⅔ cups (250 g) confectioners' sugar 1 cup, generous (135 g), powdered almonds ⅓ cup (55 g) flour 5 egg whites = ¾ cup (155 g)
UTENSILS	1 large bowl Wooden spoon 50 small tartlet pans Small saucepan Baking sheet Parchment paper

The Batter: Melt the butter and cook until it no longer bubbles. The butter will have a slightly nutty taste and be light brown. In a bowl, mix the sugar, powdered almonds and flour. Gently stir in the egg whites, then the hot butter.

Baking: Preheat the oven to 450°F (240°C). Generously butter the tartlet pans. Fill each pan halfway with the batter and place on a baking sheet. Bake in a 450°F (240°C) oven for 5 minutes, then lower the heat to 400°F (200°C) and continue baking for 5 minutes more. Turn off the oven and wait another 5 minutes before removing. Turn out while hot onto parchment paper.

To Store: They can be kept 6 days refrigerated in a tightly sealed container.

201

Rolled Almond Cookies (Tuiles aux Amandes)

PREPARATION	15 minutes
RESTING TIME	1 hour, 30 minutes
BAKING TIME	8 minutes per sheet
INGREDIENTS	*For 50 cookies* 2 cups, generous (200 g), slivered almonds ¾ cup (185 g) granulated sugar 3 tablespoons (30 g) flour 3 egg whites = ½ cup (110 g) 2½ tablespoons (40 g) melted butter
UTENSILS	Bowl Spoon Fork Ring mold, ribbed brioche mold or rolling pin 3 baking sheets Parchment paper [optional] Spatula

The Batter: In a bowl, mix the almonds, sugar, and flour, then add the egg whites and the melted butter. Mix well, then leave the batter 1 hour and 30 minutes in the refrigerator before baking.

Baking: Preheat the oven to 350°F (180°C). On a buttered or parchment paper-lined baking sheet, drop the cookies, using a tablespoon. Flatten each mound with a fork dipped in milk. The cookies have to be nearly flat; if not, the center of the cookie will not bake. Place about 16 to 18 cookies on a baking sheet. Bake each sheet, one at a time, for 8 to 10 minutes or until the cookies are golden brown. As soon as the cookies are baked, remove from the oven. Lift each cookie off the baking sheet with a spatula and roll it around the rolling pin to shape it and allow to cool. The cookies can also be shaped by pressing them into a ribbed brioche mold or a ring mold, then allowing them to cool.

To Store: These cookies will keep 6 days in a tightly sealed container.

CROSS INDEX
Basic Recipes and the Desserts that Use Them

The following is a listing of the basic recipes included in this book, along with the numbers of the recipes that they are used in. If, for example, you have made a pastry that uses flaky pastry dough and you find you have some left, you can consult this listing to determine what other recipes in the book also use flaky pastry dough.

1. **Ladyfingers:** Recipes 134, 142, 156, 157, 158, 159
2. **Jelly Roll:** Recipes 66, 67, 68, 70
3. **Classic Flaky Pastry:** Recipes 49, 54, 58, 82, 83, 84, 85, 90, 94, 99, 102, 109, 122, 132, 189, 192, 194
4. **Quick Flaky Pastry:** Recipes 49, 54, 58, 82, 83, 84, 85, 90, 94, 99, 102, 109, 122, 132, 192
5. **Succès Batter:** Recipes 92, 110, 112, 119
6. **Génoise:** Recipes 61, 64, 73, 74, 75, 76, 78, 79, 80, 86, 88, 91
7. **French Meringue:** Recipes 68, 74, 81, 86, 116, 117
8. **Swiss Meringue:** Recipes 67, 68, 69, 70
9. **Brioche Dough:** Recipes 39, 40, 41, 42, 43, 44, 51, 56, 96
10. **Short Pastry:** Recipes 37, 93, 103, 104, 105, 108, 131
11. **Cream Puff Pastry:** Recipes 87, 90, 111, 113, 114, 115, 121, 122, 123, 184, 185, 186, 187
12. **Sweet Short Pastry:** Recipes 37, 98, 100, 106, 118, 131, 133, 134, 188
13. **Chantilly Cream:** Recipes 75, 76, 77, 79, 83, 84, 85, 87, 106, 114, 116, 118, 120, 122, 124, 137, 149, 156, 157, 158, 159, 165, 166
14. **Chocolate Chantilly:** Recipe 73
15. **Fresh Fruit Sauce:** Recipes 149, 152, 160, 162, 166
16. **Caramel Sauce:** Recipe 152
17. **Almond Pastry Cream:** Recipes 37, 44, 49, 54, 56, 58, 60, 103, 108, 126, 127, 128, 129, 130, 134, 188
18. **Homemade Almond Paste:** Recipes 57, 122, 134
19. **Chiboust Pastry Cream:** Recipes 87, 90, 120, 121
20. **Butter Cream:** Recipes 64, 66, 78
21. **Coffee-Flavored Butter Cream:** Recipe 66
22. **Chocolate Butter Cream:** Recipes 66, 117
23. **Almond Butter Cream:** Recipes 66, 92, 112, 119, 125
24. **Vanilla Pastry Cream:** Recipes 44, 50, 56, 61, 66, 83, 85, 87, 96, 99, 100, 106, 111, 115, 120, 121, 123, 124, 132, 133, 136, 155, 185, 186, 187
25. **Coffee Pastry Cream:** Recipes 76, 113, 184
26. **Chocolate Pastry Cream:** Recipes 79, 113
27. **Chocolate Icing:** Recipes 71, 79, 80, 112, 113, 184
28. **Fondant Icing:** Recipes 86, 113, 115, 123, 184, 185
29. **Dessert Syrup:** Recipes 44, 61, 64, 66, 69, 70, 73, 74, 75, 76, 78, 79, 80, 88, 152, 155, 156
30. **Chocolate Mousse:** Recipes 66, 69, 72, 81, 110, 117, 153
31. **Chocolate Sauce:** Recipes 97, 137, 141, 152, 158
32. **Vanilla Sauce:** Recipes 97, 153, 156, 157, 159, 160, 161, 163, 164, 165, 166
33. **Bavarian Cream:** Recipes 66, 149, 152
36. **Almond Paste Decoration:** Recipes 61, 67, 68, 69, 70, 78, 80
41. **Brioche Mousseline:** Recipes 60, 152, 153, 154
43. **Brioche Parisienne:** Recipes 152, 153, 154, 155
47. **Croissants:** Recipe 55
62. **Basic Baba Dough:** Recipes 63, 124
179. **Apple Sauce:** Recipes 53, 94, 102

INDEX

Page numbers in **boldface** type indicate pages with color plates.

Abricots (apricots):
- *au sirop* (stewed in wine), 266-7
- *frais avec leurs noyaux* (stewed whole), 267

Allumettes glacées (glazed match sticks), 290-1, **295**

Almond(s) *(amandes):*
- butter cream *(crème au beurre praliné),* 70
- butter cream pastries *(colisées),* **193**, 194
- cake, strawberry *(fraisier),* **62**, 141-3
- caramelized, 16
- cookies, rolled *(tuiles aux amandes),* 305
- cream puffs *(choux pralinés),* 191-2, **196**
- paste, homemade *(pâte d'amandes à faire chez soi),* 66
- paste decorations *(décors en pâte d'amandes),* **12**, 85
- pastry cream *(crème d'amandes),* 65-6
- slices, brioche *(tranches de brioche aux amandes),* 118-9
- soufflé *(soufflé aux amandes),* 231
- Succès *(Succès praliné),* **95**, 163-4

Almondines, cherry *(amandines aux cerises),* 89

Alsatian Kugelhopf, 9, 110

Amandines aux cerises (cherry almondines), 89

Ambassador cake *(ambassadeur):*
- almond paste decoration for, 85
- recipe for, 123

Appareil (creams):
- *à Bavaroise* (Bavarian cream), 81-2
- *à charlotte* (charlotte cream), 82
- *à soufflé* (basic soufflé), 82-4

Apple(s) *(pommes):*
- charlotte *(charlotte aux pommes),* 256, **272**
- dartois *(dartois aux pommes),* **97**, 168-70
- sauce *(compote de pommes),* 276-7
- soufflé with Calvados, 239-40
- tart, country-style *(tarte paysanne),* 185-6
- tart, Eleanor's *(tarte Eléonore),* **142**, 179-80
- tart, St. Nicholas' *(tarte normande),* 183-4

Apricot(s) *(abricots):*
- cake *(regent a l'abricot),* 158-9
- in fresh fruit sauce, 63
- jam as a glaze, 18-9
- pineapple cake *(Singapour aux abricots),* 162-3
- stewed in wine *(au sirop),* 266-7
- stewed whole *(frais avec leurs noyaux),* 267
- tart *(tarte aux abricots),* 174-5
- tartlets *(tartelettes aux abricots),* **207**, 215

Arlesian cookies *(sablés arlésiens),* 300-1

Autumn meringue cake *(meringue d'automne),* 9, 43, 44, **72**, 151-2

Baba(s):
- *au rhum* (rum baba), 125-6
- basic dough *(pâte à babas),* 124

Bagatelle:
- almond paste decorations for, 85
- *aux fraises* (strawberry cake), 126-7, **129**

Bain-marie, 15

Baking:
- position in oven, 15
- quality of baking sheet, 16
- using baking sheet, 15

Banana(s):
- *au sirop* (stewed bananas), 268
- stewed, 268
- tart *(tarte antillaise aux bananes),* **120**, 176-7

Basic baba dough *(pâte à babas),* 124

Basic recipes:
- creams, 57-85
- doughs, 29-56
- explanation of, 9-10

Basic soufflé *(appareil à soufflé),* 82-4

Basque cake *(gâteau Basque),* 107-8

Batters, basic recipes for, 29-56

Bavarian cream:
- cream for *(appareil à bavaroise),* 81-2
- cream-filled brioche *(brioche Estelle),* 246-7
- fresh fruit sauce for, 63
- fruit-flavored *(bavarois sans alcool),* 243
- vanilla sauce for, 80

Bavarois sans alcool (fruit-flavored Bavarian cream), 243

Beaten egg, for glaze, 19

Beignets mille fruits (fruit fritters), 225-6

Biscuits:
- *à la cuillère* (ladyfingers), 31-2
- *de l'Oncle Tom* (Uncle Tom's cake), 128-9
- *de savoie* (Savoy sponge cake), 89-90
- *roulé* (jelly roll dough), 32-3
- *roulés* (rolled cakes), 130-1

Blueberry tartlets *(tartelettes aux myrtilles),* 214, **294**

Bordelaise brioche, 90-1

Bowls, 16

Bread and butter pudding, 244, **255**

Breakfast cakes, 87-119

Brioche:
- almond pastry cream for *(crème d'amandes),* 65
- almond slices *(tranches de brioche aux amandes),* 118-9
- Bavarian cream-filled *(brioche Estelle),* 246-7
- Bordelaise, 90-1
- cheese *(la chantellée),* 171-3
- chocolate mousse-filled *(brioche Estelle à la mousse),* 247
- dough *(pâte à brioche surfine),* 45-50
- *Estelle au bavarois* (brioche filled with Bavarian cream), 81, 246-7
- filled, general comments, 246, 250
- fruit salad-filled *(salpicon de fruits en brioche),* 248, **258**
- fruit sauce with, 63
- individual, 92
- molds, 27
- mousseline, **13**, 93
- nanterre, **13**, 94
- Parisienne, **13**, 96
- polonaise, 96, 249-50, **259**
- rolled with candied fruit *(roulée aux fruits confits),* **23**, 98-9
- royal pudding *(pudding royal),* 173-4

Bûche (log):
- *au café* (coffee-flavored), **48**, 133-4
- *au chocolat* (chocolate log), 134-5
- *aux marrons* (chestnut log), 136
- *fraisier* (strawberry log), **47**, 131-2

Buns, raisin *(pains aux raisins),* **2**, 114-5

Butter, 16

Butter cream *(crème au beurre nature):*
- almond *(crème au beurre praliné),* 70
- basic recipe for, 68-9
- chocolate *(crème au beurre au chocolat),* 70
- coffee-flavored *(crème au beurre au café),* 69
- pastries, almond butter cream *(colisées),* **193**, 194

Buttering pans and molds, 16, 19

Caissettes oranges (orange cream tartlets), 291-2

Cake(s):
- ambassador *(ambassadeur),* 123
- apricot *(régent à l'abricot),* 158-9
- apricot-pineapple *(Singapour aux abricots),* 162-3

Autumn meringue *(meringue d'automne),* **72**, 151-2
aux fruits confits (fruit cake), 99-100
Basque *(gâteau Basque),* 107-8
chestnut *(marronier),* 149-50
concord *(concorde),* **59**, 138-40
Easter *(gâteau de Pâques),* **71**, 146-7
French twelfth-night *(galette des rois aux amandes),* 105-6
fruit *(aux fruits confits),* 99-100
Genoa *(pain de Gênes),* 115-6
Ivory Coast *(côte d'ivoire),* 140-1
large, 121-164
layer, 19
Mexican *(gâteau mexicain),* 145
mocha *(moka au café),* 155-6
Pentecost *(colombier de la Pentecôte),* 101-2
prune or raisin *(far aux pruneaux ou aux raisins),* 170-1
rolled *(biscuits roulés),* 130-1
Savoy sponge *(biscuit de savoie),* 89-90
strawberry almond *(fraisier),* **62**, 141-3
strawberry *(bagatelle aux fraises),* 126-7, **129**
Uncle Tom's *(biscuit de l'Oncle Tom),* 128-9
upside down orange *(rosace à l'orange),* **83**, 159-60
Cantaloupe, stewed *(compote de melons verts),* 276
Caramel:
almond puffs *(choux pralinés),* **283**, 288-9
almond soufflé *(soufflé praliné),* **232**, 237-8
custard *(crème à la vanille caramelisée),* **217**, 257-60
sauce *(caramel liquide),* 64
Caramelized almonds, 16
Carolines (miniature eclairs), **283**, 285-6
Chantilly:
chocolate *(chantilly au chocolat),* 61
cream *(chantilly nature vanillée),*60
Charlottes:
apple *(charlotte aux pommes),* 256, **272**
aux fraises ou au framboises (strawberry or raspberry charlotte), 251-2
aux marrons (chestnut charlotte), 252-3
aux pêches ou aux poires (peach or pear charlotte), 254
aux pommes (apple charlotte), 256, **272**
caramel sauce for, 64
Cécile (chocolate-vanilla charlotte), 250-1, **269**
chestnut *(charlotte aux marrons),* 272-3
chocolate mousse for, 78
chocolate-vanilla *(charlotte cécile),* 250-1, **269**
cream *(appareil à charlotte),* 82
fruit sauce for, 63
peach or pear *(charlotte aux pêches ou aux poires),* 254
strawberry or raspberry *(charlotte aux fraises ou au framboises),* 251-2
vanilla sauce for, 80
Chataigneraie, 137-8
Chefs' hats, as a symbol, 9-10
Cheese brioche *(la chantellée),* 171-3
Cherry:
almondines *(amandines aux cerises),* 89
molds, 51
tartlets *(tartelettes aux cerises),* **207**, 212-3
Chestnut:
cake *(marronier),* 149-50
charlotte *(charlotte aux marrons),* 272-3
cream, 16
soufflé *(soufflé aux marrons),* 236
Yule log *(bûche aux marrons),* 136
Chiboust:
pastry cream *(crème chibouste),* 67-8
Saint Honoré, **86**, 160-2
Chocolate:
butter cream *(crème au beurre au chocolat),* 70
chantilly *(chantilly au chocolat),* 61
eclairs *(éclairs au café ou au chocolat),* 195, **196**
heads *(meringues tête de nègre),* **193**, 199-200
icing *(glaçage au chocolat),* 75-6
marquise *(marquise au chocolat),* 148-9
mousse *(mousse au chocolat),* 78-9
mousse-filled brioche *(brioche Estelle à la mousse au chocolat),* 247
pastry cream *(crème pâtissière au chocolat),* 73
rice pudding *(riz au chocolat pour Géraldine),* 263-4
rolls *(pains au chocolat),* **36**, 113-4
sauce *(sauce au chocolat),* 79-80
soufflé *(soufflé au chocolat),* **232**, 234
-vanilla charlotte *(charlotte cécile),* 250-1, **269**
Yule log *(bûche au chocolat),* **48**, 134-5
Chocolatines, 40, 41, 191, **193**
Choux:
au Grand Marnier ou au Kirsch (cream puffs with Grand Marnier or Kirsch filling), **283**, 286-7
pralinés (almond cream puffs), 191-2, **196**; also (caramel almond puffs), **283**, 288-9
Christmas log, *see* Yule logs; see also Holiday cakes
Clafoutis tutti frutti (fruit flan), 51, **77**, 167-8
Classic flaky pastry *(feuilletage classique),* 33-35
Coconut soufflé *(soufflé à la noix de coco),* 238-9
Coffee:
butter cream *(crème au beurre au café),* 69
cakes, 87-119
eclairs *(éclairs au café ou au chocolat),* 195, **196**
pastry cream *(crème pâtissière au café),* 73
Cold desserts, 241-279
Colisées (almond butter cream pastries), 40, 41, **193**, 194
Colombier de la Pentecôte (Pentecost cake):
almond paste for, 66
recipe for, 101-2
Compote:
de melons verts (stewed muskmelon or cantaloupe), 276
de pommes (apple sauce), 276-7
de rubarbe (stewed rhubarb), 277
Compressed baker's yeast, 22
Concord cake *(concorde),* **59**, 138-40
Confectioners' sugar for glazing, 18-9
Congolese cookies *(rochers congolais),* 299-300
Cookies:
arlesian *(sablés arlésiens),* 300-1
congolese *(rochers congolais),* 299-300
hazelnut *(sablés aux noisettes),* 303-4
Little Cornflower's *(sablés corn flower),* 301-2
raisin *(palets aux raisins),* 297-8
rolled almond *(tuiles aux amandes),* 305
teddybear's *(sablés nounours),* 140-1
Côte d'ivoire (Ivory Coast cake), 140-1
Coulis de fruits frais (fresh fruit sauce), 63
Country style apple tart *(tarte paysanne),* 185-6
Cream(s), 57-85:
Bavarian *(appareil à bavaroise),* 81-2
butter *(crème au beurre nature),* 68-9
charlotte *(appareil à charlotte),* 82
Cream cakes, hazelnut *(noisettines),* **193**, 201-2

Cream puffs:
  almond *(choux pralinés),* 191-2, **196**
  pastry for *(pâte à chou),* 53-5
  salambo, **196**, 208-9
  with Grand Marnier or Kirsch filling *(choux au Grand Marnier ou au Kirsch),* **283**, 286-7
Crème:
  à la vanille caramelisée (caramel custard), **217**, 257-60
  au beurre au café (coffee-flavored butter cream), 69
  au beurre au chocolat (chocolate butter cream), 70
  au beurre nature (butter cream), 68-9
  au beurre praliné (almond butter cream), 70
  chibouste (chiboust pastry cream), 67-8
  d'amandes (almond pastry cream), 65-6
  de marrons (chestnut cream), 16
  pâtissière au café (coffee pastry cream), 73
  pâtissière au chocolat (chocolate pastry cream), 73
  pâtissière vanillée (vanilla pastry cream), 70
Crêpes:
  Suzette, **220**, 226-7
  vanilla pastry cream for, 70
Croissants, **36**, 102-4, 113
Cross-indexing in this book, 10, 306
Custard, caramel *(crème à la vanille caramelisée),* **217**, 257-60

Dartois, apple *(aux pommes),* **97**, 168-70
Decorations, almond paste *(décors en pâte d'amandes),* 85
Dessert(s):
  large, 121-164
  omelette with rum *(omelette flambée au rhum),* 230-1
  syrup *(sirop à entremets),* 77-8
Diamond-studded circles *(diamants),* 292-3, **295**
Dictionary of terms and procedures, 15-22
Difficulty of recipes, 9-10
Doigts de fée, 44-5
Double boiler, 15
Dough(s):
  baba *(pâte à babas),* 124
  basic recipes, 29-56
  brioche *(pâte à brioche surfine),* 45-50
  cream puff *(pâte à chou),* 53-4
  cutting, 17
  flaky pastry *(feuilletage classique, rapide),* 33-9
  Genoise, 42-3
  hook, 45-50
  jelly roll *(biscuit roulé),* 32-3
  kneading, 18
  ladyfinger *(biscuit à la cuillère),* 31-2
  meringue, French *(meringue française),* 43-44
  meringue, Swiss *(meringue suisse),* 44-5
  pricking, 20
  refrigerating, 20
  short pastry *(pâte brisée),* 51-3
  Succès *(fond de Succès),* 40-1
  sweet short pastry *(pâte sucrée),* 55-6
Dried figs stewed in wine *(figues au sirop),* 268-70
Dutch pithiviers *(pithiviers hollandais),* 117-8

Easter cake *(gâteau de Pâques),* **71**, 146-7
Eclair(s):
  coffee or chocolate *(éclairs au café ou au chocolat),* 195, **196**
  forming, 54
  large, with chantilly cream *(gros éclairs à la chantilly),* **196**, 197
  martiniquais (pineapple eclairs), 198
  miniature *(carolines),* 285-6
  pineapple *(martiniquais),* 198
Egg(s):
  in recipes, 17
  measuring, 17
  whites, 17-8
Eleanor's Apple Tart *(tarte Eléonore),* **142**, 179-80
Electric mixer:
  for brioche dough, 49
  speeds of, 17
Epiphany cake, *see* French Twelfth-night cake

Far aux pruneaux ou aux raisins (prune or raisin cake), 170-1
Feuilletage:
  classique (classic flaky pastry), 33-5
  rapide (quick flaky pastry), 38-9
fève, 105
Figs, dried, stewed in wine *(figues au sirop),* 268-70
Filled brioche, 246-50
Fillings, 57-85
Financiers:
  almond paste for, 66
  recipe for, 304
Flaky pastry:
  classic *(feuilletage classique),* 33-5
  cutting, 17
  quick *(feuilletage rapide),* 38-40
  rolling out, 34-35, 39
  turning, 21
Flan, fruit *(clafoutis tutti frutti),* **77**, 167-8
Flan rings using, 17
Flat-bottomed bowls, 16
Flexible blade spatula, 21
Floating island *(ile flottante),* 261-2
Flour:
  used in recipes, 18
  measuring, 18
Folding egg whites, 17-8
Fondant:
  chocolate icing as a substitute for, 75
  icing *(glaçage au fondant),* 76-7
  recipe for, 18
Fond de Succès (Succès batter), 40-1
Fraises au sirop (stewed strawberries), 270-1
Fraisier, 18, 52, 141-3
French meringue *(meringue française),* 43-4
French Twelfth-night cake *(galette des rois aux amandes),* 105-6
Fresh fruit sauce *(coulis de fruits frais),* 63
Friands:
  almond paste for, 66
  recipe for, 104-5
Fritters, fruit *(beignets mille fruits),* 225-6
Fruit(s):
  cake *(cake aux fruits confits),* 99-100
  flan *(clafoutis tutti frutti),* 9, **97**, 167-8
  -flavored Bavarian cream *(bavarois sans alcool),* 243, **245**
  fritters *(beignets mille fruits),* 225-6
  mixed, stewed in wine *(fruits panachés au sirop),* 271
  salad-filled brioche *(salpicon de fruits en brioche),* 248, **258**
  sauce, fresh *(coulis de fruits frais),* 63
  stewed, *see* Stewed fruit
  syrup for stewing, 266
  tartlets, basic recipe, 212. *See also* individual fruits
  tartlets, miniature *(mini-tartelettes aux fruits),* **283**, 289-90, **294**
Fruits panachés au sirop (mixed fruit stewed in wine), 271

Galette des rois aux amandes (French Twelfth-night cake), 105-6
Gâteau:
  Basque (Basque cake), 107-8
  de madame, 143-4
  de Pâques (Easter cake), **71**, 146-7
  de semoule aux raisins (semolina cake with raisins), 260-1
  mexicain (Mexican cake), 145
Gaufres (waffles), 228, **229**
Gelée de groseilles (red currant jelly), 279
"Generous" measure, 22

Genoa cake (pain de Gênes):
almond paste for, 66
recipe for, 115-6
Génoise:
cutting, 19
fresh fruit sauce with, 63
recipe for, 42-3
Glaçage:
au chocolat (chocolate icing), 75-6
au fondant (fondant icing), 76-7
Glazed apple tart, *see* Normandy tart with royal icing
Glazed match sticks *(allumettes glacées)*, 290-1, **295**
Glazing:
beaten egg for, 19
confectioners' sugar for, 18-9
fondant, 18
oven use for, 15
procedures for, 18-9
Grand Marnier soufflé, 235
Granulated dry yeast, 22
Greasing pans and molds, 16
Gros éclairs à la chantilly (large eclairs with chantilly cream), **196**, 197

Hazelnut(s):
caramelized, 16
cookies *(sablés aux noisettes)*, 303-4
cream cakes *(noisettines)*, **193**, 201-2
Heads, chocolate *(meringues tête de nègre)*, **193**, 199-200
Holiday cakes:
Easter cake *(gâteau de Pâques)*, **71**, 146-7
Pentecost cake *(colombier de la Pentecôte)*, 101-2
Twelfth-night cake *(galette des rois aux amandes)*, 105-6
Yule logs *(bûche)*, **47**, **48**, 131-6
Homemade almond paste *(pâte d'amandes à faire chez soi)*, 66
Hot desserts, 223-240

Ice cream with caramel sauce, 64
Icing:
chocolate *(glaçage au chocolat)*, 75-6
fondant *(glaçage au fondant)*, 76-7
Ile flottante (floating island), 261-2
Individual brioche, 92
Individual St. Honoré cakes, 205-8
Individual savarin cakes, 206, 209-210
Ingredients, quality of, 11-14
Italian meringue:
for chiboust pastry cream, 67
for strawberry Yule log, 131-2
Ivory Coast cake *(côte d'ivoire)*, 140-1

Jelly, red currant *(gelée de groseilles)*, 279
Jelly roll dough *(biscuit roulé)*, 32-3

Kneading:
brioche dough, 49
short pastry dough, 52
sweet short pastry dough, 56
Kugelhopf:
Alsatian, 110
Lenôtre, 108-9, **109**

La chantellée (cheese brioche), 171-3
Ladyfingers *(biscuits à la cuillère)*, 31-2
La nouvelle cuisine française, 11
La nouvelle pâtisserie française, 11
Large cakes, 121-164
Large desserts, 121-164
Large eclairs with chantilly cream *(gros éclairs à la chantilly)*, **196**, 197
Layer cakes, 19
Lemon:
meringue pie *(tarte au citron meringuée)*, 178-9, **181**
soufflé *(soufflé au citron etoilé)*, 233
Lenôtre, Gaston:
his career, 7-9
his school, 8
Lenôtre kugelhopf, 108-9, **109**
Letchis au sirop (stewed lichees), 273
Lichees, stewed *(letchis au sirop)*, 273
Linzer torte, 110-11
Little Cornflower's cookies *(sablés corn flower)*, 301-2
Little pastries, 189-221
Loire Valley millefeuille *(millefeuille val-de-loire)*, 154

Making meringue shells, 41
Marble surface, for working dough, 21
Marly, raspberry *(marly aux framboises):*
almond paste decoration for, 85
recipe for, 147-8
Marquise, chocolate *(marquise au chocolat)*, 148-9
Marronier (chestnut cake), 149-50
Match sticks, glazed *(allumettes glacées)*, 290-1
Measure(s) and measuring:
ingredients, 22
pans for baking, 19
Meringue:
à la chantilly (meringues with chantilly cream), **193**, 199
chantilly, 43
d'automne (Autumn meringue cake), 9, **72**, 151-2
French *(meringue française)*, 43-4
Italian, for chiboust pastry cream, 67-8
mushrooms, forming, 44, 45
pie, lemon *(tarte au citron meringuée)*, 178-9, **181**
snowmen, forming, 44
Swiss *(meringue suisse)*, 44-5
tête de nègre (chocolate heads), **193**, 199-200
with chantilly cream *(meringues à la chantilly)*, **193**, 199
Mexican cake *(gâteau mexicain)*, 145
Millefeuille:
Loire Valley *(millefeuille val-de-loire)*, 154
preparation, 152
strawberry or raspberry *(millefeuille aux fraises ou aux framboises)*, 154-5
with vanilla pastry cream *(millefeuille à la crème pâtissière)*, 153
Miniature eclairs *(carolines)*, **283**, 285-6
Miniature fruit tartlets *(mini-tartlettes aux fruits)*, **283**, 289-90, **294**
Mirabelle(s):
plum tart *(tarte aux mirabelles)*, 180-1
plum tartlets *(tartelettes aux mirabelles)*, 213, **294**
Mirlitons, 112
Mixed fruit stewed in wine *(fruits panachés au sirop*, 271
Mixing bowls, 16
Mocha cake *(moka au café)*, 155-6
Molds:
size, 19
turning out from, 21-2
Mont-Blanc, 200-1
Mousse, chocolate *(mousse au chocolat)*, 78-9
Mousseline brioche, **13**, 93
Muskmelon, stewed *(compote de melons verts)*, 276

Nanterre brioche, **13**, 94
Napoleons, vanilla pastry cream for, 70
New school of French pastry, 11
Noisettines (hazelnut cream cakes):
recipe for, **193**, 201-202
Succès batter for, 40, 41
Non-stick paper for baking, 19-20
Normandy tart with royal icing *(tarte normande glace royale)*, 82
Nozzles for pastry bags, 20
Nut brittle, 16

Oeufs à la neige (snow eggs), 262-3, **284**
Omelette, dessert with rum *(omelette flambée au rhum)*, 230-1
Orange(s):
cream tartlets *(caissettes oranges)*, 291-2
tart *(tarte aux oranges)*, 184-5
upside down cake *(rosace à l'orange)*, **83**, 159-60
with grenadine syrup *(oranges à la grenadine)*, 278
Orange-flower water, 19

Oven, preheating the, 20

Pain de Gênes (Genoa cake), 115-6
Pains:
  au chocolat (chocolate rolls), **36**, 113-4
  aux raisins (raisin buns), **2**, 114-5
Palets aux raisins (raisin cookies), 297-8
Palmiers, **295**, 298-9
Pans, 19
Parchment paper, 19-20
Paris-brest:
  chiboust cream for, 67-8
  individual pastries, **74**, 202-3
  large pastry, **74**, 156-8
  shaping the dough for, 54, 55
Parisienne brioche, **13**, 96
Pastry:
  bags, 20
  techniques, 313-320
Pastry cream:
  almond *(crème d'amandes)*, 65-6
  chiboust *(crème chibouste)*, 67-8
  chocolate *(crème pâtissière au chocolat)*, 73
  coffee *(crème pâtissière au café)*, 73
  vanilla *(crème pâtissière vanillée)*, 70-3
Pastries, almond butter cream *(colisées)*, **193**, 194
Pastries, small, 189-221
Pâte:
  à babas (basic baba dough), 124
  à brioche surfine (brioche dough), 45-50
  à chou (cream puff pastry), 53-4
  brisée (short pastry), 51-3
  d'amandes à faire chez soi (homemade almond paste), 66
  sucrée (sweet short pastry), 55-6
Peach(es):
  charlotte *(charlotte aux pêches ou aux poires)*, 254
  in fresh fruit sauce, 63
  stewed in wine *(pêches au sirop)*, 273-4
Pear(s):
  charlotte *(charlotte aux pêches ou aux poires)*, 254
  stewed with honey *(poires au sirop)*, 274-5
  tart with almonds *(tarte aux poires ou aux pêches aux amandes)*, **169**, 186-7
  tartlets *(tartelettes aux poires)*, 207, 214-5
Pentecost cake *(colombier de la Pentecôte)*, 101-2
Petit fours:
  general comments, 285
  shaping meringue for, 45
Pie, lemon meringue *(tarte au citron meringuée)*, 178-9, **181**
Pies and tarts, 165-188
Pineapple:
  eclairs *(éclairs martiniquais)*, 198
  tart *(tarte feuilletée a l'ananas)*, 175-6
  tartlets *(tartelettes a l'ananas)*, 216, **294**
Pistachio soufflé *(soufflé aux pistaches)*, 236-7
Pithiviers:
  basic recipe, **37**, 116-7
  Dutch *(pithiviers hollandais)*, 117-8
Plastic scraper, 20
Plum:
  tart *(tarte aux mirabelles)*, 180-1
  tartlets, Mirabelle *(tartelettes aux mirabelles)*, 213, **294**
Poires au sirop (stewed pears with honey), 274-5
Powdered caramelized almonds, 16
Powdered vanilla, 22
Praliné, 16
Preheating oven, 20
Preparing molds for baking, 19
Pricking dough, 20
Profiteroles, chocolate sauce for, 79
Prune(s):
  or raisin cake *(far aux pruneaux ou aux raisins)*, 170-1
  stewed in wine *(pruneaux au sirop)*, 275
Pudding(s):
  bread and butter, 244
  chocolate rice *(riz au chocolat pour Geraldine)*, 263-4
  fresh fruit sauce for, 63
  rice, with eight treasures *(riz impératrice aux huit trésors)*, 264-5, **284**
  royal, 173-4
Puff pastry, *see* Flaky pastry
Puffs, almond cream *(choux pralinés)*, 191-2, **196**
Puits d'amour (wells of love), 203-4

Quantities, determining, 20
Quick flaky pastry *(feuilletage rapide)*, 38-9

Raisin:
  buns *(pains aux raisins)*, **2**, 114-5
  cookies *(palets aux raisins)*, 297-8
  or prune cake *(far aux pruneaux ou aux raisins)*, 170-1
Raspberries:
  charlotte *(charlotte aux fraises ou au framboises)*, 251-2
  in fresh fruit sauce, 63
  marly *(marly aux framboises)*, 147-8
  millefeuille *(millefeuille aux fraises ou aux framboises)*, 154-5
Red currant jelly *(gelèe de groseilles)*, 279
Refrigeration of dough, 20
Régent à l'abricot (apricot cake), 158-9
Rhubarb, stewed *(compote de rubarbe)*, 277
Ribbon, 20
Rice pudding:
  chocolate *(riz au chocolate pour Géraldine)*, 263-4
  with eight treasures *(riz impératrice aux huit trésors)*, 264-5, **284**
Rochers congolais (congolese cookies), 299-300
Rolled:
  almond cookies *(tuiles aux amandes)*, 305-6
  brioche with candied fruit *(brioche roulée aux fruits confits)*, **23**, 98-9
  cakes *(biscuits roulés)*, 130-1
Rolls, chocolate *(pains au chocolat)*, **36**, 113-4
Rosace *à l'orange (upside down orange cake)*, 9, **83**, 159-60
Royal brioche pudding, 173-4
Rum:
  as ingredient, 21
  baba *(babas au rhum)*, 125-6
  -flavored salambos, **283**, 287-8

Sablès:
  arlesiens (arlesian cookies), 300-1
  aux noisettes (hazelnut cookies), 303-4
  corn flower (Little Cornflower's cookies), 301-2
  nounours (teddybear's cookies), 302-3
Sacristains, 296-7, **296**
Saint-Honoré:
  chiboust cream for, 67-68
  recipe for individual pastries, **86**, 205-8
  recipe for large pastry, **86**, 160-2
  shaping the meringue for, 55
Saint Nicholas' apple tart *(tarte normande Saint-Nicolas)*, 183-4
Salambos:
  cream puffs, **196**, 208-9
  rum-flavored, **283**, 287-8
Salpicon de fruits en brioche (brioche filled with fruit salad), 248, **258**
Sauce:
  apple *(compote de pommes)*, 276-7
  chocolate *(sauce au chocolat)*, 79-80
  vanilla *(sauce à la vanille)*, 80-1
Savarin cakes, individual, **206**, 209-10
Saving egg whites, 17
Savoy sponge cake *(biscuit de savoie)*, 89-90
Scales, 22
"Scant" measure, 22
Scraper, plastic, 20
Semolina cake with raisins *(gâteau de semoule aux raisins)*, 260-1
Short pastry dough *(pâte brisée)*, 9, 51-3

Singapour aux abricots (apricot-pineapple cake), 162-3
Sirop à entremets (dessert syrup), 77-8
Small pastries, 189-221
Snow eggs *(oeufs à la neige)*, 262-3, **284**
Softened butter, 16
Soufflé:
- almond *(soufflé aux amandes)*, 231
- apple, with Calvados *(soufflé aux pommes)*, 239-40
- basic recipe for *(appareil à soufflé)*, 82-4
- caramel almond *(soufflé praliné)*, 232, 237-8
- chestnut *(soufflé aux marrons)*, 236
- chocolate *(soufflé au chocolat)*, **232**, 234
- coconut *(soufflé à la noix de coco)*, 238-9
- Grand Marnier, 235
- lemon *(soufflé au citron etoilé)*, 233
- pistachio *(soufflé aux pistaches)*, 236-7
- praline *(soufflé praliné)*, 232, 237-8
- vanilla *(soufflé à la vanille)*, 240

Spatula, 21
Sponge cake, Savoy *(biscuit de savoie)*, 89-90
Stewed fruit:
- apricots in wine *(abricots au sirop)*, 266-7
- apricots, whole *(abricots frais avec leurs noyaux)*, 267
- bananas *(bananes au sirop)*, 268
- cantaloupe *(compote de melons verts)*, 276
- general comments, 266
- lichees *(letchis au sirop)*, 273
- muskmelon *(compote de melons verts)*, 276
- peaches in wine *(pêches au sirop)*, 273
- pears with honey *(poires au sirop)*, 274-5
- prunes in wine *(pruneaux au sirop)*, 275
- rhubarb *(compote de rubarbe)*, 277
- strawberries *(fraises au sirop)*, 270-1

Strawberries:
- almond cake *(fraisier)*, **62**, 141-3
- cake *(bagatelle aux fraises)*, 126-7, **129**
- charlotte *(charlotte aux fraises ou au framboises)*, 251-2
- in fresh fruit sauce, 63
- millefeuille *(millefeuille aux fraises ou aux framboises)*, 154-5
- stewed *(fraises au sirop)*, 270-1
- Yule log *(bûche fraisier)*, **47**, 131-2

Succès:
- almond *(succès praliné)*, **95**, 163-4
- batter *(fond de succès)*, 40-1
- praliné *(almond succès)*, **95**, 163-4
- small, 211

Sunshine tartlets *(tartelettes coup de soleil)*, **207**, 218
Sweet short pastry *(pâte sucrée)*, 55-6
Swiss meringue *(meringue suisse)*, 44-5
Syrup(s):
- basic recipes for, 57-85
- dessert *(sirop à entremets)*, 77-8

Tartlets:
- apricot *(tartelettes aux abricots)*, **207**, 215
- basic recipe, 212
- blueberry *(tartelettes aux myrtilles)*, 214, **294**
- cherry *(tartelettes aux cerises)*, **207**, 212-3
- miniature fruit *(mini-tartelettes aux fruit)*, **283**, 289-90, **294**
- mirabelle plum *(tartelettes aux mirabelles)*, 213, **294**
- orange cream *(caissettes oranges)*, 291-2
- pear *(tartelettes aux poires)*, **207**, 214-5
- pineapple *(tartelettes à l'ananas)*, 216, **294**
- sunshine *(tartelettes coup de soleil)*, **207**, 218
- walnut *(val d'isère)*, 219-21

Tarts:
- almond pastry cream for *(crème d'amandes)*, 65-6
- apricot *(tarte aux abricots)*, 174-5
- banana *(tarte antillaise aux bananes)*, 120, 176-7
- Eleanor's apple *(tarte Eléonore)*, 142, 179-80
- flan rings for, 17
- friands, 104-5
- mirabelle plum *(tarte aux mirabelles)*, 180-1
- orange *(tarte aux oranges)*, 184-5
- pear or peach with almonds *(tarte aux poires ou aux pêches aux amandes)*, **169**, 186-7
- pineapple *(tarte feuilletée a l'ananas)*, 175-6
- St. Nicholas' apple *(tarte normande Saint-Nicolas)*, 183-4
- turning out, 21-2

Tarte, see Tarts
Tartelette, see Tartlets
Teddybear's cookies *(sablés nounours)*, 302-3
Testing of recipes, 14
Têtes de nègre (chocolate heads), 43, 44, **193**, 199-200
Time, preparation, 21
Torte, Linzer, 110-1
Tranches de brioche aux amandes (brioche almond slices), 118-9
Tuiles aux amandes (rolled almond cookies), 305
Turn out, 21-2
Twelfth-night cake, French *(galette des rois aux amandes)*, 105-6

Uncle Tom's cake *(biscuit de l'Oncle Tom)*, 218-9
Unsalted butter, 16
Upside down orange cake *(rosace à l'orange)*, 9, **83**, 159-60
Using electric mixer:
- for short pastry, 52
- for sweet short pastry, 56

Utensils, 14

Val d'isère (walnut tartlets), 219-21
Vanilla:
- custard with caramel sauce, 64
- extract as substitute for orange water, 19
- ice cream with chocolate sauce, 77
- pastry cream *(crème pâtissière vanillée)*, 9, 70-3
- sauce *(sauce à la vanille)*, 80-1
- soufflé *(soufflé à la vanille)*, 240
- sugar, 22
- whipped cream, *see* Chantilly cream

Waffles *(gaufres)*, 228, **229**
Walnut tartlets *(val d'isère)*, 219-21
Weights and measures, 22
Wells of love *(puits d'amour)*, 203-4
Whiten, 22
Wooden spatula, 18, 21
Work table, 20-1

Yule logs:
- almond paste decorations for *(décors en pâte d'amandes)*, 85
- chestnut *(bûche aux marrons)*, 136
- chocolate *(bûche au chocolat)*, 134-5
- coffee-flavored *(bûche au café)*, **49**, 133-4
- strawberry *(bûche fraisier)*, **47**, 131-2

Yeast, 22

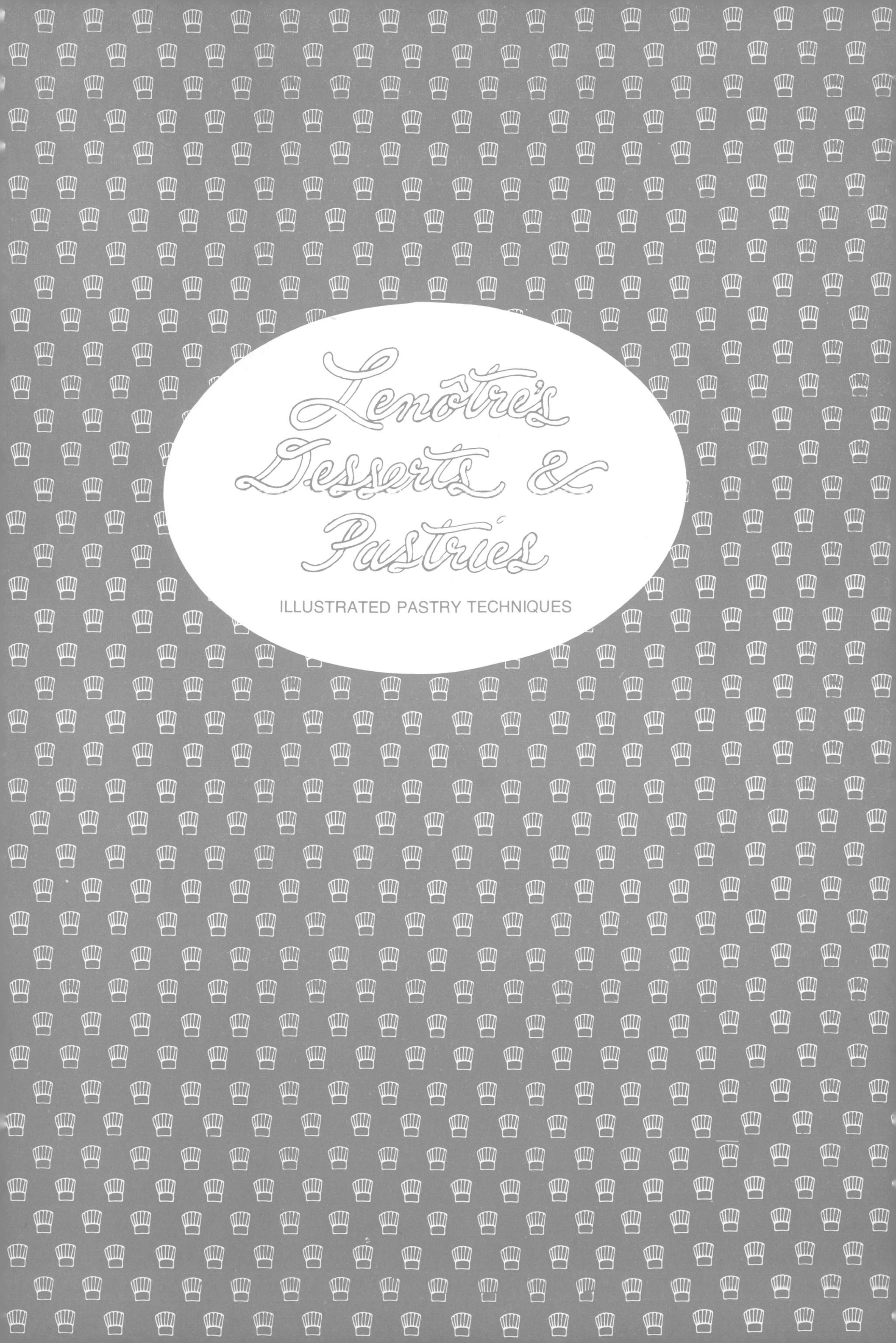
Lenôtre's Desserts & Pastries
ILLUSTRATED PASTRY TECHNIQUES

Brioche Dough

This dough should be made the night before intended use. If preferred, it can be frozen and used at a later time. Brioche dough may be mixed with an electric mixer equipped with a dough hook, but it is best to knead small quantities by hand. The illustrations following show how to knead by hand.

Have all the ingredients measured and ready for use. Place the flour on the table in a mound and make a well in the center. Put the yeast solution in the well and mix it with a little flour, then add 3 eggs. Incorporate about half the flour, then add the sugar-salt-milk mixture and one more egg, working with your fingers to mix all the ingredients together.

When all the flour has been mixed in, knead the dough for 15 minutes, stretching it and slapping it back onto the table as you do so.
When the time is up, add the remaining 2 eggs and keep working the dough until it becomes elastic and stretches easily without breaking.
Now add the softened butter to ⅓ of the dough; then add the remaining dough, half of it at a time, using the plastic scraper to cut and mix the dough together.

Place the dough in a large bowl, cover the bowl with a cloth and let it stand for 1½ to 2½ hours at room temperature. When the dough has risen to twice its original bulk, punch it down and stretch it twice.
Let the dough rise again in the refrigerator for 2 or 3 hours — it should be rounded on top like a ball. Punch the dough down as before and keep it refrigerated overnight.

For individual brioche
On a lightly floured table, use your hands to roll the dough into a thick sausagelike shape. Divide it into 16 equal pieces. Dust the palms of your hands and the table with flour and roll each piece of dough into a ball. Don't press hard on the ball of dough while rolling it.

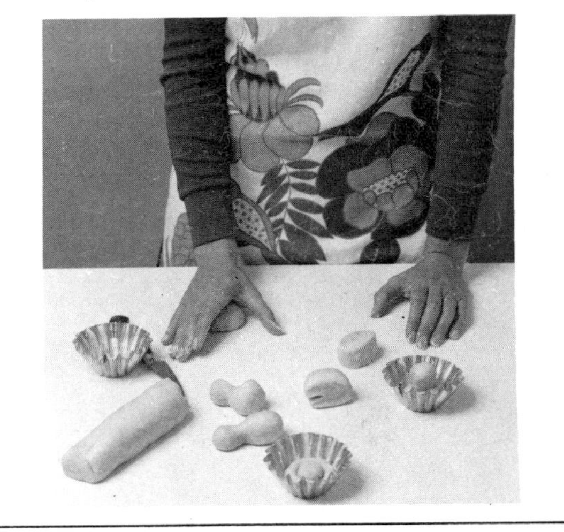

Once a ball is formed, use the edge of your hand to dent the dough and form a smaller ball or "head" for each brioche.
Butter each mold lightly with a pastry brush.
Place the dough in the molds with the small ball on top. Use your fingers and gently press down the dough all around the bottom of the smaller ball.
Let the dough rise for 1 hour 30 minutes in a warm place.

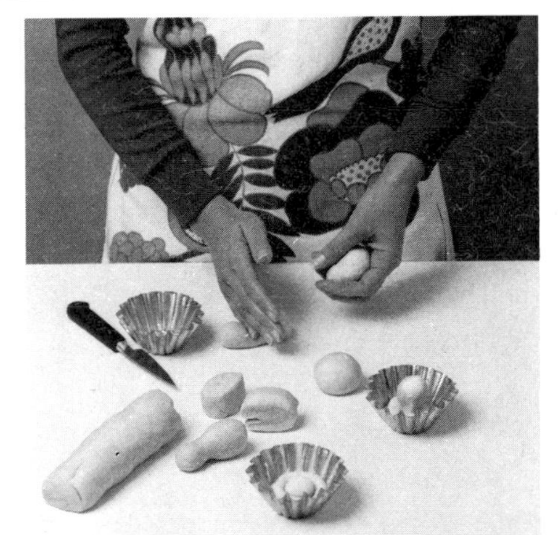

For large brioche
Place the brioche dough on a lightly floured surface. Flour your hands and divide the dough into 2 balls, one large and one small (the small ball should be a little less than one third the size of the other). Roll the bigger ball of dough gently between your hands to make it smooth and round.
Butter the mold and place the big ball of dough in it.
Roll the smaller ball of dough, shaping it like a pear. Make a depression in the top of the larger ball and place the narrow end of the smaller ball in the depression. Press lightly to make the two balls of dough stick together.
Let the dough rise for an hour and a half at room temperature or until it has doubled in volume.

Short Pastry

This pastry dough is used to make pie shells, Cherry Molds, or Clafoutis Tutti Frutti. The dough should be prepared a day in advance if possible.

Have all the ingredients measured and ready for use. Place the flour on the table in a mound, then make a well in the center of it. Sprinkle the sugar and the salt on the edges of the flour and in the well place the butter and the eggs. Mix all the ingredients together until crumbly, working very quickly with the tips of your fingers.

Then, knead the dough gently by pushing it away from you against the table with the palm of your hand. Add the milk as you do so.
Gather the dough into a ball and knead once more, working as quickly and gently as possible. Form the dough into a ball, wrap it in a floured cloth or place in a covered bowl and let it stand for at least 1 hour in the refrigerator; the dough will be easier to work if thoroughly chilled.

Roll out the dough on a lightly floured table. Roll the dough back onto the rolling pin, then use the rolling pin to lift the dough onto the pie shells or flan rings.
Line the pie shells or flan circle with the dough; either cut the excess dough off flush with the mold by rolling the rolling pin over the mold, or leave a small border and crimp it by pressing the dough against the mold at regular intervals with the blunt edge of a knife. Leave in a cool place for 1 hour before baking.

Classic Flaky Pastry

Flaky pastry is made by wrapping cold butter inside cold dough, then rolling it out and folding it several times. This produces a very flaky dough, made up of many layers, which will rise to several times its original height when baked. The photographs show the various steps to follow.

Prepare the dough, as described in the instructions for Recipe 3. Place the cold butter between 2 sheets of waxed paper and tap it several times with a rolling pin in order to flatten it slightly and make it more pliable. Roll the dough into a square on a floured surface, place the butter in the center, and fold in the sides. The butter should be completely enclosed inside the dough.

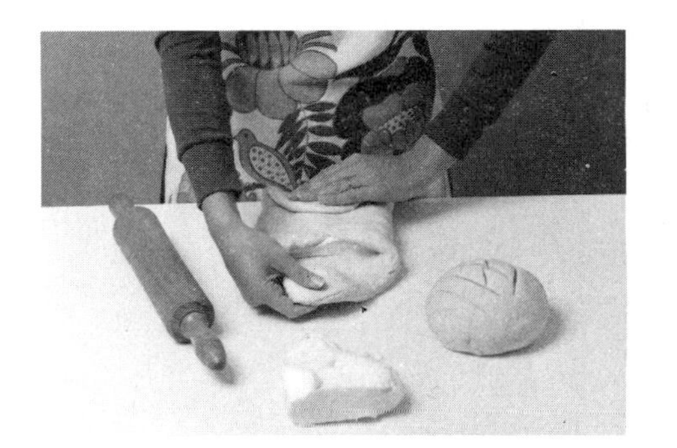

Place the folded dough so that the line of the last fold is perpendicular to you. Lightly flour the surface of the dough and the rolling pin. If necessary, sprinkle a little more flour on the rolling surface as well.

Roll the dough out into a long rectangle slightly more than ¼ inch thick, checking frequently to make sure the dough is not sticking to the table. Reflour the table and rolling pin when necessary, but do so as lightly as possible. When the desired thickness is reached, fold the dough into thirds. Give the dough ¼ turn so the line of the fold is again perpendicular to you. You should never roll across this fold, but always roll along it.

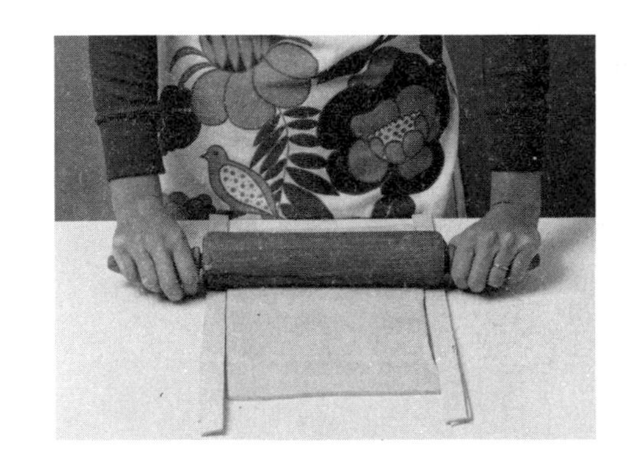

To roll the dough evenly, cut some cardboard rulers 10″ (25 cm) long. Place several of these rulers on top of each other until you reach the thickness you want the dough to be. The rulers will serve as a frame.

Give the dough 2 more turns. Refrigerate again for 1 hour. Just before using the dough, whether frozen or just refrigerated, give it 2 more turns and chill it for 1 hour in the refrigerator before rolling it into the shape asked for in any specific recipe.

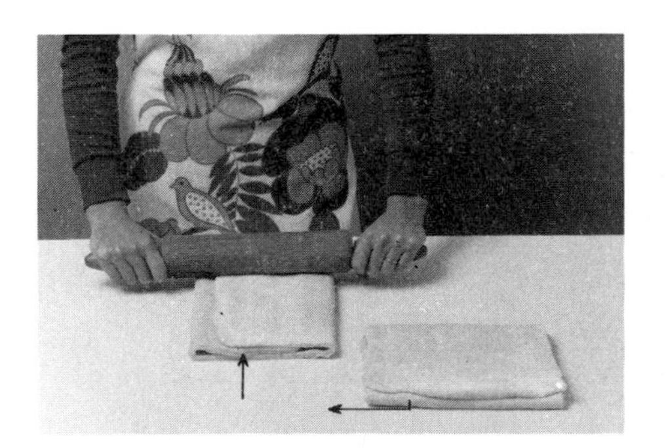

Quick Flaky Pastry

This method of making flaky pastry differs slightly from the classic method, cutting the time needed to make it almost in half. However, it does not keep as well as classic flaky pastry, so it is best to use it the day it is made.

Prepare the dough as instructed for Recipe 4. Place the butter between 2 sheets of waxed paper or plastic wrap and tap it several times with the rolling pin to make it more pliable.
Lightly flour the dough and the rolling surface. Roll the dough out into a rectangle about ¼ inch thick. Break the butter into pieces, and cover ⅔ of the dough with them.
Fold the dough into thirds, beginning with the third which was not covered with butter.

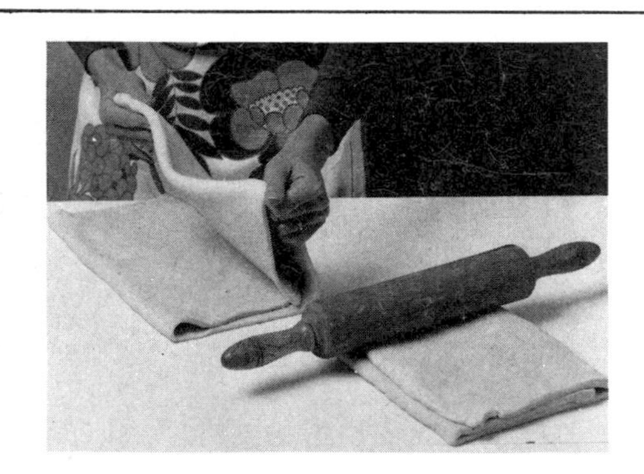

Turn the dough so that the line of the fold is perpendicular to you. Roll it out into a rectangle again — this time slightly less than ½ inch thick. Fold the dough in fourths; i.e., fold the ends until they touch in the middle, then fold the dough in half.
Give the dough a ¼ turn so the folded edge is perpendicular to you. Roll it out again and fold it in fourths again. Cover it well and chill it for 1 hour in the refrigerator.

Using the Pastry Bag

To make the Succès, meringues, ladyfingers, or cream puffs, you squeeze the batter through a pastry bag fitted with various sized nozzles. The following illustrations show the proper way of using the pastry bag to obtain the various shapes desired.

To make large meringue shells, draw an 8″ (20 cm) circle and a 6″ (15 cm) circle on each baking sheet. Squeeze out the batter in a continuous spiral to fill the circles, using a pastry bag with a ¾″ (2 cm) nozzle.
To make small shells, draw 20 1½″ (4 cm) circles on each pastry sheet. Fill each circle with the batter using a pastry bag with a ½″ nozzle.

To make meringue mushrooms, squeeze the meringue onto the baking sheet in long strips and round drops, or caps. When baked, attach the stems to the mushroom caps by pressing them together gently.

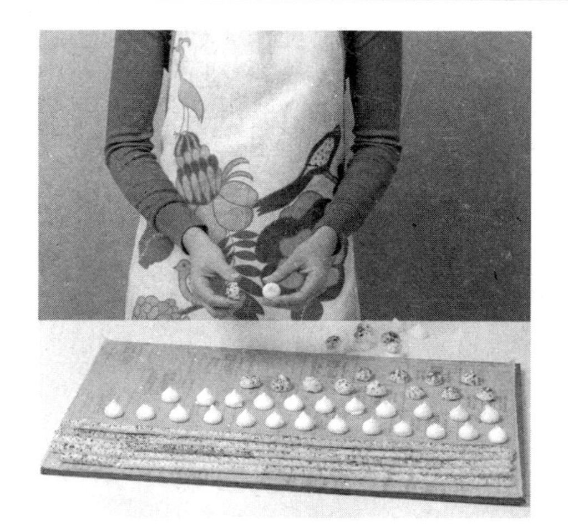

To make a large cream puff circle, such as for a Paris-Brest, fill the pastry bag with cream puff pastry and draw a circle on the baking sheet with the dough. Draw a second circle inside and touching the first one, then place a third circle on top of the 2 other circles. Dust the rings with chopped or slivered almonds.

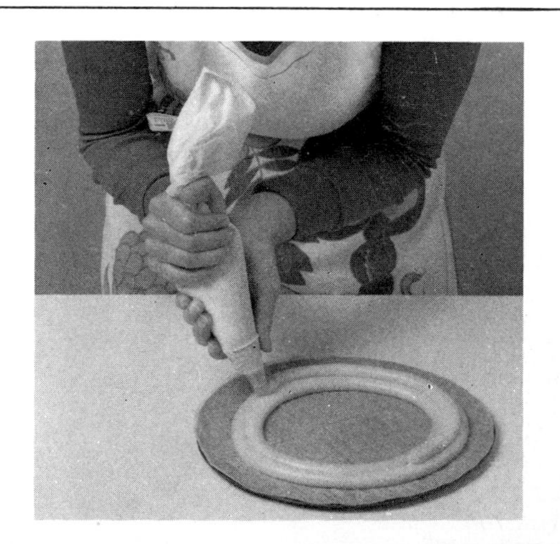

Lenôtre's Desserts & Pastries
ILLUSTRATED PASTRY TECHNIQUES